Man of Ashes

MAN OF ASHES

by Salomon Isacovici and Juan Manuel Rodríguez

Translated by Dick Gerdes

UNIVERSITY OF NEBRASKA PRESS: LINCOLN

Originally published as *A7393: Hombre de cenizas*. English translation published by agreement with the author.

© 1999 by the University of Nebraska Press. All rights reserved. Manufactured in the United States of America

⊗ The paper in this book meets the minimum requirements of American National Standard for Information Sciences—Permanence of Paper for Printed Library Materials, ANSI Z39.48-1984.

LIBRARY OF CONGRESS CATALOGING-IN-PUBLICATION DATA
Isacovici, Salomon, 1924–1998. [A7393, hombre de cenizas. English] Man of ashes / Salomon Isacovici and Juan Manuel Rodríguez; translated by Dick Gerdes. p. cm. – (Texts and contexts) ISBN 0-8032-2501-6 (cl : alkaline paper) 1. Isacovici, Salomon, 1924–1998. 2. Jews – Romania – Sighetu Marmatiei – Biography. 3. Holocaust, Jewish (1939–1945) – Romania – Sighetu Marmatiei – Personal narratives. 4. Auschwitz (Poland: Concentration camp) 5. Holocaust survivors – Ecuador – Biography I. Rodríguez, Juan Manuel, 1945-. II. Gerdes, Dick. III. Title. IV. Series.

DS135.R73I8313   1999   940.53'18'092–dc20   96–25032   CIP

To my people and to the memory of my beloved wife, Frida, with whom I shared so many days of sunshine and joy as well as gray days of bitterness. She played a fundamental role in my life, just as she does in this book that is its legacy.

Salomon Isacovici, Quito

CONTENTS

PUBLISHER'S PREFACE: Salomon Isacovici was born to a farming family in western Romania, growing up among the scents of alfalfa, hay, and clover. One day in 1940 his family woke as Hungarians, altered overnight by the changing borders of World War II. But to other Hungarians they were Jews, and week by week their world grew worse. First came indifference, then bullying, then beatings. In 1944 the Germans arrived and Isacovici, his family, and every Jew from his town were pushed into cattle cars and taken ever closer to the soot and smoke of Auschwitz. He became a man of ashes.

Man of Ashes is Isacovici's autobiography, chronicling his youth in Romania and the never ending punishment of Birkenau and Auschwitz. Lucky to escape during a massacre, he was shot, recaptured, and sent to another concentration camp, Gross Rosen. He was still there when U.S. soldiers liberated the camp.

At war's end he returned to his home only to find another family living there. To recover his life and his family he had to start anew, telling his children of their grandparents and great-grandparents, who they had been, what they had lost, how they had lived, how they had died. This is that story.

Acknowledgments: There are a number of people who deserve particular mention for contributions to the translation, and the publisher wishes to thank especially Professor Dolores L. Augustine of St. John's University, Jamaica, New York; Jennifer Comeau of the University of Georgia Press; Adrienne Mayor of Princeton, New Jersey; Professor Alan E. Steinweis of the University of Nebraska; and Jennifer Stimson de Rodríguez of Quito and Los Angeles, for their valuable advice, suggestions, and help.

In the process of translating *A7393: Hombre de cenizas*, Professor Gerdes was assisted by Salomon Isacovici and his family as he checked matters of fact and descriptive material, which resulted in a number of changes and improvements. Before his death in February of 1998, Salomon Isacovici was able to review and approve the entire translation.

JUAN MANUEL RODRÍGUEZ, collaborator and coauthor with Salomon Isacovici of *A7393: Hombre de cenizas*, is the author of a number of works, including *Jorma el predioador: El espantapájaros* (a finalist in the Premio Novadades y Diana), *Fricciones* (Aurelio Espinoza Polit prize), *El mar y la muralla, El pez perfume*, and *El pulso de nada.* He is dean of the College of Communications and professor at Universidad San Francisco de Quito.

DICK GERDES is a translator living in Washington DC. His translations of Latin American fiction include Alfredo Bryce Echenique's *A World for Julius* (American Literary Translators Association prize, Columbia University Translation Center prize), Diamela Eltit's *The Fourth World* (Nebraska 1995; Soeurette Diehl Frazier Translation Award from the Texas Institute of Letters), and Ana Maria Shua's *The Book of Memories* (1998). His translation of Shua's "A Good Mother" appears in *Prospero's Mirror: A Translators' Portfolio of Latin American Short Fiction* (1998).

Man of Ashes

1

Killing is their daily work. They killed my mother, Basia, who clung to life hoping to see her children grow up. They took the lives of my younger sisters, Blima and Pesil, before they had reached the prime of life. They destroyed my father, Hers, a skeletal somnambulist. They gunned down my adopted brother, Schmiel, whose life had been so painful. They poisoned my brother Saul, forcing him to be grateful for his hunger. They suffocated my grandfather Mordecai, a blacksmith whose beard was longer than his age. Cousins, friends, neighbors—all of us—faced death.

I am Salomon Isacovici, a Jew from Sighet, Romania. I am a witness. I have endured it all. Voluntarily exiled to Quito, Ecuador, I now return to face that same darkness of the caves of Mount Solovan in the Carpathians of my youth. Before, we were like countless grains of sand in the Negev Desert; now we are but pebbles scattered about the field, lost and eroded, with misfortune tattooed on our skin.

A light-skinned, blond nurse pushes me on the stretcher toward the operating room. Before I go in, the doctor says loudly to me, "Hang in there!" In the operating room, the aseptic silence recalls the winter nights when the moon would rise over the Carpathian Mountains. The glare of the operating lights is like the spotlights in the camps. The instruments, lined up two by two on white gauze, glisten in deadly silence.

Open-heart surgery. How many acts of madness have already seared my heart? More than a thousand? Paradoxically, I don't ask myself if I can survive a second operation. Perhaps I have more memories of facing death than most. In my case, in the concentration camps of Birkenau, Auschwitz, Jaworzno, and Gross Rosen I would wake up every day with the same feeling of death, reliving the agony and unable to shake it—even in my dreams.

The surgeon approaches and whispers in my ear again, "Hang in there." They cover my face with an oxygen mask cold like the skin of a frog. Inhaling deeply, I gasp desperately for one last breath. My mind wanders uncontrollably, dredging up bits and pieces of memories that rush headlong into each other. One of the assistants rubs my left arm in order to give me a shot. He stares at the tattoo: A-7393. I drift back in time: 1985, 1960, 1947. The years slip by like a log raft floating on the Tisa River of my birthplace: 1945 . . . 1943 . . . Quito, Italy, France, Auschwitz, Transylvania, Sighet, Mount Solovan . . . the caves, the darkness . . . a paralyzing darkness that begins to take control of me, finding its way into my consciousness. Finally, there is sleep.

Flanked by the Tisa and Iza Rivers, my native city of Sighet lies along the border between Romania and Czechoslovakia. Winters were bitterly harsh. Chilblains always left red spots on the skin of my hands and feet. I always preferred summertime: the reflection of light on the rivers, the picnics and swimming, the warmth of the air, the fragrance of apple trees.

My family was one of the few Jewish farming families in the region. Small farms formed a patchwork quilt all the way up to the Carpathians. The countryside turned green every year, and we'd harvest the extensive fields of alfalfa, hay, and clover in order to feed the cows and horses that the army would buy from us. The apple crops from our orchard were so abundant that my father would export them, before the war, to Germany. At the time, no one could have predicted what was going to happen; the only threats to my childhood were the icy winters that we faced when we had to get up early each morning and brave the bitter cold on our way to school.

Our house was old and sat about three hundred feet from the border guards' post. The bridge over the Tisa led to another country: Czechoslovakia. The pitched pinewood roof of our house shed the rain and snow easily, preventing leaks. In the summertime, the front porch was always filled with red and

white flowers. We'd gather there at dusk to refresh ourselves
from the heat that rose from the earth. As the moon began to
rise in the sky, we'd get together with other families to sing
ballads in Yiddish and laugh about the day's events. We could
hear the dogs barking in the distance, and the yellow cat would
stretch out lazily at our feet.

Inside the house, a hall led to the bedrooms and the kitchen,
where there was an oven with a huge, black door that looked like
the entrance to the caves of Mount Solovan. Donning her flow-
ered apron and scarf, my mother used to bake *cholent*, made of
beans, barley, and meat, and *kugel* noodle cakes for the Sabbath.
In the winter, we would always sit near the oven while the wind
blew over the icy surface of the river; soon we'd grow drowsy
from doing our homework and we'd gaze at the flames of the
fire twirling and twisting, trying to escape up the chimney.

In the morning, as I got out of bed, I could still feel the faint
warmth of the embers emanating throughout the house. I used
to look curiously through the frosty windows at the cold, clean
countryside. I'd put my hands on the windowpane and let my
fingers trace the fanciful designs of stars and fir leaves that had
formed from the steam of our breath and made ice crystals on
the panes during the night. Putting on a heavy jacket and a
woolen cap and then loading up the sleigh, I would race down
the snowy hills with my brothers and friends.

When I was four years old, my father told me that I was to go
to the *cheder*, the Jewish school. At the time, the word *cheder*
meant adventure and growing up, although I was still no taller
than a kitchen stool. My parents wanted me to start learning
the Hebrew alphabet, our religion, and our customs. And so
it happened that, one morning in autumn, I began attending
the *cheder*.

I knew about the school because it was located next to the
rustic old synagogue, where the Jewish elders spent long hours
studying and reading works handed down to them from their

elders. The two entrances to the synagogue, which were separate, permitted access for the men through the right door and for the women through the left door. The main room was large and had a podium in the middle surrounded by worn wooden benches. A chest holding the scrolls and manuscripts of the Torah was at the back of the room. I couldn't see the women because they would sit in an adjacent room, and the wall that separated us was very high, with a curtained opening at the top through which they could hear the prayers.

The playground at the *cheder* was made of dirt. A leafy walnut tree, usually filled with squawking birds, provided shade on sunny days. We'd climb two plum trees in our search for fruit, always tearing our woolen pants. Rabbi Moshe would talk to us about the Jewish doctrines that had been handed down by our ancestors, and he'd sing *zmires*, ritual songs for the Sabbath. Old Moshe's face was as wrinkled as a newly plowed field, but his expressions were surprisingly noble, like the images from a sacred book. His movements were slow and slight, and he would only smile when he watched us play games on the dusty playground or throw snowballs during the icy winters.

The *cheder* was located about a mile and a half from our house, and we had to cross the train tracks to get there. During the winter we'd walk in single file like tame geese along the banks of the Tisa. My oldest brother, Paisi, always went first, making tracks in the snow that created a path for the younger ones behind him. Bringing up the rear, I'd follow the trail between the walls of snow, anxious to reach the large room of the *cheder* where a stove filled with firewood released its inviting warmth.

The classes were taught by levels. A faded blackboard hung on one of the walls. The silence and the discipline in the school were as rigid as the bamboo cane that Rabbi Moshe would brandish at us.

Recess was at ten o'clock every morning. I still associate those times with my first feelings of guilt. My friend Ernö Wiener would sit there and eat buttered bread; while I watched him fill his mouth, my own drooled with envy. I'd wonder why my parents always sent me to school without a slice of bread like Ernö's. Since there were so many of us, I concluded that perhaps my parents didn't have enough money to buy bread for everyone.

My friendship with Ernö never earned me a single bite of his bread. But one day he invited me to his house, where neatly lined up on the hearth were ten coins. I stared at them with envy and, when Ernö was looking the other way, I snatched one of them. After I left his house I went straight to the bakery and bought a sweet roll. But when I came outside and stared at the roll I had purchased, my heart started pounding. Guilt had overtaken my desire to eat the roll. Without taking a single bite, I headed straight for home. I didn't dare go inside with it, so I went to the barn and tossed it to the dog. Wagging his tail gratefully and ignorant of my anguish, he devoured the roll. For several days, my torment became a nightmare; somehow, though, new adventures helped to dissipate my guilt.

When I was six years old, I began attending the public school as well as the *cheder*. In the mornings I learned to be a Romanian, and in the afternoons I learned to be a Jew. But I never went alone; since I had six brothers, at least one of them was always present.

I didn't find out that Schmiel wasn't my real brother until I turned fifteen. My parents had adopted him, following the Jewish tradition of taking in children who had lost their mothers. Normally, the closest relatives, if they were financially capable, would take charge of such children, who would return to their father's house only if he married the deceased mother's sister. Because his father had married a different woman, Schmiel became our brother. To me, Schmiel was always unhappy, a person who suffered for reasons that no one could explain. Even his attempted suicide and his hopeless heroism fighting as a partisan in the war seemed to be a natural part of his personality.

There were eleven of us in the family, including my parents

and two sisters; that is, we were a total of eleven until the war began. Then we were separated, one by one, like sheep scattering in the presence of a wolf. Some of us were taken to the slaughterhouse or lost forever, like my father, whom I saw for the last time dying of typhoid in the camp at Gross Rosen. Before those bitter events, however, my life was as peaceful as a dove's.

Those birds always seemed to be so blissful, perched on the roofs of our house and barn. Their feathers were as splendid as a rainbow appearing behind the Carpathians. And there were different species. The homing pigeons were mostly gray, and their purple breasts would change with the light of the sun, with a beautiful iridescence that would have made them the envy of the greatest of painters. Two colorful bands crossed their wings, and when they walked they looked like sergeants wearing shoulder stripes. The queen doves seemed so elegant; their white color gave them an air of distinction. Although they were awkward — they could hardly fly from one rooftop to another — they possessed a radiant magnificence. I still miss them very much. However, not all was peaceful for those rooftop inhabitants: sometimes when they would fly up into the sky in flocks, shrinking to the size of little turtledoves, a hawk would suddenly drop down on them like a deadly flash of lightning. Scattering, the birds would take refuge in the pigeon loft or on the patio, but there were always victims.

One afternoon a hawk descended from the clouds and attacked a flock of pigeons. There was one that could barely fly, and it fell prey to the hunter's claws. When I approached the hawk, it released its prey. The pigeon's feathers were bloody: it was trembling like a leaf and already dying. I made a nest out of grass and buried it in a coffin of straw; I thought it would sleep better in a nest similar to the ones abundant with those eggs freckled like a child's face. That incident taught me that life wasn't what it appeared to be, and, although I knew nothing about how life really was, it seemed to me that in growing up and coming to understand things, there was something repugnantly secretive about it.

Experiencing my first great flood taught me something more about what the pigeon's death had meant, for I learned that pain and misfortune, the same as laughter and the brilliance of the sun, were a natural part of life. One afternoon, gray clouds that had been floating aimlessly by began to loom menacingly in the vast sky. It grew dark, hastening nightfall. Earlier, swallows had been flying around announcing the arrival of the spring rains, but now they were scattering chaotically, seeking shelter from the impending storm.

On Friday it began to rain. The initial slow, steady rainfall turned torrential; now it was beating on the roof with such force that it seemed like a drum pounded by a lunatic. Flashes of lightning pierced the sky. Gusts of wind drove the heavy rain against the windowpanes, while the force of the downpour bent the trees. Outside, the Tisa roared and became swollen, and the rising waters of the river began to spill over the surrounding dikes.

The patio turned to mud. My father and older brothers put on their big capes and gathered up the hens and chicks. From the window I saw the chickens standing like statues with their feet sunk into the mud; they were easy to catch. The birds were put in the attic of the barn, and my father closed the door to keep them inside.

The water surrounded the house and reached the first steps of the porch. The house was already saturated with humidity, and we paced back and forth, having to jump over the puddles. We were all tired. My brothers Idel and Isaac were dozing off at the kitchen table, for the beating of the rain on the roof had left us in a stupor, unable to hear a thing. My mother tried lighting a fire, but water kept running down the chimney and snuffing out the remaining coals. After countless attempts, she managed to get a feeble flame going, and the water-soaked wood began to crackle loudly. I could sense the damp air permeated with the odor of lichen and moss. I could feel the clammy, heavy emptiness of the rooms, smelling like bitter almonds. I could even feel the pain of the drowning apple trees.

The river reeked of misfortune. The news arrived without warning: "The Tisa has flooded. Several houses have already collapsed." Numb with fear, I sat on the edge of my bed for a long time, watching a candle burn out. Our maid, Anita, a gentile who limped of a dislocated hip, went around the house making the sign of the cross. By four o'clock it was already dark.

The rain besieged us until our prayers began to sound like the repetitious beating of the rain on the tin roof. Fighting off drowsiness, we prayed into the night. I went to the window before going to sleep and looked outside: water was swirling madly and had reached the highest step of the porch. I kept my shoes on, wrapped myself in the covers, and fell asleep.

By daybreak the inside of the house had been flooded. With water up to his knees, my father draped the tallith, or prayer shawl, over his shoulders with pronounced reverence and began the prayers of the Sabbath. Then we went up to the attic to look out at the countryside. A watery blanket had covered the patio and the fields; it even covered the trees up to their branches. Ducks swam around and dove happily in the immense lake. The houses that were partially submerged in the raging water looked like boats anchored on a lake.

By Saturday afternoon the rain had stopped. On the other side of the river, a family had gathered on the rooftop of their house and were hollering, beckoning, begging for help. Some small boats tried to get close, but their struggle against the current was in vain. The house started to crack under the pressure of the water, then it crumbled to pieces like cake, and the family disappeared under the waves of the Tisa River.

On Sunday the floodwaters began to recede. A high sea of dirty water had dragged along logs, uprooted trees, and drowned donkeys and cows. When the water on the patio had retreated, we immediately started to work: my mother cleaned the mud from the floors, the older children repaired fallen fences, and the younger children picked up branches left in the wake of the flood.

A few days later I visited the river dikes where different kinds of birds had built their nests. The nests had been flooded and lots of small birds were dead. I used to play around there, trying to catch the birds when they would seek refuge in their hiding places. I'd block the entrances with stones and mud and wait for hours and hours to see if they could get out. After the flood, not a single trace of life was left in those niches.

That flood made me think about the way death touches living things when nature explodes in all its fury. Since I had grown accustomed to seeing foals and calves being born in the stable, life for me had meant birth, not death. After witnessing the storm and the destruction that was left after the water had subsided, I thought that God ruled the forces of the world in order to make us understand his dominion over all beings. When they talked about war and death at school, I could never imagine men dying at the hands of other men. How could men reappear again and again in the world committing the same pernicious acts? Death was a great flood through which the hand of God had executed his plan. Only he made things live and die.

Yet these matters were still not clear to me. Once I thought I had seen a dead bird, but after a few months I observed the same bird alive, revived and fluttering in the same branches as before. That's the way I saw it: spring meant birth and winter meant death.

Even the winters brought new games such as tobogganing in the snow and ice skating at the lake. But with winter also came shortages and hunger. I remember one winter in particular. Snow was falling gently. We were gathered in the kitchen when we heard the dogs start to bark loudly, then a knock at the door. My father left his spoon in his soup and went to open the door. A white gust of snow and wind swept into the room. Coughing and covered with snow, our young neighbor Beril was standing on the porch. While my father was letting him in, my mother brought another bowl to the table. The young man had come to ask for some food for his invalid mother. Beril had been supporting his mother as a tailor. Suffering from tuberculosis, he always seemed to be coughing all over the few pieces of clothing he would be working on.

His mother, Pesil Slomovici, had become a widow just a few years after she was married. An illness had left her disabled and her only son would sew until his index finger and thumb were swollen like leeches ready to burst with blood. The young man barely earned enough to cook a pot of mush once a day. The house they were living in had been given to them by a Hungarian family named Strinbelyi.

That evening my mother gathered up some goose fat, corn, and firewood and set out for the old crippled woman's house. Neither my father's pleas nor the storm stopped her from making the trek, for she wanted to help the poor invalid woman. Amid blowing snow and cold, my mother and oldest brother accompanied the tailor back to his house. They gave food to Pesil, lit a fire, and straightened up her room. From that time on, my mother always gave food to that unfortunate pair. After the old woman died, my mother named my youngest sister after her.

When summer came around, things changed. A youthful and lively spirit spread throughout the hills. The winds that had bellowed across the Tisa were transformed into refreshing afternoon breezes. When I was eight years old, I had a most exciting adventure: my parents let me move to the hayloft in the barn, which made things more comfortable for everyone else in a house that was not large enough to accommodate eleven people. In the mornings, I would go fishing with my brothers in the Tisa. Since we hardly used the oven during the summer,

my mother would light the coals on the patio in front of the
porch. Upon our return, we'd fry up the small fish and devour
them for breakfast.

Squawking, the geese would always come up to the house
and demand something to eat. Since we only ate kosher things,
we did not use pork lard for cooking; hence, geese were quite
desirable for their fat. My family took meticulous care of our
geese because they also helped protect the property; living near
the border, we never knew whom to expect.

Summertime was also great for hiking. One day when I was
ten years old, I went with my father to the caves of Mount Solovan, high up in the peaks. Taking me by the hand, my father
explained that those tunnels and caverns had been lived in by
people of the Stone Age. As we entered, the caves seemed enormous, but little by little they grew smaller in size. On the walls,
we could make out the black marks that my father said were
made by the fires that the people had learned to tame. I tried
to imagine how one goes about taming fire. I envisioned some
gypsies, like the ones who taught bears to dance, juggling
flames. But it was pitch-black inside; with each step that took
us farther and farther into the thick darkness, I squeezed my
father's hand all the harder. He must have noticed because he
started shouting, which not only lessened my fears but also allowed me to appreciate the sound of the echoes. Then I began
to shout too, and while our voices were distinct, the words that
echoed back to me seemed to come from only one voice.

That same night I looked out from the window of my room at
the well on the patio. Why did I associate it with the caves? I can't
remember why, but I know that I looked at the well for hours on
end. An owl had landed on the rim and, seemingly mesmerized,
it stared with its big straw-colored eyes into the well. A young
hare approached the well, most likely searching for water, but
the owl pounced on it and started pecking at its neck. Then,
grasping it with its talons, the owl flew off while the little feet of
the hare pattered to find ground. That scene, and the visit to the

caverns, left me disturbed that night. I dreamed about the mice that nested near the barn and would travel single file toward the edge of the well. The owls would prey on them, killing them one by one. When I woke up, new thoughts had already dissipated my dreams. Still, those images have stayed with me throughout my life.

When I turned twelve, I could no longer fritter away my time because I had just entered high school. But if I wanted to study, I had to make some money to pay for it. My father did not pay me for helping with the apple harvest or planting corn and vegetables; he said that I was well paid with the food and lodging I received at home. So I had to find a way to earn money for school. I didn't have a cent to my name and my needs were as great as my growing despair: I needed to buy books, a school uniform, and shoes as well as pay the tuition. My decision to continue in school led me to become a small-time smuggler. Without giving it a thought, I readily accepted the idea that taking risks was necessary at times, especially if I were to become a grown-up.

2

That summer, before classes started, I spent some time thinking about how to make money. I thought about Sighet, in the
province of Maramures in Transylvania, which lies on the border. From our small farm, located on the banks of the Tisa that
flowed into the Danube, we could see the Carpathians in the
distance. To cross the bridge over the Tisa, which served as the
border, was to enter into Czechoslovakia. Inhabitants along its
banks lived by smuggling, mainly food, which was less expensive in Czechoslovakia than in Romania.

One morning I went to my brother Idel, who was working as a
barber, and begged him to lend me some money. He questioned
me repeatedly, wanting to know what I was up to. When he
finally understood my plan, he agreed. With the money tightly
knotted in my handkerchief, I crossed the border alone for the
first time in my life. I bought some goods in Czechoslovakia and
returned across the bridge, trying to blend in with the others.

Thus began my life as a small-time smuggler. I quickly discovered that smuggling food—chocolates, preserves, sausages,
and small delicacies, which were important items for house-
wives—provided the most profits. In two weeks, I was able to
pay off Idel's loan and double my savings; hence, I came to believe that the lucrative ends would justify the dangerous means.
During my first year as a smuggler I had no problems hiding
the small packages of goods in my clothes. Since I was still a
youngster, the guards did not pay much attention to me. I tried
not to draw any attention my way, and getting across the border
without being noticed always took time and resourcefulness.
The best way to avoid calling attention to myself was to cross
with a group of adults and act as if I were merely a part of the
scene and not its protagonist.

Little by little I learned the trade well; for instance, I would
always carry herring with me so the guards wouldn't search
me. The stench nauseated them. I'd also smuggle across about

twenty pounds of rice per trip, and I hid the more valuable items — silk and cocoa butter — in the rice.

When I'd shop for herring, cocoa butter, taffeta, lemons, and shoes, I'd make friends with Jews from the neighboring city of Solotfina. At the time, I didn't think how valuable these contacts would be when we began to take clandestine revenge against the Hungarians.

With my job as a smuggler, in addition to my studies, I had more than enough to cope with for a person my age. In school there were always problems because I was a Jew. Isaac, the most quarrelsome of my brothers, always defended me; he'd pick a fight with anyone who got in my way. When he wasn't around, though, I had to stand alone. In school I was harassed a lot with insults, but what hurt the most was to hear over and over again that I should go back to my homeland. I had learned in school that one's homeland is where one is born, and I had been born in Sighet. I didn't understand the meaning of the word "wanderer" until my father explained it to me. Moses had been a "wanderer."

"Ever since we lost our land," my father said, "we have had to live without a homeland. For many Jews, the only homeland is Palestine. But one can still be a Jew anywhere in the world."

I had learned in my history classes that conflicts between nations usually broke out over the possession of land, and I never could understand why the Jews didn't fight for their lands. Without realizing it, I was becoming a little Zionist. At night I would imagine being an army commander going out to reconquer our lands. But I never showed any hostility at school; my father had taught me that the use of force only created more problems. I always tried to follow his advice faithfully. But not so with my friend Baruch Farkas: he used to walk around punching out anyone who confronted him.

The matter of not having a homeland really bothered me when we sang the Romanian national anthem. I loved the land where I had grown up. The Romanians used to say that when we had finally left for good, my parents' property would be turned

over to them; but I always responded that this country was not
just theirs—it was my homeland too. The orchards where we
grew apples, the fields of hay and clover, and the plots where
we planted corn and wheat had become my homeland. In those
days, when I'd sit by the river, I thought less about the birds
that nested on its banks and more about having to defend our
territory where the cattle grazed because it was my country too.
But my army was no more than my younger brothers Saul and
Samuel, who would participate in imaginary battles and carry
out territorial conquests with me. One day we'd convert the
barn into a fortress, the next day the horse corral became an
unknown land that we would discover and conquer. Deep down
inside, however, I felt as Romanian as those who threatened to
take our farm away from us. Ironically, the matter of not having
a homeland would be felt by the Romanians themselves when,
years later, they witnessed the cession of Sighet to Hungary with
one stroke of the pen.

Once, on the school playground, a gentile spat on me and all
the other boys just laughed. Red with rage because the uniform
that I had worked so hard to buy had just been contaminated, I
lunged at him. We tumbled to the ground. I managed to get on
top of him and punch him in the face before the other gentiles
pulled us apart. As I was brushing the dirt off my uniform, the
boy came over to me and offered to shake hands. After that
incident, Alexander Nedelcovici became a good friend. I think
I've regretted that punch in the face ever since because he was
the most loyal and unwavering Christian friend I've ever had.

One Friday, upon arriving at the bridge from Czechoslovakia
with my clandestine purchases, I discovered that the large gate
separating the two countries was closed. It was only five o'clock
in the afternoon but it had been barred shut; neither wagons nor
people were allowed to cross. I didn't know what to do. After
some indecision, I rearranged the bundle on my shoulder and
sought shelter at an aunt's house. Although surprised to see me,

they welcomed me. My uncle, who was my godfather, tried to make me feel at home.

It was the first time that I had been away from home over-night. To make things worse, it was the eve of the Sabbath, when the family would assemble for dinner together. I was in bed by nightfall, but I couldn't sleep. Our houses faced each other, only the Tisa separated us. I observed the window of my house for quite some time. I could see the candles that my mother had blessed as, one by one, they burned out. According to tradition, on the Sabbath the candles were allowed to burn themselves out. After my house finally grew dark, I went to sleep.

When the border opened at daybreak, I crossed the bridge and went straight home. Although my parents remained wor-ried, Idel had already told them about my smuggling; yet they never said anything to me about it. Like other border towns, half of Sighet's population made a living by smuggling. The border guards tended to look the other way. After that particular in-cident, I managed to improve as much on my little delinquent practices as I did on my judgment. Although the guards would change every so often, they began to recognize me with so many comings and goings. To avoid them I had only two alternatives: crossing underneath the bridge between the steel crossbeams or swimming across the river. Both ways were dangerous, but I tried them immediately. I made a bag from oilcloth, tied it to my waist, and swam from one bank to the other. I'd get up at dawn when the guards were still drowsy and make my way to Czechoslovakia. My return route depended on the time of day. When shopping took less time, I'd swim back; but when I finished at dusk, I would crawl silently through the framework under the bridge.

For three years I crossed back and forth, until events in 1940 brought a halt to my studies and ended my profession as a young smuggler. Under pressure from the Germans, Transylvania was handed over to Hungary, anti-Semitic persecution worsened, and I had to quit school. The Romanians who had harassed me saying this was not my homeland found themselves in the same situation: they were not Romanians anymore, now they were Hungarians.

Animosity against Jews had always been present, but when the Hungarians arrived, the hostilities reached alarming proportions. Before their arrival, a Romanian political party espousing German racist ideology had already begun to disseminate anti-Semitic propaganda. For this reason Isaac was constantly involved in fights on the streets or on the school grounds; he had gained a reputation as a tough guy and a troublemaker around the city, and many people began to fear him. I respected his bravery but was ashamed of his viciousness.

One day, as we were walking through the streets, I asked him why he was always so irritable: "Sanyi, I fight back to make them afraid of me," he said. "If they're afraid of us, they'll leave us alone."

With my high school studies cut short, I went directly from being a student at school to apprenticing as an auto mechanic with a specialty in soldering. Soon the instructor and the other apprentices, all of whom had been contaminated by the spark of anti-Semitism spreading so quickly with such fiery vehemence, began insulting me and acting abusively.

The soldering instructor, whose name was Lazslo Pastor, was an inveterate drunk. He mocked me for being a Jew and did everything possible to prevent me from learning the trade. Every day he would send me out to buy him brandy. I'd get on my bicycle and ride to the nearest tavern. No sooner would I return than he'd send me out again to get more. He never sent a gentile out on those errands. And that's not all: even though he knew that working on the Sabbath was against our religious laws, he would make me clean the workshop on Saturdays.

Since I wasn't learning much about soldering or auto mechanics but was gaining a lot of experience at getting around on a bicycle, I began to play tricks on my instructor. On Saturdays, I would drag my feet in order to extend my cleaning chores into the next day, so I could be alone at the shop. After the bell would ring for Mass, I'd go to the workshop and quickly finish up the cleaning and then use the rest of the time learning how to solder. It wasn't long before Lazslo Pastor became suspicious, so one day after attending Mass and then spending some time at the tavern taking shots of liquor, he showed up unexpectedly at the workshop. He walked straight over to the soldering iron and touched it to see if it was hot. Since I had already learned not to be taken by surprise, and suspecting that behind those frightening beady eyes he was up to something, I would always place wet rags on the soldering iron to cool it down.

Since he made me buy the liquor in small bottles, I had to make at least four trips to the tavern every day. He never called me by my name; he would only say, "You, Jew bastard" and tell me to do this or that. The other apprentices ridiculed me because he had made me a slave to everyone. At first I took the humiliation, thinking "This, too, shall pass"; but after a long time of martyrdom and putting up with fistfights with my fellow apprentices, I rebelled, decided to abandon the training program, and returned home to help out on the farm.

During that time, however, not everything was all grief and pain. On Saturday afternoons, several young people would gather at Sighet's main park, then go to the movies and dancing afterward. That's when I met Leah Gitel. We started to meet each other after work. We dated for about a year, until my parents began to oppose the relationship whose beginning had coincided with the beginning of those turbulent times. After Leah moved to Budapest, I was very lonely. I'd sit on the banks of the Tisa, watching the rafts floating down the river, pulled along by the current.

Looking back, I'm sure it was for the best, because events could have made it hard on us had we remained committed to each other during those years of the war's uncertainty and persecution. When I saw her again after the war, we were mere ghosts

of a nightmare that Europe had witnessed but refused to acknowledge. In its silence, Europe had become an accomplice of
the Holocaust.

Like many others, the Jews had been the inhabitants of
the Maramures region in Transylvania for several generations.
There were Hungarians, descendants of the Huns who had arrived from Mongolia in hordes; Romanians, a nation that came
into being with the union of the Dacians and the Romans during the Roman conquest; and Jews, who were descendants of
migrants who had arrived several centuries later. Transylvania
was inhabited by some 380,000 Jews and 18,000 lived in Sighet,
comprising more than half of its population.

Basically, we were a city within a city; among us there were
several social levels, from artisans and merchants to professionals. One distinctive caste was composed of the Hasidim,
that is, the strict Orthodox Jews, known for their black, wide-
brimmed hats, long black coats, and earlocks. As I think back
on it, I can visualize a small kingdom in which the rabbi, with
his family, was like a king of the Hasidim. As the spiritual leader
of the community, he would dedicate himself to the study of
the Talmud, the authoritative body of Jewish tradition, and the
Cabala, the mystical interpretation of the Scriptures. Special
judges, known as *dayanim*, rarely gave verdicts outside their
own jurisdiction. The Hasidim fulfilled their religious obligations by supporting the rabbi and his family.

The symptoms of what was to come began to be felt even
before the German occupation; it was like an air of indifference,
something tepid that seemed to emanate from the river. The
gentiles refused to acknowledge our presence. We used to be
friendly despite our religious and cultural differences; now they
no longer greeted us as before. At first their gestures were less
friendly, then the waves or hellos disappeared, then there was
barely a whisper when we'd pass by each other, and finally, nothing. Jewish families stopped socializing with friends of other
religious beliefs. Prayers were reduced to murmurs. Despite the

hot summers, homes remained tightly closed, and the window shutters that were used only during the winter months now remained permanently fastened like extended accordions.

Even though work routines and religious activities continued, Jews socialized only among themselves now. And despite all the differences among us, the rabbi managed to keep our community together. Many of us were opposed to the passive apathy that was overtaking us, but others believed they were guilty of something about which they knew nothing. Silence overtook the porch where we used to gather in the summer evenings to talk while the darkness spread over the house's once sunlit hardwood floors.

Our elders proceeded with sacred serenity, but some of us became rebellious and formed clandestine groups under the command of a leader. It was then that I began to feel isolated from everything, and at the time I thought that to be born in Sighet, which means "island," had more meaning than I could ever imagine. Before, being a Jew had never alienated me from those good people who lived in our city. With the passing of time, though, I came to realize what it meant to be a Jew; for some implacable reason, our heritage seemed like some congenital, incurable disease that segregated us from the others. My parents, who had always been cheerful and happy, had turned mute. At night, I would go over and over the word "Jew" that began to echo in my brain with the same force as that echo I had experienced in the caves of Mount Solovan. Clutching that word and whispering it to myself repeatedly, letting each letter take shape inside me, I would fall asleep with the sensation that the word was suspended over my neck like a guillotine.

3

By 1939, Germany was militarily well prepared and began its devastating march through Europe, trampling everything in its path with its nail-studded boots. Having already annexed Austria and occupied Poland and Czechoslovakia, the Germans ceded part of the latter country to the Hungarians, who took the region adjacent to Romania. Now the bridge over the Tisa joined Hungary and Romania. All this was disconcerting to everyone, but the only one who didn't seem to care much was my cousin David Isacovici, for he continued to smuggle between the two countries with the same audacity as always. "Smuggling between Romania and Czechoslovakia," he would say, "is the same as smuggling between Romania and Hungary."

When the hostilities began, the border area became tightly guarded. Even though I was always able to talk with the picket of Romanian soldiers at the border because they had taken a liking to me, I grew ever more apprehensive just being around them. Meanwhile, David continued to smuggle brandy. His earnings permitted him to support his family—until one day he was arrested. No one would have known about the incident had my father not been involved.

It was Saturday and we were at the synagogue. The tallith adorned his shoulders and my father was chanting passages from the Torah. Suddenly, soldiers stormed into the room, dragged my father into the street and, with the tallith still in place, took him to jail. We didn't know what to do; no one could understand why they had acted so irreverently. Not long afterward, we learned that they were looking for my cousin who had been accused of spying for the Hungarians.

My father didn't know anything of David's whereabouts; nevertheless, they suspected that he was helping my cousin because we lived near the bridge joining the two countries. My older brothers and my mother went to inquire about my father at the military command post. Even though it was Saturday, I was told to go to the barn to feed the cows. I opened the door, which always made a creaking sound. Pitchfork in hand, I climbed the ladder to the loft where the hay was stored to keep it dry and ready to be tossed below into the stalls. As I went around gathering up clumps of hay with the pitchfork, I discovered David hiding in the hay. I immediately leaped upon him and shouted, "How could you do this to us?"

Bewildered, David just looked at me. After I told him what had happened to my father and blamed him for it, he explained that he had to hide from the soldiers.

"This must be kept a secret between you and me. They're not after me because I'm a smuggler, they know I'm a spy. About three months ago I was apprehended by the Hungarians during one of my smuggling trips to Solotfina. They said they'd let me go and even let me continue my smuggling in exchange for something they wanted from me. They wanted information about Romanian military activities. Before they let me go, they warned me that if I tricked them, they would kill me. On my fourth trip, I was apprehended by the Romanians! They interrogated and beat me. They wanted to make me confess to crimes I hadn't committed. Thank God they didn't know I was spying for the Hungarians. They beat me until I was unconscious, and then it occurred to them that I should do some spying for them. My knees turned to rubber but I took them up on the offer so I wouldn't be sent to jail. You see, I was now a double agent, free to cross the border either way without any hassles. I would give both sides a little information — it was like my passport to continue operating. Things were going along pretty well until the Romanians became suspicious. They had noticed that the Hungarian border guards just looked the other way every time I crossed the border. One night, a Romanian agent followed me and figured out that I was spying for both sides. So two days ago they arrested me, but I managed to escape when they were walking me to the jail. That's why they've taken your father in, so he'll tell them where I am."

He told the story calmly, while he nibbled on a piece of dried alfalfa. Then he said, "Don't worry about your father. Since he doesn't know anything, they'll have to let him go." When he saw the worried look on my face, he gave me a big hug. By the time I was able to collect my thoughts, David had already gone down the ladder and was waving good-bye from the barn door.

He was right about my father. At dusk they let him go. His only defense was that after having lived so many years on the border, the guards knew him well enough to know that he had never become involved in smuggling or collaboration with foreigners.

David's life became a road full of potholes; he continued to get himself into all kinds of trouble. I remember the time he created a big ruckus in front of the judge who made David declare his complicity in a swindle that involved his own friends.

Since David was familiar with the ins and outs of smuggling across the border, he took advantage of his experiences in order to deceive some other smugglers he knew. When he learned that a cargo of brandy would be coming through at a particular place, he hid in the bushes early one morning and waited. Before long he heard the smugglers going past, and, shaking the bushes, he yelled out in Romanian for them to stop: "Stuy! Stuy!" Believing the loud cries were coming from border guards, the men set their goods down and fled. David came out from behind the bushes, snatched up the booty, and then went out and sold it.

But his sham was soon discovered by the victims. When they asked around who had been selling liquor, everyone said it was David. The victims demanded justice from the *dayan*. In the synagogue, my cousin was insolent and flatly denied any wrongdoing to the judge, until finally the judge placed the tallith on David's head, wrapped the tefillin around his head and left arm, and made him swear on the Torah that he had nothing to do with the theft. Wrapped in the tefillin with his left hand on his chest, David let out a burst of nervous laughter and admitted his guilt. He was reprimanded in public and ordered to return any money made from the sale to his victims. Nevertheless, his adventures continued relentlessly until the vicissitudes of the war made border crossings almost impossible.

In the fall of 1940, the Germans put on pressure to bring the region of Transylvania under the control of the Hungarians. A single command changed our nationality and the name of our land which, under the Hungarians, became known as Erdely. No longer Romanian but now Hungarian, we were governed by the laws of a new regime.

That winter was very cold. Two opposing feelings circulated among the Jewish population. For those who were truly or only seemingly optimistic, ceding to Hungary wouldn't really change things much; in other words, it was business as usual. For others, the event meant confusion and disorder. The news on the radio was so perplexing that many people still did not know which side to take—now there were Zionists, Anarchists, Bolsheviks. My older brother Paisi, who was swayed by the Communists, believed that the war was going to establish a new Socialist order in Europe.

Thinking about my old schoolmates, I could laugh to myself because they, who had treated me as a foreigner, were now suffering the same humiliation under the Hungarians. Yet they were always better off than us, and if they had become second-class citizens, then we had dropped to third.

War brought many anomalies to daily life. People everywhere —artisans and professionals alike—were going hungry. In order to obtain rationed bread, it was necessary to wait in line from six o'clock in the morning until the afternoon. The Bulgarian baker had a daughter named Minda who was very pretty. I never tried to flirt with her because I was still hurt from my separation from Leah. There's a certain morbidity in suffering alone, but that's the way I was. Still, the baker's daughter was friendly to me. Despite boots and two pairs of heavy socks, I suffered excruciating pain from the cold standing in line in the middle of winter. Even breathing was difficult.

One morning, when the gray clouds were hanging low, the baker's daughter saw me standing in line. Yawning and rubbing those deep, dark eyes after baking bread since daybreak, she came over to me and said, "Sanyi, you don't have to wait in line, just come at five o'clock every day and I'll have bread waiting for you and your family."

As she walked away, I saw the steam radiating from her clothes as if she were an angel walking through the snow. I knew that angels came down to earth as human beings but, numb from the cold and half asleep from getting up so early, it all seemed like a dream. However, the pain of freezing feet kept me from dreaming very long. I don't think I ever thanked Minda for her kind gesture, but that afternoon she gave me the bread and repeated, "Don't forget, every day at five."

If it hadn't been for Minda, I would have had to wait long hours in line, freezing to death. The bread was always waiting for me, but not long after that I was drafted.

The Hungarian army took the city without firing a single shot. One winter morning I could see the constant movement of trucks crossing the bridge in front of our house. Like conquerors, the Hungarians were in a festive mood at first, but soon they began to ride roughshod over us. Upon their arrival, the Hungarian military immediately armed the local Hungarian population who had been living in Sighet, and they, in turn, began to harass us.

I became aware of the Hungarian cruelties when my brother Isaac told me that a young Jewish girl had been raped and murdered by eight Hungarian men. While the prayers in the synagogue and the predictions of the elders were hopeful, the taunting and humiliation had already become widespread: one day they would beat up an old man, on another they would assault young Jewish girls in public. Insults and abuse became an everyday occurrence.

It wasn't long before I, too, experienced the violence firsthand. One day, some Romanian friends and I were at the park with our girlfriends when some young Hungarians began to shout obscenities at the girls. One of the ruffians insulted Alexander's girlfriend and Alexander pounced on him, not expecting the guy to pull out a gun, hold him at bay, and make fun of his cowardice. I managed to calm Alexander down. We backed off and started to leave. They called us chickens. This taught me that not even the Romanians, such as my friend Alexander, were free from being pushed around.

A few days later, I was walking on the street with Farkas when three Hungarians cornered us and pushed us up against a wall for not walking single file. One of them cocked his pistol and pointed it at my head. I couldn't remember being so afraid. He shouted insults into my face. Cautiously, Farkas drew nearer to them and, with indifference, asked them why they would want to bother themselves with a stupid, uneducated peasant Jew. Those words, coming from a Jew, must have seemed funny to them. I had become the butt of their jokes and they let me go.

One afternoon, while I was at my brother Idel's barbershop waiting for five o'clock to come around so I could pick up the bread, I saw my father walk in front of four soldiers. They could tell he was a Jew because of his beard and the way he was dressed. We had not yet been forced to wear the yellow star that would be pinned to our clothing. The soldiers pushed and shoved him from one side of the street to the other. When he fell to the ground, they began kicking him viciously. He didn't cry out once.

"They're attacking our Dad!" I screamed.

Idel abandoned his customer, whose face was still lathered, grabbed his razor, and charged into the street. I followed him out. My temples were pounding with anger. A lopsided fight ensued because the soldiers were unarmed. Brandishing his

barber's razor, my brother leveled blows and slashes at whom-
ever was in sight. One soldier was cut on the arm and blood
began to spurt out everywhere. That gave us the advantage and
the soldiers fled. Trying to stand up, my father said, "Let them
go, it was just a fall."

We helped my father up and brushed off his clothes. Idel
calmly returned to work and continued shaving his customer
as if nothing had happened.

That evening, however, a military patrol showed up and broke
down our door with guns and bayonets. As they entered the
house, they told my mother that they had come to arrest Idel
for attacking Hungarian soldiers with a razor. They had barely
spoken when the seven of us brothers were already pouncing
on them. We disarmed them with blows to their heads with fists
and sticks, marched them out of the house at gunpoint, and kept
their guns.

An hour after the incident, while we were discussing it nervously and fearing retaliation, the military commander, who
was polite and pleasant, came to the house. "If you'll return the
weapons, nothing will happen to you," he said.

Although we were distrustful and my brother Emil was opposed, my father ordered us to return the weapons. We learned
some days later that the patrol that had come to our house had
been arrested by the commander because they had let "some
Jewish simpletons disarm the occupation forces."

That night the senior members of the family met to discuss
the situation: things were getting worse for Jews and the vivid
events of that day were an indication that something had to be
done quickly. However, my father was of the belief that things
would calm down once the war was over. "It will be over soon
and things will return to normal. We have always been a peaceful people and it is forbidden for us to kill."

My father, though not highly educated, respected the Talmud
and Jewish precepts to the letter of the law. Paisi, with revolution
gleaming in his eyes, would argue with my father. After a long

discussion that evening, it was decided that the best option for the moment was to send Idel into hiding in order to avoid retaliation; hence, he went to live for several weeks at my aunt's house across the river. He would still come home late at night and my mother gave him special things to eat and he'd take cheese and smoked meat back with him in a pouch. My sisters Blima and Pesil asked my mother where he was and she'd always tell them that he had gone on a trip.

Every Thursday, without exception, my mother would prepare cornmeal mush and seasonal dishes for about twenty indigent people, a work of charity that became so normal for us that we didn't even pay attention to those who came to eat on the patio at the house. Even after the war had started, her work continued, despite the lack of certain foods that were rationed.

My account of my relationship with Leah hasn't been as exact as it might have been. There's always something in a first love, so clear and diaphanous—painful too—that we try to hide it, to keep it from being sullied. Those experiences are like a bouquet of flowers that we want never to wither. To invoke these memories is to crumple the petals and toss them away forever; but I am compelled to recount certain things as dispassionately as possible.

My memories of Leah are associated with my own nakedness and vulnerability. As victims, we feel shame; yet if executioners felt shame they wouldn't be executioners but victims themselves. The difference lies in feeling shame.

Once my work was finished at the shop, I'd walk along the edge of the river on my way home. On warm days, I'd take the path down to the river to wash off the grime and sweat. I would undress near a pool of water that was protected by the foliage of nearby trees. At dusk, after washing off and refreshing myself, I would get dressed and continue my path back home.

At a dance held at the community hall one Sunday, a young girl came up to me and said, "I've seen you naked."

I gasped, then I turned red. I hadn't had much opportunity

to be around girls my age because my sisters, the ones who were the closest to me, were still small children. The mystery of the opposite sex was like a sea that had been barely traversed by only a few conversations and the suggestiveness of some movies I had seen.

I didn't even know the girl who had just spoken to me. Curious, I pulled her aside and asked, "What's your name?"

"Leah."

She looked at me with her beautiful dark shiny eyes. Again I blushed. Even though the conversation didn't last long, it seemed that she wanted to continue to play on my timidness. The music left me swaying to the beat of the couples crowding the dance floor. Leah nudged me to join in. I felt less embarrassed. Not only had I just learned her name, but I had discovered that she used to spy on me when I swam naked in the river. Her revealing awareness of my body made me fall in love with her. I wonder if we fall in love with someone who knows us the best.

Before we met, Leah used to watch me from the other side of the river. After we got to know each other, she would wait for me at the workshop gate near the river. We fell in love and she'd cross the bridge so we could be with each other. Soon we began to swim naked together in the river and I'd always get home late. Although my parents had learned from my older brothers what was going on, they didn't say anything to me until life for us had become so difficult that living itself was becoming dangerous. One evening my parents forced me to make a decision—the first painful decision of my life. My mother said to me, "We know you're involved with Leah Gitel and we wouldn't object to it if we knew that something long-lasting and permanent would come of it. But this is not the case. What if the girl gets pregnant? Have you thought about that?"

I listened but avoided looking at her.

"And Leah's aunt is very poor," added my father. "Your mother feeds her every Thursday."

"I know they're poor," I rebutted.

My mother sat down in front of me and took my hand. "Your father doesn't want you to think that their economic status is the problem, but you must understand that he's trying to make you understand that these are difficult times for all of us. Not being financially secure would just make things worse. These days, even well-to-do Jews are going hungry. Shortages are widespread. No one knows how long the war will last. For you, less responsibility means less agony. Don't think about the future right now, because we don't have one."

My mother spoke with gentleness, although she knew I was rebellious and generally ignored anything imposed on me. "If you consider what's best for her and really care about her, then you'll end this relationship right now. You're too young to get married. Under the present circumstances, your marriage would probably become a calamity: war can separate all of us."

I thought about it all night long. The problem didn't only involve us. In my decision, perhaps a selfish one, Leah had no say. When I finally told her that it was best for both of us to break off our relationship, she resigned herself to the decision without really wanting to accept it. Even though I was destroying a relationship that had made me happy, events were already occurring that cut short my sorrow over breaking up and forced me ruthlessly down paths I wouldn't wish for anyone.

It was raining and it had turned dark. Pedaling my bicycle hard, I hurried across the city in order to meet with a group of young people at ten o'clock. We had formed a clandestine Jewish organization in Sighet, and the leader had decided on retaliation. I wasn't completely aware of what specific wrong had been done to us; all I knew was that I had received an order through a companion of mine to meet at ten o'clock. We were going to get rid of an anti-Semite.

While I pedaled in the rain, I was feeling no regrets, for I hadn't chosen this path that my life was taking. Ever since the arrival of the Hungarians in Sighet, cases of anti-Semitism had become widespread. An anti-Semitic activist group supported secretly by the army had been committing hostile, even murderous acts, yet its members went unpunished. Young Jews, organized into small groups of six plus a leader, would carry out a basic principle of the Bible: An eye for an eye and a tooth for a tooth. Each member of the group was assigned a number and would carry out his order, be it execution, transportation, surveillance, or providing backup in case of retreat.

Hardly any lights in the city were on; ever since the war had begun, electricity was rationed and, fearing air raids, the city was left in darkness. As I rode along, I kept checking my pocket to make sure I still had my brass knuckles. When I arrived at our meeting place a few minutes before ten, my companions were already waiting for me. From our hiding place, I could see inside the tavern: candelabras with tallow candles provided light and I could hear music playing.

The six of us, all Jews wearing kerchiefs to cover our faces, took up our posts near the tavern. No one said a word. We each had our brass knuckles ready and only the executioner carried a club. The technique for executing an anti-Semite who had killed a Jew was simple: a blow to the back of the neck. We weren't allowed to use metal objects. A blunt instrument would not only bring instant death but also give the appearance of a fall or some drunken street fight.

A group of Hungarians staggered out of the bar. We didn't move. The guilty person was not among them. Then one of us said a prayer, but I never knew who it was. The prayers seemed to cleanse our guilty consciences. It was barely drizzling now. Just as my heart became heavier and heavier, the tavern door opened again and a slovenly soldier stumbled outside, hanging onto a prostitute. No signal from our leader. Even though I was getting drowsy, I went over what they had told me to do: "When you strike the enemy, never look at his face."

It must have been midnight when someone nudged me. I tensed up and looked at the fogged windows of the tavern. A silhouette came out of the dim doorway, turned the corner, and started singing some Hungarian ditty. We approached him silently, but his singing muffled the sounds of our movements. We got so close to him that we could have picked his pockets. Thump, the sound of the blow. Like a falling tree, the Hungarian collapsed on the wet pavement. Unaware that he was being followed, numbed by the alcohol, he didn't even moan. Dislocated neck. No one looked at his face. We shoved his body into a jute sack and four of us picked him up. Crossing the city with a dead body in a sack was risky business. Even though darkness favored us, night patrols were always out and about. I led the group on my bicycle, scouting for danger. After seemingly going around in circles, we finally got out of the city. We cut through some trees and finally arrived at the river's edge, whereupon we threw the body into the river. From the light of the moon, I could see it float away like a tree trunk. The river's swift current was our guarantee that our victims would eventually end up in the Danube.

But then a plan to disperse our clandestine groups was put into effect, and our reprisals ended. The men who had reached eighteen, or who were already older, were drafted, and those of us who were younger had to attend premilitary training. During one day and two nights each week we were ordered to guard strategic places—public buildings, bridges, and churches. We had been taught to sound the alarms in case of an air raid, and we had been trained in civil defense in the event of air bombings, fire, or sabotage. Blackouts had become more frequent and curfew was set for eight o'clock in the evening. While on guard one night, I heard footsteps nearby. I shouted "Halt!" and asked the person to identify himself. Like every other response, the only thing I heard were insults in Hungarian. I landed a blow to the Hungarian's back, sending him to the pavement where he lay sprawled out for a few minutes. That incident sent me to jail for two days. I had not complied with my obligations: I was supposed to protect the Hungarian population, not attack it.

Overt discrimination against the Jews led us to realize that we had to defend ourselves at all costs and that we couldn't wait for others to help us. As Jewish men were sent off to boot camp, the clandestine groups disbanded. Now everyone had to fend for themselves and for their families.

One morning I was waiting my turn for a medical examination that was a part of the required premilitary training. I was seated with several others. Suddenly the office door swung open and a large man, dressed in civilian clothes, entered the room. He was exceedingly arrogant. Everyone stood up except me; I thought someone would call my name first. Suddenly the man kicked me in the leg and shouted, "Haven't they taught you to salute? Stand up!"

So I stood up, but I punched him in the face so hard that he fell down. He got up and went into the office. After a while, they called me in. As soon as I entered the room, they closed the door and six Hungarian soldiers savagely set to work to put an end to my disrespect: they repeatedly kicked my legs, my body, and my face. Between each blow, I could hear him saying, "I am Second Lieutenant Vigola Yanchi, you Jewish pig. Every Jew must salute Vigola Yanchi. The disobedient ones, like you, end up in the gallows."

During the beating, I struggled to remember the name and face of my tormentor. Frantically I tried to protect my body from the blows, but soon I went limp like a sack of wheat. Defenseless, I fell to the ground, but then they would lift me up again and continue beating me until I finally lost consciousness.

When I came to, I found myself lying in the snow on the grounds of the barracks. Jewish friends had notified my family that I had been arrested and beaten for not saluting Second Lieutenant Vigola Yanchi.

I was thirsty and my head buzzed like the blades of a windmill. I crawled over to a wall and curled up to get warm. Each time I tried to move, the pain was so strong that I can't remember how long it took me to get to that wall. Since my body was numb, the pain became concentrated in my head, but something like electric shocks throughout my nerves told me that I was still alive.

I was shivering all over and felt nauseated. Clots of blood had dried on my face. I was miserable. I took a handful of snow and rubbed it on my face. It burned. I looked around to see if I was alone. The world around me had turned dull gray.

Then two soldiers carrying rifles with fixed bayonets came outside, put me on all fours, loaded me down with twenty-four pairs of skis, and ordered me to crawl. I tried to stand up but only fell to the ground. Again they lifted me onto all fours, but this time they tied the skis to my back with a rope. Pricked by the tips of the bayonets in my loins, I began to crawl. By then it was daybreak.

Escorted by the two soldiers, my march began by leaving the barracks and going through the streets of Sighet. Everything was closed — the park, the synagogue, the pharmacy, the tavern. Some early risers, on their way with their coupons to stand in line for bread rations, scarcely looked at me. Romanians and Jews alike, they had the same pain of war etched into their faces. I hunched over under the weight of the skis. My hands were freezing as I clung to the wooden tips of the skis to keep my balance. With each step, I felt pain in my hips. The early morning sun tinted the houses in Sighet a yellowish hue.

We walked out of the city. The countryside was white and the trees extended their shadows over the snow. Trying to take my mind off the pain, I imagined that my shadow looked like a donkey's. At the beginning of our march the two soldiers were on either side of me, but outside the city they walked behind me. My destination was a military post some ten miles away.

We had been walking about two hours when the Hungarians took some pieces of smoked bacon out of their backpacks and casually began to chew on them. I began to count each step I took, but that only made the pain worse. While the guards sat down to eat their breakfast, I just kept walking straight ahead

until I couldn't see them anymore; even though I stopped to rest,
I was unable to sit down with the skis strapped to my back, so
I stuck them into the snow and leaned up against them, which
gave some relief. I scooped up some snow and ate it. Those small
comforts—the short rest and the snow—seemed like heaven
to me.

When I saw them beginning to approach me, I started walking again. I felt a little better. The soldiers spoke in Hungarian
and acted as if they didn't even see me. For them, the walk was
an excursion outside the barracks. When I couldn't bear the
weight anymore or had to climb a hill, I got down on all fours
and crawled like an animal, until my hands froze in the snow.
The fields were deserted, and I could see farmers' houses off in
the distance, encrusted in the snow like jeweled inlay.

Now the sun was beaming down from overhead and the sweat
had begun to seep into my contusions. The stinging was fierce.
We stopped. While they ate lunch, I managed to rest while still
standing up. When one of them tossed me a piece of bread, I
devoured it in silence.

When nightfall came, icy winds started blowing hard. At that
point, I think I was about to collapse, but we finally arrived at a
small military post called Hoszumezö in Hungarian, or Campulung in Romanian. They unloaded the skis from my back but
the weight clung insistently to my shoulders. I felt sharp pains
in my ribs when I coughed, like Beril, who had suffered from
TB. Cold and shaking all over, I had a fever. But I continued to
stomp the frozen ground with fury, trying to bring feeling back
to my feet. Each time I jumped up and down, the name of Vigola
Yanchi echoed in my head. As my eyes clouded over, darkness
set in.

By the time I returned to Sighet, I was all but dead. The name
of Second Lieutenant Vigola Yanchi had been etched into my
brain. For three straight weeks, my mother nursed me back to
health, and by the time I had recovered from the ordeal the first
detachment of German soldiers had been assigned to the city.

4

My grandfather became the first victim. His image had long faded from my memory until, many years after the war, it came back to me when I visited Rome in 1973. Earlier, in Jerusalem in 1968, I had searched for someone whom I had nearly forgotten while I was in the concentration camps. Despite our prayers and love for him during the good and bad times, my memory of him had been blocked out as if a handful of ashes had been thrown into my eyes, blinding me.

In 1948, I left Europe forever, and suddenly I found myself living in one of the most beautiful countries of South America: Ecuador. During my years in this Andean country, I have worked hard not only to survive but also to forget my nightmares; yet, no matter how hard I would try to erase the Holocaust from my mind, the expressionless faces of the Indians constantly reminded me of those times of interminable torture. On a hacienda where the barren lands reach over twelve thousand feet, the Indians, whose daily lives are nothing more than pain and suffering, would remind me of the affliction that I had experienced in the German concentration camps. My decision to leave my job as administrator of the hacienda and to take up residence in the city of Riobamba, where I worked as a traveling salesman, helped me to escape those faces tortured with hunger and slavery. The Indians' hapless state and the magnitude of their physical and mental suffering made me wonder if I were not once again trapped in the camps at Auschwitz and Jaworzno. It seemed as if the demented faces of the Holocaust would follow me wherever I went. I was continually tormented by those images of life in death, but I always attempted to mitigate that miserable situation.

I hadn't returned to Europe since my departure in 1948, so I decided to travel there with my wife Frida in 1973. Somehow I was still alive, when so many others had died in the camps; I needed to overcome feelings of guilt. I hadn't even considered returning to Europe; perhaps I was afraid to confront my memories. My children, however, convinced me that returning to my origins would be healthy for me.

In 1973, finally, Frida and I flew to Rome. After we were settled at our hotel, it was a matter of simply becoming another tourist in the capital of the gentiles. Italy was not unfamiliar to me: I had been there in 1946.

My search through a labyrinth of memories didn't consist of reliving the past, which would have been masochistic; rather, it consisted of discovering whether God continued to be persecuted in Europe. I was obsessed with the idea of discovering God through others, through all those images, the dogma, and so many beliefs and old traditions surrounding that Being who had been destroyed in my heart. God, for me, had been crushed in Europe and now I was searching for Him, the One who had been so close yet so distant from me.

Despite Frida's protests, there wasn't a church, synagogue, temple, sanctuary, or tabernacle that I didn't manage to visit. She preferred to go shopping, visit museums and art galleries, attend shows, or walk along some famous avenue. Although she wasn't entirely convinced, Frida agreed to accompany me in my meandering through those religious mazes.

When I visited the catacombs and saw the wrapped, parchment-like bodies of the sacred mummies, I thought I was reliving visions of Block 8 in Auschwitz. Frida said I was only tormenting myself. I hadn't realized that those visions of persecution could not be exorcised from my soul. I had lost my faith in humanity. My faith in God was on shaky ground, but I continued to pray that I would meet God once again.

After a few days in Rome, we went to the Vatican and entered the monumental basilica where Saint Peter is supposed to be buried. Pious Christians were there demonstrating the strength of their beliefs and respect, the very same virtues that I was struggling to acquire. Suddenly, in one of my wanderings through a church permeated with mystic warmth, I came face to face with my grandfather, Mordecai Hers. Directly in front of me, I saw his messianic beard, that stony face, those penetrating eyes. As I grew pale, Frida took me by the arm and whispered, "Is there something wrong, Sanyi?"

I couldn't respond. We were standing in front of Michelangelo's Moses and the vision of my grandfather had just reappeared in my memory. I imagined myself standing next to the old man and I then could see him clearly at the *cheder*, giving me an apple that he had bought from an old woman who used to stack them in pyramids down at the corner.

That vision brought back the memories of his ill-fated death. It happened for no reason at all. My grandfather was living in the village of Iapa, about three miles from Sighet. At the time, he must have been about seventy years old. He had been a blacksmith all his life, and even in old age he possessed that strength required of blacksmiths who gave shape to red-hot metal. After retiring, he would trek back and forth to Sighet to see his daughters. It was the natural thing for him to do, for it kept the old man busy. He would visit us often, whiling away the time with his many grandchildren. Watching them grow up while he grew old provided a world of peace for the man, who was like the old tree from whose branches new buds had sprouted.

One morning, on his customary walk to Sighet, my grandfather was brutally knocked down by a Hungarian soldier who hit him with his rifle butt. The blow shattered several ribs and damaged a lung. Gasping, he was taken to our house. His face was the color of white marble and his long, abundant white beard that had turned yellow on the ends rested flatly on his chest. During the few moments that the pain would allow him to breathe consciously, he prayed in Hebrew in a low voice. A few weeks later, he died. Although we didn't realize it at the time, his death was the first in a long, painful succession of deaths in my family.

By 1941, German troops were arriving in Sighet, now a strategic point for crossing the Carpathians to the Russian front. A German detachment had taken over the local military barracks

and soon they began giving orders to the civil authorities and
the Hungarian military.

The Germans had devised a plan to destroy our clandestine organizations. On their arrival, the Nazis gave orders to round up young Jewish men who were eighteen years or older. This order directly affected my brothers Paisi, Idel, and Isaac, as well as my adopted brother, Schmiel. As a result, very few young people ever managed to head off in other directions by crossing the border and the Black Sea. Once they had been rounded up, they became part of an unarmed military squadron that dug ditches and antitank trenches on the Russian front. Near the end of the war, the Hungarians turned these young men over to the German army, after which they were taken to the concentration camps. Very few survived.

One morning, Schmiel was ordered to appear at the barracks. The reaction of that strong, hard-working man, who had helped support our family, was unpredictable and tragic. It was noontime and everyone was preparing for lunch. Suddenly, the sound of thunder resonated throughout our wooden house. When I heard the noise outside, I ran to the porch and into the house. The spectacle was horrible: his face was turning blue and his bloodshot eyes were popping out of their sockets as he swung back and forth, kicking his legs, hanging by a rope from a beam in the attic. I ran over to him and tried to push him up so he wouldn't choke. I screamed for help, but it seemed as if my voice had become stuck in my throat. Schmiel was just too heavy for me to hold, but I pushed up on his legs, closed my eyes, and started screaming again with all my might. My voice filled the entire attic and the echo rebounded everywhere like grotesque laughter. My father appeared in the door and lifted up the body. He told me to cut the rope with a knife, then we placed Schmiel's unconscious body on the wooden floor.

While he was convalescing, I didn't dare go into his room to see him. I was terrified to look into his death-filled eyes. When he began to wander around the house in a morbid trance, I avoided him and made sure never to find myself alone with him. Once he began to feel better, he joined us at mealtime, but I wouldn't dare to lift my eyes from my plate. Schmiel was miserable and he hated me for saving his life.

After that failed suicide attempt, his hatred for life was what stood out about his reclusive personality. Years later, my friend Baruch Farkas told me that Schmiel had been sent against his wishes to the Yugoslav border, where he was recruited by the partisans. He would always volunteer to take the lead into battle, risking his life with the slightest excuse, hoping to die. And he did — on the banks of the Danube, at the Iron Gate Dam on the border between Romania and Yugoslavia, ending what he had started when he tried to commit suicide in our house. Having no respect for life is something I've never understood, and I hope his hatred doesn't follow me through eternity. Paradoxically, while Schmiel chose to die for not being able to find meaning in life, many Jews who loved life were sent to their death.

It all began with a German decree: the Jews had to provide documents proving their identity. Although we didn't understand what it meant, that first step set in motion the disappearance of a first wave of people, especially those who were not from Sighet, such as Jewish refugees from Poland and Czechoslovakia, and other undocumented residents who were deported to Polish Galicia. So one morning all Jewish foreigners were taken to the train station. They walked slowly, submissively, in icy silence. Carrying only small bags, they had given up all their possessions. Their faces communicated the worry and fear that had supplanted the laughter and enjoyment they had experienced living in Sighet. The Romanians-turned-Hungarians looked at them with distrust and exulted in their own good fortune. But I saw children crying of thirst and grasping their parents' legs in desperation. As for the Jews who were from Sighet, I saw in their faces relief that they were not the ones being deported. I saw abandonment, resignation, and helplessness in from departing. But I also heard others express hope:

"They'll have a better place to live."

"Sighet is so full of poor people. Now they'll have the opportunity to travel."

"They'll get work and have bread for their children."

But few actually believed those empty promises. The truth of the matter was that they were not leaving to find a better future, but rather they were being denied their future forever.

They were escorted to the train station and crowded into cattle cars. Overwhelmed and crushed by the ensuing chaos, family members clutched each other for fear of being separated or lost among the multitude. But no one dared break ranks either; that would have meant suicide because everywhere machine guns were pointed at them. Unable to comprehend what was happening, the frightened, sobbing children followed their parents. Once everyone was aboard, the doors were locked from the outside. As the train huffed and puffed to pull away, the squeaking train wheels signaled a bad omen. Under a cloud of smoke, the train started to move. The onlookers dispersed and went about their business. But, like a thick fog, an impenetrable feeling of doubt and despair permeated the air.

No one had time to continue thinking about those poor souls, for they were forgotten amid the urgency of our own problems. The movement of German troops and the growing—and ever more bloody—hostilities against the Jews fueled our panic. Images of the deportees lingered—the grimaces; the crying children, desperate to satisfy their thirst; the agony in the sullen eyes of the deportees; the smoke of the train; the long line of cattle cars; the futile good-byes, now frozen in time; the prayers in the synagogue; the sheer hopelessness emanating from the silence of that procession of shadows.

Totally unaware of what was actually happening, everyone seemed unconcerned. But then, unexpectedly, it happened: first, the sudden banging on the door at night; then people going around spying on each other; still others listening silently to the radio; those trying to eat but getting choked up; and everyone living on empty stomachs. Finally, the anguish and desperation became so strong that not even the soothing flow of the Tisa or prayers could allay our worries.

It became normal to trust no one, to hoard foodstuffs, to anticipate the worst, to feel shivers down one's spine because of confusing news that brought both hope and fear. As we were drafted into premilitary training, the cancer of the war extended to those of us who had not yet turned eighteen. As Jews, we no longer knew what the concept of homeland meant, for the place where we were living had been converted into a living hell.

The soldiers charged with guarding us during the premilitary training used fear as a mechanism of control. The most common form of breaking us down consisted of hitting us with rifle butts and stomping on us with their boot heels. In extreme cases of noncompliance, one of us would be hauled up with his hands behind his back and hung from a tree with his toes barely touching the ground. It was impossible to withstand that position for more than five minutes. When the young person would faint, they'd throw a bucket of water on him and string him up again. And so the torture would continue mercilessly.

While this was typical of the way the young Jewish men were treated, old people were persecuted in other ways: their stores were ransacked, their windows were broken, they were yelled and screamed at, they were denied knowing where their children were, their food was rationed, they were prohibited from going to the synagogue and speaking in Yiddish, the women were insulted, and both men and women were questioned and jailed without cause. Their homes were broken into, they were never to look up, they had to greet the invaders in friendly fashion, they had to breathe in fear and let it flow through their blood.

Time passed like a slow unavoidable blindness; darkness was taking over our lives. The only brief moments of peace seemed

to come when our parents would repeat, "This, too, shall pass.
Let us not lose faith in God. We are still alive and we are still together."

One night, however, a Jewish family of five who had escaped from Galicia came to our house. Veiled in agony, their faces were marked with death. Between coughs and deep sighs, the father explained how they had survived. After the train crossed through Hungary into Poland, they were loaded into the backs of trucks and taken to a forest near the city of Kolomea. Every last one of those deported Jews was forced to dig a common grave with picks and shovels. They even had to scoop out the dirt with their hands. Pointing their machine guns at them, the ss used them for target practice. After the rat-tat-tat of the machine-gun fire had ceased, there came isolated pistol shots here and there to finish off those who were still alive. Nothing else could be heard.

One member of that family was the father's beautiful sixteen-year-old daughter. The ss raped her, beat her, and left her unconscious, but her parents and their two small children managed to escape, crawling among hundreds of the victims of the massacre, whose bodies were still warm. After hiding in the trees nearby, they were able to rescue their daughter. For months afterward, still together, the family wandered aimlessly. They avoided getting caught by traveling at night and resting during the day. In a state of desolation, they showed up at our house and told us their painful story. Now they wanted to escape by way of the Black Sea and tried to convince us to go with them.

Confronted by the prospect of leaving Sighet and abandoning our home and fields, we all just stared at each other. My three older brothers and Schmiel had already been drafted and we had no idea where they were. Our parents told us that soon the war was going to be over and my brothers would be returning home. After that family had finished talking—their eyes were full of terror and their souls destroyed by the eternal condemnation of being Jews — my father explained to us that the possibility, which was highly remote, of escaping from Sighet was not an option. He said it was not a choice open to me, even though I had been considering it.

Since my older brothers were gone, I told my father I would help on the farm, and I assured him that I didn't intend to run away or abandon my mother and younger siblings, Saul, Samuel, Blima, and Pesil. I have never regretted my decision, even though I didn't know what those responsibilities would involve.

It was early winter 1942, and with the help of my father and Saul, I began to oversee the farm operation: trimming the trees, protecting the apple crop from rabbits, feeding the cattle, drying the animal feed, repairing the farm tools, and taking care of a million and one details that took me away from other important responsibilities. With my brothers gone, I was the oldest in the family and I had to carry out my obligations to the best of my ability.

Whenever I'd go into town I'd run into a wretched old man who seemed to have gone crazy. He would talk to passers-by about the horrors committed in Galicia. Though no one wanted to believe him, his words seemed to touch raw nerves.

Secretly, we would listen to the radio about the advances and retreats at the battle front. With each hint that the Germans were close to surrendering, our hopes soared. But on the Russian front, the fighting was fierce and my mother would imagine that her sons were either dead, buried in the snow, or wounded in some unknown faraway place. Unable to help them, she would break down and cry.

Despite the harassment from the Christian population and the Hungarian police, our farm kept us from going hungry. But we made do without many things. The majority of the gentiles believed that once they were rid of the Jews they would inherit our possessions; and, indeed, they began to benefit from our misfortunes.

The year 1944 started off well: the German army had retreated from Russia. That spring we'd hear people repeat over and over, "Soon the war will be over." However, such hope didn't translate into positive changes for us; on the contrary, it wasn't long before Saul and I were drafted. By then, my mother had said good-bye to five of her sons. Since we had already received some premilitary training, it wasn't difficult for us to begin to take orders.

After getting settled into our barracks, we received orders to march some thirty-five miles to Korosmezö, a town nestled at the base of the Carpathians, where we were to set up quarters in the town's schools and synagogues. We went to sleep early that night because we had to rest up for the work that faced us the next day.

It was early when we were awakened with curt, threatening orders:

"Five minutes to wash up!"

"No yawning in rank!"

"Stand straight!"

"Are you deaf, you Jewish shits?"

I was assigned to construct kitchens, while others built latrines and organized work camps. Now, on top of the tiring and unending work, premilitary training meant insults, endless orders, and even physical abuse.

The purpose of that military activity was nothing more than a pretext to separate us from our families with the least resistance; also, it was to build the ghettos—fenced-off areas of a city where Jews were forced to live. Soon, however, we discovered their true intentions. Every day we transported boulders from the river and moved them from place to place for no apparent reason. The officer in charge assured us that the rocks were necessary to build trenches and other fortifications for the rear guard. "You people are building the second front. You will save the nation from invasion." But these and other meaningless statements didn't generate much enthusiasm.

Despite the deplorable—and scarce—food, and the little time we had to rest, we were not treated too harshly. Put together, the three daily meals they gave us didn't even add up to a single breakfast. Saul and I had set up sleeping quarters in one of the synagogues and, between the two of us, we tried to make the best of things. Fortunately, because of the hard work we were used to on the farm, our bodies withstood the harsh labor. At night, there wasn't as much vigilance because sleeping time was as important as the air we breathed. Also, no one would have tried to escape; the fear of being caught was too great. We couldn't abandon the camp altogether because of the reprisals they would take against family members back home or against friends in the barracks.

Nevertheless, I left the camp one night in search of food. My nocturnal adventure depended upon my returning without their noticing my brief absence: to be discovered by a patrol would have meant the end for me. But I left the camp anyway and followed the silvery river that was reflecting the light of the moon. After walking about three miles I came upon a small village. I walked cautiously down the dirt streets, trying to make sure no one was watching. I knocked on several doors but no one showed a face. The barn doors were wide open, and there were no signs of any animals. Amid the silence, only a sick and hungry dog was sniffing around for something to eat.

Then I saw a light coming from a hut off in the distance, so I went up to the door and knocked lightly. After a few moments, a small, hunchbacked man appeared, bearing a club. When we saw each other, both of us jumped back in surprise. Hoping he wouldn't attack me, I offered him a few coins. I explained to him that I had come in search of food. He grumbled, "You're not going to find anything here, sonny."

I explained that I had escaped from the encampment up the road and, like him, I was a Jew. His clothes gave him away. Speaking in Yiddish, I asked, "What has happened to the people in this village?"

He told me that everyone was dead. They had been buried at the edge of the river. An icy jolt penetrated my bones, petrifying me. The old man had survived a massacre because he had fallen asleep in the barn, and during their search, the soldiers hadn't discovered him. When he awoke to the noise of gunfire, the riddled bodies of his grandchildren, children, and neighbors were strewn about on the ground, spurting blood from their wounds. He was the only witness.

I left the village in a trance of fear. The few potatoes that the old man gave me bounced around in my woolen pouch. As if to smirk, the moon's reflection danced on the waters of the river. The others who bunked in the synagogue with me were still asleep. I got into bed but I was unable to close my eyes. The next morning I told Saul about what had happened. Refusing to believe me, he stuck to the illusion that we were really working to build a second front.

One night my friend Farkas appeared at the synagogue as if he were one of the new draftees. He had brought some cheese and smoked goose legs from my mother; he also had news from home. After we talked for about half an hour, he had to leave, so I asked him to tell our family that we were still alive and well.

After making his care package last over two weeks, we finally had to finish off the cheese because it had acquired such a foul odor. That day a guard stomped into the synagogue and shouted my name. "Who is Isacovici from Sighet?"

I went over and identified myself. He said he had a message for me from my friend Alexander Nedelcovici, the schoolmate who had once spit on me. "Alexander Nedelcovici says not to worry about your parents and the rest of your family. They're fine. They're in the ghetto."

As the guard walked away, the word "ghetto," the meaning of which I didn't know at the time, sent my mind spinning. Naturally, my concern for my family began to grow. All kinds of confusing visions swirled around in my head. I didn't understand the new path upon which I was embarking.

After three months of going hungry and doing routine work, we were ordered to return home. We packed up our belongings and made preparations to leave. With our little bags on our shoulders, we began our march at dawn. I thought about our farm and the work that awaited me. "In wartime, the only thing that's important is land," I repeated to myself. I gave a lot of thought to what lay ahead upon my return to Sighet.

My sisters' faces came to mind; by now they were old enough that I could depend on them to help out. Saul, who was walking next to me and had grown taller than me, talked about how he was going to help me on the farm.

5

In the early spring of 1944 the Fascists seized power in Hungary and the government immediately sanctioned German occupation of the country. With the same swiftness that Nazi troops and their heavy equipment, along with the implacable ss, began to arrive in Sighet, news about Nazi assaults on Jews in Budapest spread throughout the city. Just days before, rumors that had generated hope about impending disaster for the Germans quickly evaporated, giving rise to widespread panic among the Jewish population. Sighet, the gateway for crossing the Carpathians, was overflowing with military personnel and war materiel.

Their shiny black uniforms made the ss officers look like crows or sinister gravediggers. Their impeccable dress, self-confidence, steely gaze, and stolid expression, topped off by their peaked officer caps, contrasted with our frail humanity—timid, fragile, insecure.

The presence of the ss, famous for their dogged obedience in carrying out executions, terrified us. Life for the average person became precarious. Soon the order was sent out for all Jews to wear a yellow star in a visible place on their clothing. Then Jewish businesses had to display in their shop windows an ignominious sign in the form of the fateful word "Jude," along with the Star of David. Hungarian soldiers, almost always accompanied by their Germans counterparts, would enter those stores and ransack them. To them, a Jewish business meant the freedom to loot it and take whatever they wanted. Owners who hid their merchandise were treated even worse: they were beaten and forced to reveal their cache.

Prohibited from frequenting public places or mixing with the gentiles, Jews were soon confined to their houses. Windows were nailed shut. Barbed wire became a familiar sight, and then wooden fences were built around certain sectors of the city. Guards were placed at the entrances. The ghettos.

Passover came and went before I returned to Sighet. With

the Nazi skull and crossbones insignia everywhere, our people stayed in their homes and celebrated our forefathers' liberation from Egyptian bondage. On a Friday, mass confinement was initiated.

That same morning, as my mother was kneading dough for the Sabbath challah, three Hungarian policemen carrying clubs and sporting feathers in their caps forced their way into our home. They crossed the patio, went up the steps of the porch, and stomped into the house: they were there to arrest my family.

My mother, whose first gray hairs were hidden underneath a kerchief that covered her head, would not be intimidated. She stood up to them with more courage than strength, defending her possessions — her home and the memories contained therein. But the policemen continued to strike her until she could no longer fight back. With a few small bundles of clothes, blankets, and food — only the "essentials," she was told — my family initiated its journey to the ghetto. My sisters Blima and Pesil, who were still so young, didn't understand what was happening; they just held onto each other, sobbing and hiding behind my parents. As he walked, Samuel felt angry but powerless to do anything.

They walked under guard past curious Hungarians who watched the procession of Jews marching toward the ghetto. The period of skirmishes, reprisals, and pretense was over. A new stage had begun: massive deportation. At first it took on the look of a simple excursion for the purpose of conducting preliminary evictions, but it quickly became open, institutionalized extermination.

Samuel told me about it when I arrived from the encampment. It was early one morning. The house had been left wide open. The street sweeper calmly walked in and took the bread my mother was kneading. The coals in the oven were still red-hot but, like the presence of the persons who were living in the house, the coals soon died out. I asked him straight out, "How could you have let this happen?"

Saul and I had left the encampment before dawn. The march back was boring and tiring. Our hopes had been dashed. As we passed through Korosmezö, I began to feel so sad and tired that my senses were numb. The empty streets were under heavy guard by Hungarian soldiers. The principal thoroughfare, which was about five miles long, was devoid of civilians; only the wind dared to explore the alleys and back streets while at the same time battering the shutters of the empty houses. A barren sight, it was as if the city had been decimated by plague. The sense of utter devastation made me apprehensive as we marched through that uninhabited, lifeless city.

Our impressions of Sighet were even worse. The windows of the Jewish houses had been painted with lime. The stark white color reminded me of the eyes of a person who was dying, like our city. The inhabitants of Hungarian homes would part the curtains in the windows and watch us march glumly—enigmatically—through the city. As we arrived at the ghetto, they opened the gate and we passed through like sheep returning to the fold. Once inside, the recent arrivals—groups of young men, all of whom were less than eighteen years of age—began searching for their families. Despite the happiness of the reunions, our embraces and brief conversations communicated an unsettling and sorrowful mood. The gloom was marked by fear emanating from everyone's anguish.

The Nazis had planned everything down to the last detail: the young Jewish men had been drafted, the leaders of the clandestine movements had been assassinated, the reserves had been ordered back to duty, and others were to report back to the barracks. Only old men and women and children remained behind in order to keep the German enterprise operating. During the time we were gone, all of our people from Sighet and the surrounding towns had been rounded up and sent to two principal ghettos. From that moment on, trains pulling their cattle cars began their daily departures.

Saul and I went around asking our neighbors if they had seen our family, and although outside spring was in the air, we found them crammed into a depressingly small, dim room. Even though my four older brothers weren't there to be with us, we greeted each other happily. Despite the scarcity, my mother used the food that she had jealously guarded to prepare a meal for us.

Anxiety had accumulated in the ghetto until life became unbearable. Privacy had all but disappeared: several families were forced to live together in the same house and share the same bathroom, kitchen, and living areas. Compliant neighbors, weakened by the fear of death, became informants and collaborated with the Germans. Taking advantage of the new situation, the Hungarians became the new owners of a large part of the city. They took over shops, stores, houses, and farms, acting as if they were the conquerors of a war that had been won without firing a single shot. Soon the ghetto began to empty itself of large numbers of people, but only to be replenished with others. Every day groups would be taken away and every day new families would arrive from nearby towns; while some were leaving the ghettos and forced to walk to the cattle cars, other convoys of Jews were arriving. Like some bizarre boarding house for foreigners, entire families came and went ceaselessly.

The Jewish Council, or *Judenrat*, would enforce the German orders. Without knowing, or wanting to know, the council ended up collaborating with the Germans' plans. The trains ran night or day. Council members propagated the rumor that we were being transported to work on farms and factories in Germany in order to remove us from the battle front. In spite of the hopeful predictions of the Jewish Council, which some people tended to believe, we still became frightened by other rumors concerning the real purpose of the trips. The strong believers clung to hope; the incredulous ones prepared themselves for an uncertain destiny.

In order to fill each cattle car with the exact number of people that was required, some families were separated. Those left behind would wander aimlessly about the ghetto as if one of their

limbs had been hacked off and they were trying to find it. Those
who tried to escape were gunned down along the fences as a
lesson to others who might try the same. Together, the lack of
space in the ghetto, the growing fears, and the outright distrust
allowed no one to make friends. As new people arrived every
day and others left, faces were constantly changing.

The anxiety crippled us. My younger sisters were the only
ones with enough energy and will power to play in the dirt with
an old, faded doll. The women spent their time mending winter clothes, and the men, humiliated by worry that paralyzed
them from taking action, wandered about trying to get news of
what was going on; by finding out, they reasoned, they could
speculate and make predictions about what the future held for
them. But the news and the rumors were so contradictory that
no one had any real idea of what was going on. To avoid becoming despondent, we clung to false promises about an attractive
future.

My family was on one of the last shipments to leave; but since
I had been at the military camp, my own stay in the ghetto hadn't
lasted more than a week. We looked at each other without ut-
tering a word. I thought about the best and the worst that could
happen to us. I looked at my cherished loved ones with grief
and apprehension. I wondered what I could do for them, and my
helplessness only served to exasperate me more. I contemplated
my mother, whose hair had turned a dull gray. As I looked at my
father, he saw in me the same feeling of frustration that I saw in
him. Blima, now ten years old, had blond hair and blue eyes,
while Pesil, who was six, had brown hair and brown eyes; while
they played in silence, I could see that the smiles on their faces
had been snatched away. Samuel, still a teenager big for his age,
paced back and forth, vexed by his inability to understand the
adult world. Saul, for his part, was extremely nervous.

During those days in the ghetto, I remember being confused
about a lot of things. I thought that if they took us away to work,
the four men of the family could work very hard in order to

support the family. I had been swayed by what the Jewish Council had said, so I didn't realize at the time that they had propagated nothing but vain illusions and were leading me down a path away from reality. During my stay, I managed to talk to one of our neighbors, Moses Fischer, who told me to flee the ghetto quickly. "Now that you are the oldest child of the family, pack a few things and gather up your younger brothers and sisters, along with my son Alter, and flee to the mountains. No matter what happens out there, you will manage to survive. I would go with you but, you see, I'm old and I've got TB. I cough all the time, and one of my coughing fits would give us away. You know very well no one is going to survive this. What are you waiting for?"

Old Man Fischer, who had made a living through organized prostitution, had two sons. But Alter was mentally retarded. Because of guilt perhaps, guilt that he couldn't admit to himself, the old man placed all of his worries on his slow-moving, abnormal son. I answered him very simply. "I will not abandon my parents, nor my brothers and sisters. I will not do it. I prefer to take my chances with them. God is merciful and he will never let them kill innocent people."

My conviction, or fear, ended our conversation. I really didn't give much thought to what he had said before I had answered him so abruptly. As I reflected on it moments later, I thought that if we decided to flee the ghetto, we ran the risk of falling into the hands of the guards who would probably cut us down with their machine guns. I decided to use caution and wait. Deep inside, a spark of hope emanated from my conjecturing. I told myself that I had always obeyed the divine precepts and that if I could talk to God I would ask his advice. But he hadn't come into the ghetto with us. The feeling that God might have abandoned us festered in me but, nevertheless, I was still hoping for a miracle. Like the departure of someone who had always been present, but who rejects us and begins to distance himself like a wisp of smoke dispersed by the wind—that is how my faith in God began to wither.

I was thinking about all those things as if I were at the bottom of a deep pit or drowning in a river. In an effort to save myself, the only thing I saw myself able to grasp in desperation was a flimsy piece of straw.

It's Alexander Nedelcovici! Our savior! At dusk that day, Alexander, my best friend from childhood and schoolmate—the one who had spat on me—found us in the ghetto. He was a Catholic whose father was Yugoslavian and his mother Romanian. He had come to save my life. He had become a guard at the ghetto and it was easy for him to come to our room and take me outside. We hid in the shadows of a street corner, and, after explaining the situation, he said, "Sanyi, pack up and come with me. I'll take you to Sugatag where my aunt lives. You can work in the fields and no one will know who you are. In just three days from now, you and your family will be deported to Poland. They are going to kill you."

Paralyzed with terror by the categorical way he presented those facts, I couldn't refute him. Immediately a feeling of surrender overtook me like the claws of the owl digging into the back of the hare at the well.

"The people who were deported before you are already dead. They don't exist anymore. I want you to live. You have twenty-four hours to think about it."

I was stunned; a raging sea of tears filled my eyes. All through the night and the next day Alexander's words kept going around and around in my mind. As I looked at my parents and brothers and sisters, I became even more convinced that I could never change my mind. Their destiny was my destiny.

The next evening, Alexander led me outside again to talk. We blended into the shadows. When I explained to him that I had decided to remain with my family—no matter what our fate might be—Alexander extended the invitation for some others in my family to escape with me. "All right, you can take Saul with you."

"Can't do it."

"All right, all right, you can take both Saul and Samuel."

"No, no. It won't work."

After three hours of trying to convince me, my stubbornness won out and he said, "You win. You can all come. The whole family gets out of the ghetto."

How lucky I felt at that moment with that tiny spark of warmth still in my heart: God had listened. We went back to the room and Alexander explained the situation to my parents and how we could escape from the ghetto. He needed our decision immediately. They listened attentively: the plan seemed to represent a path back to life.

My parents looked at each other in silence. My father stroked his beard, choosing his words carefully. "We will share our common destiny. I do not believe that God will permit innocent people to be killed."

I'll never forget those words. When I heard him say them with such solemnity, strength, and serenity, all I could do was simply repeat them, just as the echoes of our words had become one voice in the caves of Mount Solovan so many years before.

Alexander didn't prolong the conversation. Before he said good-bye, however, my parents looked at me and said, "Sanyi, you are a man now. You must decide for yourself."

Their words touched my soul. My decision was firm and I didn't hesitate to say that I had decided to remain a part of their destiny. I believed that we would be saved by God because he would never permit innocent human beings to be killed.

"I'm staying," I affirmed boldly.

With relief and hope, we immediately embraced Alexander. Even though tears were rolling down our cheeks, the affection we felt for him, who was now our brother, became the embodiment of the risk that he had taken for us. I think he suffered more than we did, for when he left us there, alone together, he saw that we were united by the strength to fight and the determination to overcome our adversity. I felt that our family had suddenly melded into a single being with great courage and a single purpose: to resist calamity.

Just as Alexander had predicted, one morning we received orders from the Jewish Council to prepare for our departure. During the night, my mother had baked bread made with goose fat, salt, and wheat. She distributed that tasteless bread among us and we put it in our colorful woolen satchels. We were ordered to carry only what was necessary for a two-day trip. After packing our little bags of provisions and some clothing, we marched to the synagogue courtyard. The ss looked on while the Hungarian soldiers searched us, one by one. We were people from all walks of life—poor farm laborers, middle-class city dwellers, and well-dressed, rich people—but the scene must have seemed like a carnival of dusty, decaying mannequins.

I saw Rabbi Samuel Danzig, the spiritual leader of Sighet's Sephardic Jews, directly in front of me. He was dressed impeccably, sporting a top hat and wearing his tallith and tefillin. When a Hungarian soldier saw the tefillin, he started asking questions. "What's in the little boxes?"

"They contain passages from the Bible. We use them for our morning prayers."

The rabbi spoke Hungarian and German fluently. Finally, noticing the soldier's indifference toward him, he added, "I am Dr. Samuel Danzig. *Lelkesz vaqyok.*"

To add that he was the "one who attends to the needs of the soul" didn't stop the soldier from sticking the tip of his bayonet under the tefillin and tearing the parchment. The rabbi tried to protect them, but the soldier hit him with the butt of his rifle. The rabbi's top hat flew off and fluttered to the ground like a wounded bird. Then it was my turn to be frisked, but they wouldn't find anything on me.

Objects of value had different destinies. Some Jews who were actually expecting a new life in Germany had sewn gold and jewels inside the lining of their coats. Others, thinking they were going to return home one day, had buried valuables under patios, inside walls, underneath floors, or in the deepest recesses of the basements of their homes. Some left their possessions with gentile friends with the understanding that everything would revert back to them when they returned. But no one ever returned and their possessions were never reclaimed.

We had left our scant things with two neighbors: a Romanian family by the name of Ulici and a Hungarian family whose last name was Balcsák. The Romanians must have made good use of what we gave them because they kept it all, while the Hungarian family did eventually return the few things we had left with them. But at the moment, the only prized possession that each of us was thinking about was his or her own life.

We were escorted from the synagogue yard to the train station. The piercing silence would only be interrupted from time to time with the sobbing of thirsty children; fearing reprisals from the guards, their parents quickly quieted them. This vast funeral procession of frightened, muted beings was being witnessed by the citizens of Sighet as they spied on us from behind their curtains, while the latticed windows remained tightly closed.

Sighet had become a specter of itself. I can't begin to imagine what the gentiles must have thought about us—a long line of defenseless, unarmed, frightened people. As we walked toward the train station there wasn't a single smile among the whole lot, no gesture that might have indicated happiness. Death was encircling us. As it closed in on us, we shook with fear.

At noon we were loaded into cattle cars. There were eighty of us in each car, all crammed together, standing. Soon we were gagging from the heat and fear. It was impossible to move. Light from the outside seeped through the cracks between the boards of the walls of the boxcars. With only four small barred windows, there was no ventilation. Hospital cars were at the end of the train, carrying the sick and even some who feigned sickness in the hope of saving themselves.

It was going on four o'clock in the afternoon when the train finally started off toward Poland. The screeching wheels and the chugging of the engine threw everyone into panic. The ensuing hysteria became contagious, passing from boxcar to boxcar. The women went into a frenzy and began screaming and pulling out their hair. The men tried to console them by squeezing them tightly against their bodies. Children were crying. While each family clung together, the parents surrounded their children, giving them space so they wouldn't be asphyxiated.

In time, the monotonous clickety-clack of the train wheels seemed to calm everyone down. Fresh air blowing into the boxcar made us feel better, if it's possible to imagine feeling better under those conditions. The train left the city, following the course of the Tisa. No one had been at the station to give us a farewell, but now the weeping willows along the banks of the river fluttered in the wind as if to wave good-bye. Suddenly, as she stood next to the barred window, my mother saw our house.

"There's our house. Take a good look, for this will be the last time I see it."

It was our new house that the Hungarian government had built a year ago, after urban planners had ordered the old one destroyed because it butted up against the bridge crossing the Tisa. We had scarcely moved in when we had to abandon it forever.

6

My mother's voice reverberated around us: "There's our house. Take a good look, for this will be the last time I see it."

As my father tried to console her, the wind-tossed trees began to block our view of the house. It was 22 May 1944. The countryside was in bloom and the leaves on the trees seemed to dance in the breeze. New life was burgeoning all over the land.

Meanwhile, the train kept following the course of the river. My heart had shrunk fearfully and my soul anguished over what awaited us. Suddenly I grasped the full meaning of my decision, and it was then I realized that the train was taking us to die.

In the summer breeze, the branches and leaves of the willows along the banks of the river waved farewell to us. Mute witnesses, they seemed to weep for us as we departed our lands. As we passed through Campulung, not far from Sighet, the train crossed a bridge and left the river behind, the same river that had been our friend for so long.

Beyond the insanity of our situation, life elsewhere continued in a normal fashion. I peeked through the slits between the boards of the cattle car and I could see a farmer looking up at us as we passed by, wiping the sweat from his brow. Birds were fluttering about happily, seemingly enthralled with the sunlight and the wide-open spaces. The brilliance of springtime was reflected in every leaf of the poplars and birch trees. The clamor in the bird nests, the intense clarity of the sky, and the buzzing of the grain stalks swaying in the fields already belonged to a distant, forbidden world.

Inside the cars, it was a different story: we were surrounded by funereal silence and oppressive shadows. Everyone's face had turned grim, tense, devoid of expression. From the very moment each family had entered the cars, they sought to defend themselves against the others. Now there were no neighbors, no feelings of ethnic harmony, no religious unity — only the desire to survive at all costs. Once we had gotten into the cars, we became animals. Just as horses, when they sense that wolves are

about to attack, stand head to head in order to defend them-
selves, kicking the enemy with their hooves from the rear, as families, we also stood together guarding our space, staring severely at those next to us, and always pushing outward to gain a few more inches of territory.

The silence became thick, almost palpable. The straining locomotive and the clickety-clack of the wheels on the tracks made us drowsy. From time to time, the loud shrill of the train whistle would jolt us back into reality. When the train slowed down or stopped to let another train pass, as if by collective decision hysteria would explode in one car and spread to the other cars. It was the desperate screaming of human beings trapped in lunacy. In the same way it began, the hysteria would quickly dissipate due to fatigue and the deadening sound of the train, only to rear its ugly head again when we were least expecting it.

Soon the stink of having to relieve ourselves spread throughout the boxcar; unable to hold it, the children began first, followed by the old people, and, finally, all dignity lost, everyone ended up relieving themselves on top of each other's excrement. Spattered and stained by feces, urine, and sweat, we began to grow accustomed to our animal-like condition. Unable to move about, we stood in our own excrement. But it wasn't long before everyone seemed oblivious to the sickening stench.

I began thinking about my older brothers who had been taken away, which left a huge responsibility on my shoulders. Everyone remained silent and exchanged looks of foreboding: we knew we were going to die. Yet none of us seemed able to accept it. The mental conflict between premonitions of death and denial, because God in all his mercy would save us, preoccupied all the adults. But we knew that a messianic miracle would take time; hence, pessimism grew in our hearts with renewed strength. The children, on the other hand, only complained about how tired or thirsty they were. The adults cursed their own helplessness to free the youngsters from their suffering.

As night came on, the cattle car became freezing cold, but the putrefaction of the excrement on the floor initiated a process of fermentation which, in turn, kept our feet warm. The filthy gases rose to our nostrils, and, even though we had been practically anesthetized by it all, we longed for clean air.

We had been traveling for twenty-four hours. A stop was made in Kasa, Hungary. By then it was afternoon. They unbolted the door and opened it. Everyone started yelling, "Water! Water!"

But it was to no avail, for a German officer began screaming orders at us. He told us to turn over any jewelry we had, saying that if anyone tried to escape they would retaliate by killing everyone else who was on board. Ironically, no one was thinking about material possessions at that moment; we were only thinking about water, which had become the most precious commodity in the world. It occurred to me that things—both necessary and luxurious—that are coveted by human beings are as ephemeral as life itself. Then I remembered the rebellious, singing waters of the Tisa that used to run alongside our house; not until now had I ever appreciated its true value, for now water's importance was as great as life itself.

They filled the water tanks of the locomotive to the brim, but there wasn't a single drop for us. That machine was worth more than all those human lives put together; we were worth nothing. Although I was demoralized, I told myself that I was going to resist, if only I could manage to think about other things; nevertheless, it was impossible to erase from my mind the image of the fresh, moving waters of the Tisa River.

The long hours in the cattle cars awakened more anxiety among the already frightened people. Our eyes drooped and our legs were lead weights. Remaining stationary for so long was numbing, but our primary senses were assailed by thirst, hunger, muscle spasms, the need to relieve oneself, asphyxiation, the stench, nausea. Then, as we'd pass through some city, we'd hear the train whistles and ringing bells, which only

triggered another panic; the screaming easily drowned out the
clickety-clack of the train wheels. Even though everyone would
settle down again, the very tranquillity seemed ominous.

Although we had lost our conscious will power, an unconscious, powerful instinct overtook us, that is, the necessity to
resist at all cost. Before climbing into those cars, we had been
respectable, civilized human beings; now we were but caged
animals. In fact, we were worse than animals, for our awareness of impending death pulled us apart. We feared death, and,
knowing that with each turn of the wheels we were getting closer
to it, we found ourselves not only physically but also mentally
exhausted. Our spirits had been destroyed, but if we remained
firm about anything, it was our belief in a miracle from God.
Everything we valued had disappeared—education, promises,
action, love, and concern for others—and we were filling the
void with pure instinct, thoughtlessness, rage, and humiliation.

We traveled north for two days and three nights. We would
sleep standing up, we would scream standing up, we would suffer from thirst in the same position, always standing up. From
the beginning, they had not allowed us to take along water. My
sisters were crying, so my parents tried to console them by lifting them up to the barred windows where the wind refreshed
them a bit. Then they would doze off, falling into a fitful sleep.
When we would get hungry, we ate crackers made with goose
fat that we could barely swallow because our throats were so
dry. Many people were suffering from fever and dizziness. Our
muscles were starting to lose their stamina. We were tortured
by the loss of feeling in our legs and arms and the pain in our
necks and bodies. And, clearly, it was impossible to think about
anything pleasant.

The train stopped. From the window we could make out a
sign that said "Auschwitz." During our long wait there, I saw another sign nearby whose words I have never forgotten: "Räder
rollen zum Sieg" (The wheels are rolling to victory).

When they opened the door, we saw ss officers pointing

machine guns at us. Those impersonal figures, like expressionless machines, looked at us impassively, showing no hatred. We started screaming for water but the prison guards didn't make a move. Even our deplorable condition—we were filthy, our clothes stank, and we were crying in animal-like desperation—didn't kindle any sympathy.

We were told that we had arrived at a work camp, and soon they would assign us to our barracks where we would spend the night. Then they closed the door and, once again, we just stood there facing each other—anxious, restless, and in pain.

A train from France arrived on the tracks next to us and we exchanged glances. The people in those cattle cars were our mirror image—some were sobbing, and others were passive, with cold, distant expressions on their faces. No one could speak, and our glances were nothing more than paralyzed gestures of death.

At midnight, the train started to move again and chugged slowly out of the Auschwitz station toward the Birkenau extermination camp. Thick smoke permeated the sky. The piercing spotlights in the camp streamed through the car windows and turned us into ragtag, fragmented puppets.

Worried and uncertain, I couldn't sleep. Outside, men were shouting orders and dogs were barking. When they started to bang on the doors, I trembled. The closer the noise and confusion got to us, the louder it became. One by one, the soldiers were opening the doors of the other cars, and, since ours was one of the last to be opened, we could hear them getting closer and closer. After us came the hospital cars.

The heavy bolts of the doors banged and clanked. As they threw open the doors, we were blinded by the powerful spotlights. At first all I could see was a pale gray area outside, but then I could discern a large open area with long lines of people who were all stooped over. The whole area was lit up as if it were the middle of the day. We were herded out of the cattle car as if we were the animals for whom the cars had been meant. We

were lifeless from fatigue and thirst. Our sacks and bags containing wheat and goose-fat crackers had to remain on board.
While I was at the Birkenau-Auschwitz camps, I found out that
nothing went to waste; the crackers would be used to make soup
for the prisoners.

My heart was beating out of control. Instinctively, I followed
the other prisoners outside. Now we really were cattle — on our
way to the slaughterhouse. While some of the ss officers forced
us into formation with their rifle butts, others sent shivers down
our spines as they shouted for us to get out: "Raus! Raus!"

It seemed like they would never stop hitting us. Our bodies
wanted to fight back but not even a whisper of protest could be
heard from anyone. Our fears had become much stronger than
our dignity, our thirst, our desire to resist. Trying to protect ourselves from the blows and the constant hounding, we squeezed
together. We had already been beaten into submission by the
fatigue and panic. No one dared defy them.

"Raus! Raus!" they kept screaming.

One poor man, totally frightened out of his wits, ran around
wildly trying to locate his family. A desperate woman, horrified
by it all, wandered aimlessly among the condemned. Then she
looked up to the sky and extended her arms upward in anguish,
but the immensity of the universe thwarted any attempt to reach
God. As she was being pushed along with the others, the blow of
a rifle butt from a German thug brought her back to reality. No
one understood what was happening. We couldn't make sense
of anything. We could only respond to the fear of the lashings,
the blows, the insults. We bolted like a herd of sheep being attacked by a pack of wolves. Where was God? Would he protect
us? Give us counsel? Give us solace?

"Men to the left, women to the right," the loudspeakers
blurted out.

Instinctively, my father, Saul, Samuel, and I surrounded my
mother and little sisters. The first whiplash struck me in the
face like a lightning bolt in a violent storm. The blows on our

backs from their clubs finally separated us. My body had lost all sensation; I felt nothing.

The blows and whiplashes sent us to the ground like apples falling from trees. Kneeling, we were kicked and smashed with rifle butts until we were nothing more than a pile of flesh, stinking and bruised. They seized my mother and sisters and dragged them toward the line for women.

I could see my mother walking away as she held my sisters' hands. She had been subdued. The definitive separation had begun, but there were no good-byes and no tears from eyes that had been hardened by sleeplessness and fatigue. We stood up and fell into line, holding hands in impotent rage.

As my mother and sisters faded into the endless shadows, I thought I perceived a cleft in the darkness. Illuminated by a dim light, I could barely make out what, today, I think was the symbol of my people being extinguished. But in that ray of light, as hard as I tried, I could not discern the countenance of God. Perhaps I was not worthy of it; instead, I only saw the faces of the children, men, and women who, rising through the smoke, had multiplied into a chaotic montage of mutilated grimaces.

During that night of never-ending punishment, the stars of the heavens descended over the death camp at Birkenau. They broke loose from their eternal moorings like lightning that opens the sky for a second and then plunges it back into darkness, leaving in their wake the unremitting silence of death. The sparks that scattered about the camp disintegrated and then went out.

Each star had been at one time a defenseless, hopeful human being who thirsted for life but who was forced to die, asphyxiated by the poisonous gas. To say that today their memory lives in the Sanctuary of Yad Vashem, in Jerusalem, is not enough. For I believe that they would have preferred the opportunity to continue living with their own memories, no matter how happy or sorrowful.

That night never seemed to end. The sobbing of desperation

and the gunshots of the ss increased my panic. My fears were so great that I was unable to shed a single tear. Some of us prayed. To whom would we appeal for mercy if God was not present? The silence inside our souls was absolute. The silence of death had taken control of our beings.

The chimneys gave off an acrid stench and the night breeze scattered the ashes of the cremated bodies upon us.

One of the families—two women and a man—would not separate despite the blows of the guards. The stubbornness of those three poor souls was stronger than the pain of the whip. Finally, the guards jerked them out of the line, took aim, and fired at them point blank. When the shooting stopped, the little family was lying in a pool of blood but they were still holding hands. Their bodies were loaded onto wagons and hauled off to the incineration pits, where the flames would crackle as they gnawed away at the flesh. The rest of us continued walking forward, paralyzed by fear, senses blunted, and choked with anguish. All hope had been lost.

I just couldn't continue to endure what I was seeing—a virtual heap of ghastly nightmares. Insensitive to physical pain, the torment in my soul intensified with each new incident. With the small scrap of humanity that was still left in me, each thing I saw brought to mind grotesque visions of even greater brutalization.

Trucks rolled up next to the hospital cars. Special agents removed the crippled, the sick, the paralytic, the dying, and the dead. They grasped the bodies by the hands and feet and tossed them into the trucks like bags of garbage. Piled one on top of another, the bodies of some prisoners muffled others' moaning. Unable to move, many of them were asphyxiated. While others fought to climb to the top of the heap, they would only be met by another body being thrown on top of them. Submerged into a sea of flesh—sick, healthy, and dead—the moaning faded away.

One of the sick prisoners who was still in good physical shape got up and stumbled across the other bodies to the edge of the truck where he attempted to jump out. One of his legs got stuck between some bodies, thwarting his escape. An ss officer saw him and shot him in the head. His body was left hanging over the edge of the truck. The middle-aged man's beard—now life-less—was parted in the old way like the tail of a swallow, and his black felt hat was still on his head. Blood dripped from his neck and trickled down the side of the truck. The image of that Hasidic man, along with the sick people thrown from the hos-pital car, has left an indelible mark on my memory. And other images continue to teem in my mind—the families assassinated for refusing to separate, the biting Alsatian dogs, the children machine-gunned to death, the human bodies tossed into the incineration pits, the blows from gun butts, the screams, the insults, the whiplashes, the never-to-be-forgotten horror.

I have no feeling. I can't think. I tell myself I want to feel, I want to cry, I want to scream. But I can't. Blima and Pesil are clutching my mother's skirt. As she pulls them along, she herself is dragged by the special command officers; then she fades into the multitude. She doesn't look back. Without saying good-bye or waving, she seems lifeless. My mother and sisters disappear, expunged.

The smoke smells of burnt flesh. Like soot, it sticks to my lips. The taste of hot, salty sand parches my mouth. My heart is destitute and racked with pain. My efforts are in vain. Death reigns the world. I am in an abyss of night made day by those spotlights that blind me. But it's all deception; night enters into our souls with the pretense of day. We've all been duped. And I collaborate in all this by continuing to lie to myself. I tell myself that I must be dreaming. This is like looking into the well from the eyes of the owl sitting on the edge. From his position, I am the hare. There he is, ever present, and yet I insist that it is an apparition. My soul tries to avoid reality. My eyes search in vain for something to change it. I'm awaiting a miracle. I pray to God with all my might and invoke him with certain joy that lasts a matter of seconds. I look up to the sky: the lowering cloud from the chimneys shields his existence from us.

Where is he? Why are my prayers drowned out by the barking
dogs and the snarls of the ss? Oh, God of the armies! But which
army? God of the ss? Oh, my tormented soul!

Is prayer possible when one's mouth is parched, when one's
heart is overflowing with abhorrence, when one's unleashed
wrath is like a flock of birds trapped in a storm?

. . . like the wounded prey that agonizes in front of the merciless eyes of the hunter. Is that the way you see us, unwilling to
lift a hand to free us from our executioners?

. . . like grains of sand that the sea's waves push and pull,
lifting us up and dashing us against the rocks. Is that the way
you treat us, unwilling to show pity for our sorrowful situation?

. . . like babes torn from their mother's arms. Is that the way
you see us, feeling no compassion for our tears, our mourning,
the pain of the bullets, or the torture that jostles about inside us
like wheat in a sieve?

. . . like the stormy wind that blows away the leaves, sweep-
ing them into the mud, humiliating them, and then burying
them in the mire. Is that the way you send us to oblivion?

Are you like the man who drinks too much wine and falls into
a drunken stupor, overcome with sleep while the corpses float
in the air, the screaming punctures our eardrums, and the cold
blood flows into the fissures of the night?

Wake up! Come! Look!

We are stunned by the shock of what we see. Our tears dry
up into nothing, our hands quiver in the air dense with victims.
Our souls have died without a burial. With the night, in darkness. Forever.

Under the watchful eyes of the guards, the line of five men
in front of me continued forward involuntarily. The commotion, shouting, and choking from the smoke of the incinerated
corpses have become increasingly commonplace. With every
step of the way, the moment of selection got closer. We gripped
each other's hands with all our might. We dragged our feet, not
because we were so fatigued but rather to delay our encounter

with death. Ten yards, nine, eight, seven . . . now only five separated us from "The Angel of Death." His steel-gray uniform shone in the glare of the spotlights. He was almost six feet tall, thin, with fine facial features and a piercing stare. Without saying a word or altering his expressionless face, Dr. Joseph Mengele was making the decisions with a slight movement of his hand: "Right, Left."

Life, Death. Suitable, Unsuitable. Useful, Worthless. Concentration Camp, Gas Chamber and Cremation.

Suddenly, Samuel, Saul, and I were shocked into action—our father was being sent to the gas chamber. The three of us leaped toward him and the guards' blows rained down on us, but we were already deadened to pain by punishment and horror. Numb as we were, we managed to pull him back to life. Life? The concentration camp awaited us.

Our desperation impelled us to bring him with us. The guards, who were tired, acquiesced. They let him stay in our line. They surely must have been thinking that the old man with the rabbinical beard wouldn't last more than a month in the camps. Their arbitrary decision had saved him for the time being. No firearms were called into service and our father was motioned toward the barracks.

Immediately, we were ordered to undress. Our clothes fell to the floor around our feet. They told us to tie our shoes together so they wouldn't get mixed up with the others. Each order was carried out in silence, automatically. Our thoughts had been vanquished from our minds, so they didn't get in the way. Electric lights shone above our heads. At the back of the room, the buzzing sound of the electric shavers could be heard.

We moved forward to where members of the special command forces were waiting to give us a shearing. With my head drooped, arms hanging down, submissive, giving no resistance, I was shaved bald. Whenever a mole was in the way, it was simply clipped off with the hair. But another injury to the body didn't cause pain anymore. I lifted my arms and my armpits were quickly shorn. The barber shouted at me to spread my legs, which I did without realizing it. The shaver was warm and the pubic hair quickly fell to the floor.

Then I walked a short way over to a man who grasped me like a stuffed doll and applied a cloth soaked in liquid disinfectant to my head, underarms, and pubic area. My body burned.

Then I was sent into the showers. A gush of hot water made me feel better briefly. I continued forward and passed through a cold shower. My body quivered but I raised my head and drank from the shower head. I could feel the water flow into my stomach. I saw my father and brothers doing the same thing.

After we left the shower area we were given clothes to wear: cap, striped shirt, undershorts, undershirt, white slippers, striped pants. We were getting dressed when a sudden attack of panic seized all four of us. We immediately hugged each other, possessed by the sensation that death was taking us forcefully into its arms like a metal vise that was beginning to squeeze our souls, until only a scream of horror could alleviate the tension. There's no doubt in my mind that because of some extrasensory link, we realized that my mother and sisters had just died. Since then, I have experienced joy and happiness that have momentarily permitted me to forget that moment, but like oil floating on water, for more years than I can count, that image and our terrible screams have been present, without fail, in my memory.

Those screams of terror closed a chapter of suffering for our family, but soon new chapters were opened. When I finally became aware of what was happening, I saw to my chagrin that they had given me a pair of wooden shoes that in the future would cause me such torture that I ended up almost dying from it.

We were ordered to leave the barracks. I looked at my father and brothers. They were a deplorable sight. It was still nighttime and we stood in line watching the flames spew out of the chimneys. A flash of consciousness sparked the image of my mother and sisters fading into the multitude, walking toward the gas chambers. Even though we were unable to imagine it, the four of us knew that they had been killed. No prayers, no words of affection, no mourning, no farewells.

The Birkenau-Auschwitz complex in southern Poland consisted of two separate concentration camps, but both had the same mission: extermination. As I would learn years later, that diabolical plan had been described by Adolf Hitler to Hermann Rauschning, president of the National-Socialist party in Danzig in the following way:

"We must devise a technique for depopulation. If you ask me what I understand depopulation to mean, I will tell you that I foresee the eradication of certain racial groups and I am committed to it because in general terms it will permit me to fulfill my fundamental mission. If Nature is cruel, then we too must be cruel. If I send the cream of German youth to war without lamenting for a moment the spilling of precious German blood in the inferno of war, I also have the right to destroy millions of members of inferior races that are multiplying like parasites."

At Auschwitz we realized immediately what was going to happen to those designated to die. From our concentration camp we could see the chimneys of the cremation ovens and it was impossible to avoid the macabre awareness of what was going on there. Proceeding in groups of five, my mother and sisters had been taken to a barracks. A German soldier had ordered them to undress and my mother must have obeyed. The shame of exposing their bodies to the watchful gaze of the soldiers would have deterred my sisters, but my mother's reassuring words and seeing her undress with motherly dignity must have convinced them to continue. My mother's arms would have enveloped her children. Upon crossing through the gigantic metal door, my mother would have looked back and seen that life was nothing more than a long line of hopeless creatures.

Human beings of all ages would have been bunched in groups of five inside an area that held about two thousand people. When the room would hold no more, the metal door with its little window would have been shut behind them. Many would have looked up waiting for the showers to turn on. The wait lasted no more than the time it took for the prisoners to be showered with Zyklon в pellets that became a poisonous gas, quickly enveloping the bodies as the terror of death precipitated massive hysteria.

Vomit, urine, excrement, tears, and sweat. Screams and gasps for air from the prisoners would be heard from the outside. Overwhelmed by fear and panic, many would scratch and bite those next to them. Before beginning to inhale the poisonous gas, many unfortunate souls would throw themselves against the door trying to open it. But some would asphyxiate others, creating a pyramid of human corpses that would be heaped up at the entrance.

Everything was over within fifteen minutes, and, shortly thereafter, electric pumps would suck out the air containing the poisonous gas. The door would open and men from the special command units wearing gas masks and rubber boots would move in quickly with powerful water hoses to wash away the vomit, urine, and excrement, leaving the corpses—many of which were still standing like white statues—clean and glistening.

Afterward, other special command units under the vigilance of German soldiers would begin examining each corpse, one by one. They would open the mouths of the dead and, using large pliers, yank out gold teeth. Then, wearing surgical gloves, they would use their fingers to explore the anus and vagina to make sure none of the corpses would go to the ovens carrying jewelry, gold, diamonds, or other objects of value.

When the examination was over, the special command units would begin to remove the corpses. The bodies would be pulled along by the wrists toward some endless corridors along which the corpses would then be transported on carts to the cremation area. The cart pusher would also help in the evacuation and cleaning of the gas chambers. Seven or eight bodies at a time would be loaded onto the carts and taken to the ovens. That night, my mother and little sisters, along with two thousand unfortunate souls, died that way.

For us, however, the nightmare was just beginning. At dawn they made us march toward Auschwitz and in half an hour we were standing in front of a gate with a sign in large German letters: "Arbeit macht frei" (Work will set you free). We went inside. We didn't believe for a second this was going to be our slogan during the time we would spend there, not after what we had gone through the previous night.

On 22 May, a total of 3,490 persons had been shipped out of Sighet; by now, our number had been reduced to half that. When dawn came to the concentration camp, it signaled a new day: 25 May 1944.

7

The crematorium was functioning nonstop. The early morning light gave shape to the sharp-edged columns of the smokestacks. As the sun began to rise above the flames of the ominous chimneys, the smoke and soot enveloped us in a dense fog. Our prisoner uniforms became covered with a thin film of grit. Some part of that black, sooty shower must have consisted of the particles of the bodies that were once my family. Instinctively, I tried to smear some on my hands as I ran my fingers over my clothing. The soot turned my palms black, making the lines noticeably visible. It seemed paradoxical to be able to make out the lines that indicated one's life, destiny, and luck. Human life was so fragile and fickle, so wretched and ephemeral, that it all fit into the palm of my hand. The souls of the dead continued floating in the air, making themselves everlastingly present, despite the vast eagerness of our executioners to obliterate our presence.

Silently, we fell into line. With heads hanging low and our arms extended over our bodies, we were but skeletons lined up in rows like repugnant statues. Hunger was devouring us. On our march, we passed the gas chambers and then the concrete pits, which looked like places to dump garbage for burning, but they were for cremating corpses. I saw the cart pushers throw load after load of the lifeless, broken bodies onto the flames fed by fuel. Like giant octopuses, the carts were laden chaotically with naked corpses whose arms and legs were hanging over the edges.

Enduring insults and beatings from the Nazi guards, the special Jewish command units would park the carts by the huge incinerators and dump out the contents. The faces of those cart pushers, who were Jews like us, were devoid of any expression. Their constant contact with death and their role in the massive extermination had so dehumanized them that their behavior was totally irrational. Like robots, they carried out their orders efficiently, dying a thousand deaths with their own people.

We advanced along the railway platform and saw lines of the newly condemned waiting to be selected. The sobbing, the praying, the orders, the whipping, the loudspeakers—everything was exactly the way it was the night before. We realized we were still alive and our mutilated feelings led us to believe, with a faint glimmer of false hope, that we had somehow survived the gateway to hell. This was our miserable consolation. We never imagined that our trip to Auschwitz was only the beginning of an ongoing struggle to postpone death.

Looking at those small barred windows of the cattle cars parked nearby, we could see ourselves the night before: people trapped inside were weeping, crying for water, displaying affliction in their faces. Now it was daytime and the spotlights had been turned off. Bundles of clothes, shoes, glasses, purses, and suitcases were piled on the train platform.

In the daylight I saw something I didn't want to see: A Jewish woman, about thirty years old, was holding a small child. Suddenly, she stepped out of the line, placed her child on the ground, and began to undress. Despite her fatigue, she seemed to move with a certain elegance. I saw her clothes falling down on top of her child, covering him entirely; her dress, slip, and jacket concealed him inside a pile of abandoned clothes. Naked, she arrogantly took five steps away from the line. Then I saw the bundle of clothes start to move. A soldier, alerted by the cries inside the clothes, went over and kicked the bundle repeatedly. The small child, wrapped inside, rolled down the path like a ball. I saw his head smash open against the cement. I heard the woman scream and then I saw her charge at the soldier. He stuck the muzzle of his rifle into her chest and fired two bullets. I saw the woman, still alive, crawl toward her child, leaving pools of blood all over the platform. I couldn't watch the rest.

The light of the new day seemed strange to me. The dead were resting in peace, but I was paralyzed by the idea of dying and seeing death all around me.

We walked less than a mile to the entrance to Auschwitz. The sign "Work will set you free" was not only ironic, it also was paradoxical to see ourselves wearing those striped clothes in that jungle of shadows with death stalking us like an attack dog. While it must have been terribly ironic, it was as real as the wooden clogs that battered and bruised the toes of my feet and the stinging, purple blows that began to cause me great pain.

Upon entering Auschwitz, we were detained in a large, open compound. The first thing I noticed was that the ground had been covered with sand. There wasn't a weed growing anywhere. Suddenly, I realized why they had covered the entire area of the work camp with it. When the resident prisoners saw us arrive, they started throwing pieces of bread to us over the barbed-wire fences. All sense of obedience and order vanished immediately, everyone lunged in desperation for a morsel. We knocked each other down, showing no mercy for the weaker ones. Amid the disorder and confusion, I was separated from my father and two brothers.

I think it was when I saw Saul being trampled by so many starving people that I persuaded myself to leave them. He had been able to catch a piece of bread in the air because he was taller, but no sooner did he catch it when numerous prisoners leaped on him, knocking him to the ground, and yanked the bread out of his hands. Saul was so severely trampled that he never even came close to tasting a crumb of that bread.

That vision of my hurt and bruised family in captivity was stronger than my will. It occurred to me that if I ever got separated from them, it might be easier to survive because I wouldn't have to see them suffer. We were unable to help each other, so I decided it would be better if each one of us took care of ourselves. The wretched piece of bread had been reduced to crumbs. My intention to remain with them had likewise crumbled to nothing.

The bread incident launched me in a new direction. My

father, Samuel, and Saul were assigned to the concentration camp in Buna, but I was kept at Auschwitz. The first thing they did was to tattoo everyone. I bared my left arm and a low-ranking soldier of the German Nazi National-Socialist Army went to work: using a needle, he inscribed A-7393, which has been a permanent part of me ever since. My punctured skin was inflamed for about ten days, after which scabs formed and then peeled off, leaving clear, dark blue, indelible numbers on my arm. Like branded cattle, I had been branded for life. From that moment until we were liberated, I would not hear my name again, only the four numbers etched into my skin reminding me that our existence on this planet is enigmatic and hopeless.

The distribution of prisoners in the camp began in that same courtyard. A German soldier went around identifying the plumbers, mechanics, and electricians. Then an officer assigned everyone to separate barracks. I quickly realized that it would be better not to know how to do anything, so after practically everyone else had been assigned to their barracks, there were only a few of us left. We were assigned menial tasks. I had to peel potatoes and was assigned to Barracks No. 8. During the month that I remained at Auschwitz, I peeled potatoes on the graveyard shift.

Barracks No. 8 was the same as any other barracks, but it was an absolute privilege having access to the kitchen; there, one would find mounds of bread and other food that the victims had brought with them on the trains going to Birkenau. The crackers and bread were used to make soup. Although I rarely went hungry then, I always made an effort to hide something in the lining of my uniform. The nights weren't so cold anymore because summer was just around the corner. Since the work was so monotonous I was always fighting drowsiness. If I'd fallen asleep, I would've received more beatings and whiplashes.

The prisoners who worked outside the camp installations used to return every day to the sound of classical music being played by other prisoners. The marching tunes completely destroyed what little bit of morale was left among us. It was bizarre to see that ragtag, skin-and-bones troop of laborers march back from work, maintaining their step at all cost; if not, they were beaten until they did.

The Moskowitz brothers from the village of Yod, which is near our city, were the musicians. I knew them because in better times they would play folk music at weddings and parties. The strangest aspect of that eccentric group of musicians was the fact that their family was composed of seven brothers and two sisters, and the men were all dwarfs and the women were normal.

During the month I was at Auschwitz, the Moskowitz family was in charge of harmonizing the prisoners' uneven steps. Someone had said that when Dr. Mengele saw them clutching their instruments in desperation, he became intrigued by the family and assigned them to play music for the inmates. I have since heard that some of the Moskowitz family survived the tortures of Dr. Mengele's medical experiments and now live in Israel.

Most prisoners at Auschwitz didn't have the same luck as the Moskowitzes. Some worked in the laundry area which, during the winter, was pure torture; others worked as tailors making the white and blue striped uniforms. There were cobblers, office helpers, and chain gangs. The worst jobs, speaking from a moral standpoint, were the ones involving special command units. Trained to carry out the orders of the ss with scrupulous accuracy, they were the executioners of their own people. They were the ones who annihilated us, cremated us, dragged and pushed us, beat and tortured us — all under the watchful eye of the ss.

The worst work of the special command units was done by the cart pushers and the millers who crushed human bones into powder. The milling operation ran around the clock, pulverizing bones of the corpses that had not been cremated in the ovens. The dust of death stuck to the millers' very souls, and they themselves looked like living corpses. The prize they received for their work was to be sent to hell—twice—the first time, when they were forced to execute their own people, and the second, when they themselves were gassed and incinerated in order to eliminate witnesses or to get rid of those who had become too weak to carry out those diabolical orders.

To explain what would happen on a typical day at Auschwitz seems too difficult for me now. Much of the time, my mind was blank due to the continuous onslaught of images that challenged any logical understanding or reason. Life in the concentration camp was an unconnected series of distorted visions. Because of that spiritual blackout, I think I spent at least three days drugged by horror. I was reliving fragments of nightmares while I was either awake or asleep. Like a zombie, I understood not one iota of what was going on around me; somehow, in order to avoid the beatings, I did manage to do what I was told. Although I felt hypnotized, in time I managed to elude that semiconscious state. I began to learn something about life in that camp from other prisoners.

I remember that hardly anyone would speak. There was an epidemic of silence. Every prisoner was governed by only one concern—survival. But first and foremost were our efforts to avoid the beatings. Anyone could have been clubbed to death instantly. Next, when one was subjected to a beating, one had to try to protect his head and teeth. Survival meant demonstrating strength, stamina, and durability. With one's health and strength, it was possible to think about the next day. They silenced us and kept us submissive by pounding in the idea that the next day we might face death. A day in which one avoided that particular moment was a lamentable but tranquil day. Without consciousness or memory, each day seemed like one continual nightmare interrupted only by sleep. I would dream only about mealtime on Saturdays back in Sighet. The obsession with food was common among us. Whenever a prisoner would talk or scream in his sleep, he would always make allusions to food. Sexual desire had been totally extinguished. It was said that they put chemicals in our food to eliminate those desires in order to keep our minds on our work.

One thing was certain: we were always at risk — like ships that could sink any minute. German jails had been emptied in order to distribute criminals, known as Kapos, throughout the concentration camps. A good number of depraved savages had arrived at Auschwitz to supervise the kitchens, organize the guards, and oversee the work details. These thugs were frightening. They harassed us day in and day out, and many prisoners died from their sadistic torture. They lived in special barracks where they slept with young boys chosen from among the prisoners who, unfortunately, let themselves be perverted in order to receive better treatment.

Naturally, it was difficult to get accustomed to living at Auschwitz. After that apocalyptic night in the depths of hell at Birkenau, the happiness to be alive that I had once felt was extinguished forever. The strange sensation of being dead yet still able to move around was always a paradox in my mind. Wandering among all those destroyed beings — that horde of ghosts, bewildered, wounded, hungry, and dressed in rags — I was just another phantom.

When I became lucid again, I tried to recognize familiar faces but I could only see the abomination, the endemic fear, the contorted expressions, the glassy, unexpressive eyes, and the inertia and suffering that had been injected into our souls. When I finally came out of the trance and returned to the reality of the concentration camp, I discovered that I had been tattooed with the number A-7393 and that I lived in Barracks No. 8.

Now that my soul was exposed to outside reality, I saw that the main streets of Auschwitz had been paved. I saw the wire fencing and the human traffic of demented people stumbling along like sleepwalkers in the immutable darkness. The main thoroughfare had been constructed in the shape of a T. Entering Auschwitz through the main entrance led to two open areas separated by barbed wire. The platform for the musicians was a few yards to the left of the entrance. The storehouses and kitchen were located beyond the open areas to the right. The prisoner camp and barracks were situated behind the open area to the left. The administrative buildings, the ss living quarters, the experimental hospital, and brothels for the Germans were located along the two arms of the street.

My memory has struggled to dredge up the details and recreate the past, that is, the daily routine of the month I was in Auschwitz. Although it had been indelibly etched into my mind, to bring it back to life when I have spent my entire life trying to forget it requires an effort fraught with much anxiety.

A typical day for me would begin at seven in the evening; that's when I'd pass through the electric fences that separated us from freedom and go to the basement underneath the kitchen. During the short walk, the ss guards would constantly remind me that I was a military prisoner. Upon arrival at my place of work, I'd sit down next to the other unfortunate souls and begin to peel potatoes until dawn. Directly in front of us was a huge cement receptacle into which we would throw the peeled potatoes, ready to be washed. From where I was sitting, I could look up through a skylight and see a guard patrolling back and forth. The ss guards watched us so closely that it was difficult to hide even a potato, but we spent a lot of energy looking for ways to avoid being caught.

Eating a raw potato was a rather unpleasant experience. I would have to chew it for a while and then swallow it with the juice, because to swallow a piece by itself is murder. It would scrape our throats but, given our hunger, we'd do anything to get a piece of food into our stomachs.

By six o'clock in the morning we would have already fallen into formation for roll call in the open area of the concentration camp. The head count was a part of the routine as much for those who worked during the day as for those who worked by night. Before the head count began, they'd allow us ten minutes to get up, make our beds, use the bathroom, and wash up.

Every day we would wake up to the commands of the guards who would scream at us to get dressed: "Anziehen! Anziehen!" And they would go around hitting those who had dozed off, or were lazy or sick. Then they would order us to make our beds: "Bettenbau!" Next, we would go to the latrines and leave the barracks in order to receive a cup of water with some common herbs mixed in. Then we fell into formation, in squads of five, next to the barracks. A German army officer would stand in front of us and order a soldier to initiate the head count. While we would stand at attention, he'd order us to remove our caps: "Mützen ab!" With our skulls bared, the officer would walk down the line counting each head as he tapped it with a stick. Shouting loudly, the prisoner at the head of each line would begin the count: "First." Then the second in line would continue, "Second," and so on until every one had been counted. If someone was missing, it would have been for one of two reasons: he had fallen back asleep or he was dead. In the first case, he would receive a severe beating from one of the thugs; in the second case, the corpse would be dragged outside and plopped into formation, counted like just another shadow among the other shadows, then thrown onto a cart and hauled off to the incinerator.

For the purpose of forming work brigades, each Kapo would get his group together and have second head count, upon which the group headed for the gate. Outside, an ss officer would then take charge of the group and direct it to the work place. For a full day's work the prisoners would receive a little soup, a small piece of bread, a pat of margarine, or a tiny piece of foul-smelling *guargel* cheese.

After the other prisoners would leave to go to work, I'd head back to the barracks to sleep. My mattress was made of straw. Our reprieve from hunger and dire circumstances was nothing but brief. The barracks had only one entrance and the latrines and wash basins were at the far end. Bunk beds occupied the rest and we slept with our feet pointing toward the central aisle down which the Kapos would walk with their whips.

Auschwitz: that's how I remember it. When the end of June came around, I was loaded onto a truck and sent to the concentration camp at Jaworzno.

8

Since the memory of my mother and sisters was still strong in my mind, getting out of Auschwitz so quickly gave me new life and helped me escape my subhuman, distressing condition. As the packed truck of prisoners left the compound, I involuntarily looked back. The same black smoke was pouring out of the chimneys: there was no truce in their efforts to annihilate us. I tried to calm down and reason things out. I told myself that I had to adapt to this new reality, I had to rise above these circumstances, and, above all, I had only one objective: to fight for my freedom.

While I was concentrating on those thoughts, I didn't notice that the tall chimneys and buildings of Auschwitz had slowly dropped out of sight. The old, dilapidated vehicle barely rolled along, unable to get up much speed; it just coughed and spewed as if it had TB. And the roads were atrocious. The SS guards, who stood at the back of the truck, never once took their watchful, harassing eyes off of us. It was a long ride, and we began to doze off and lean against each other. Innocently believing that our luck would change by our departure from Auschwitz, every one of us tried to sleep in order to regain our strength.

Four hours later we arrived at the new prison camp: Jaworzno. It was located near a coal mine in the industrial region of Upper Silesia in Poland. No sooner had we gotten settled into our barracks when another prisoner came over and spoke to me. "There are two prisoners who have been here a long time and they have been looking for you."

That new twist worried me. I had become so accustomed to misfortune that I spent a good part of the night laboriously considering the calamities that I might have to confront. I could only come up with gloomy, tragic thoughts that kept me in deadly turmoil.

The next morning, the Kapo's whiplashes woke me up; the welts marked my skin as if they were strips of red meat, and the idea of fighting for life took on the violent color of pain. I got up as swiftly as I could, made my bed, and washed up. That day I began my new life as a miner. We walked to the mine entrance where ventilator towers clattered ceaselessly. After going down about 150 feet, we were handed shovels and picks. A guard warned us that to lose one of those tools meant automatic death.

At the far end of the mine, between the passageways, the air became scarce. In spite of the summer weather above ground, the humidity down below sapped our weakened, ill-fated condition. Work never let up for an instant and we were fed only at the end of each eight-hour work day. Thirst tortured us the most, and some miners even passed out. So whenever a Kapo wasn't watching, we would drink the brackish water mixed with coal that seeped from the fissures in the walls of the mine.

Our job was to extract the coal with a pickax, shovel it into carts, and take it to the surface. The long hours never seemed to end, and we never knew if it was night or day outside. That darkness has always reminded me of the well at our house in Sighet. My humbled, defeated consciousness would rebel briefly to remind me that I had to fight for the one purpose that had been imposed upon me: survival at all cost. I could never get that image of the rabbit trapped by the owl in the dark well out of my mind.

Despite working alongside other prisoners in the mine, I was always terrorized by the loneliness and silence among us. Our silence was heightened by the sound of the pickaxes striking the walls. At times I felt as if I were the only person left in the world, trapped in darkness and anguish by the ominous future. I was reduced to a mere shadow in a world of shadows. Perhaps because of that feeling of total helplessness, instead of tumbling into my wooden bed after work, I'd wander about the grounds around the barracks. I didn't look up much and I dared not speak to anyone out of fear and distrust. Instead, I would meditate on how my life had changed since the war had started. It was a war that I didn't understand; similarly, I couldn't understand why men felt compelled to persecute and assassinate other men.

More than anything, I used to think about what I was going to do when I eventually left the concentration camp. I had to keep the faith, kindle my confidence, and believe that I would be able to escape from this horrible situation.

By taking those walks along the avenues of death, I got to know the camp better. In terms of its layout and buildings, Jaworzno was quite similar to Auschwitz. It was designed to hold about fourteen thousand prisoners. The installation was surrounded by two rows of barbed-wire fencing about 15 feet high. The ss had constructed their watch towers between the two rows of barbed wire. Each tower was about 30 feet high and equipped with a machine gun and four powerful gyrating lights, one in each corner of the tower. A German guard was stationed in each tower and they would stand watch for eight-hour stretches. The lights kept the whole camp lit up at night. Since the grounds on the inside, as well as an area 150 feet beyond the fences, were covered with sand, the reflection of the lights at night created an image of a beach illuminated by the moon.

I had made those observations when I first arrived because my initial reaction was to escape at the first opportunity. I considered getting out underneath a vehicle or under a train car. But in time I began to realize that such action would be impossible because of the tight security and the perpetual head counts; in fact, it was a Jewish friend from Poland who dissuaded me from attempting such folly.

One afternoon, after my first day of work, two rather healthy-looking strangers came up to me. They wanted to know if I knew anything about their families. They were from Sighet. I immediately asked them their names.

"Our name is Herstick," answered one of them.

I was completely taken by surprise. For the first time since my stay in the concentration camps, I had run into some of my relatives. The two robust young men were my cousins, sons of one of my father's sisters. Then I became worried about this encounter because, in that world of shadows, family relationships and feelings for one another were nonexistent. Affection and concern were so strange and so inappropriate that it became difficult to accept the presence of relatives. In truth, there was nothing human about that infernal place.

But I quickly regained my composure and agreed to go outside the barracks with them to talk about a world that was already forgotten, something like trying to remember a book I'd read years before. I responded to their questions with what little I knew. I knew that their mother had died about two months earlier and that the rest of the family was safe in Budapest. Apparently they already knew about their mother because they didn't show much emotion when I told them. But they got upset when I told them the rest of their family was out of danger in Budapest.

"Nowhere in Europe is anyone out of danger," said one of them.

But they quickly changed their tone and said how pleased they were to have found a relative. I couldn't empathize with their feelings of warmth and love; frankly, it was difficult for me to share their feelings of happiness. I simply feigned enthusiasm, for none of it meant anything to me. By that point, my idea of survival didn't allow for happiness. Happiness had been erased from my memory with the cruel blows of that indescribable night at Birkenau. I had no desire to share my ill-fated experiences with anyone, but my cousins let themselves get carried away on a whirlwind of talkativeness and expressions of hope. As they spoke, I was thinking that my life in the mine was nothing more than another path leading to death.

When I learned that they didn't work in the mine, that their life was not so bad, I couldn't help but feel a mixture of envy and suspicion. "Could they be spies or torturers?" I wondered to myself.

They described how they had acquired a life with certain privileges, whereas my life was a world in which just a small breath of air was cause for celebration. Three years ago, they told me, the two of them had been deported to Auschwitz. Shlomo, the youngest, was a trained wrestler and boxer. That knowledge saved his life because he was assigned to train the ss in those skills. At both Auschwitz and Jaworzno, where he had been sent several months before, he had managed to live quite comfortably. Then, using his influence as a trainer with the ss, he helped his older brother Isaac land a job as a foreman with a hydroelectric project. Due to their important positions in the camp, they were receiving special treatment, even to the point of eating the same food as the German soldiers.

Everyone had to be inside their barracks by seven o'clock so we said good-bye, but before departing they promised to help me out as soon as the opportunity presented itself. That night, I thought about it and decided I shouldn't get my hopes up; prisoners take care of themselves, and, for me, real feelings of solidarity, even among relatives, didn't exist. While harboring few illusions, I was still hopeful that my life at Jaworzno would get better. Then I fell fast asleep.

The harassment and hunger that I experienced in the mine over the next few days destroyed any notion that their promise would come true. Deeply fatigued, I began to think that those persons with whom I had spoken were simply snatches of a broken dream. Meanwhile, the perpetual spectacle of death terrified me. No day went by without corpses, stacked like cords of wood, piled up at the mine entrance. A bullet in the back of the head was waiting for everyone — those who fainted from the work, the ones who stabbed their foot with a pickax, the others who got trapped under the wheels of the carts, or those who became too weak to work. And they were replaced immediately. Nary a tear of affection would be those unfortunate beings' farewell. But were they really so unfortunate? More than one hanged himself from the beams in the mine shafts. It was no coincidence that I would remember my adopted brother Schmiel. However, whenever I thought about him and his lack of respect for life, some empty cavity inside my soul would fill up with the weary desire to continue resisting by any means possible.

Despite those images of suffering, I led a life of monotony, for even the most horrible sights now seemed natural after seeing them on a daily basis. At dawn every day, the Kapos would enter the barracks yelling at us to get dressed. Then the torture would begin: "Bettenbau!"

The whiplashes would split our skin, and, scurrying like frightened rabbits, we would try to cover ourselves with our arms as we ran about trying to avoid the punishment. The ones who were still alive jumped out of their beds with sleepy eyes and swollen faces. The ones who slept near the side door would receive the most lashings. I had the advantage of sleeping at the far end of the room which allowed me more time to get up and put my clothes on. But day in and day out, the prisoners with bunks nearest the showers were beaten mercilessly. After washing, we would run outside to stand in formation and receive breakfast, that same sugarless, watery tea or chicory served in a small tin saucepan that was used for our soup in the afternoon.

Then it was time for the head count. Every last one of us was counted until they had the correct number, including, as I said, the dead prisoners who were counted as if they were still alive. When I would finally come out of the mine and sniff the breeze from the countryside, I felt as free and sturdy as a walnut tree, despite the deathly watch of the guards. During those months that I worked in the mine, I had no sense of how much time had passed. The most bothersome aspects of my life as a miner were the darkness that depressed my soul and the sickening dust that we had to inhale. The only advantage to working in the mine was that we were given an extra ration of bread.

As time passed and I was able to overcome the emotional turmoil that had left me mute, I began to associate with some of the other hapless prisoners. That's how I came to know a young Jew from Poland. He was among those who had been there the longest. One afternoon, I conveyed to him my secret plan to escape. But he whispered in my ear not to discuss the matter again because it was ludicrous. He told me stories about confused young men who had tried to escape and only ended up swinging from a rope. He felt so strongly about the matter that in order to curb my intentions to escape, he admonished me, "If you continue to insist on trying to escape, I'll be the first to turn you in."

I put my plans on hold; but my desire to stay alive continued to grow with the encouragement we would give each other. Having to face death on a daily basis only spurred my desire to continue living. The two of us were able to convince each other that the best way to leave the concentration camp alive and through the main gate was by conserving our energy and avoiding the beatings.

Then, after some time had passed, during a head count by an ss officer, I was called out of line; immediately, my companions from the barracks began to encourage me in Yiddish. Like me, they thought my time had come because I was no longer able to continue working in my job. The fate of those who are pulled out of line was known by all: instant death. But the ss officer simply told me I wouldn't be working in the mine anymore. The news produced not only surprise but also fatigue. At first, I thought it was all a hoax and that my desire to live would soon end. With little hope left, I followed the officer to another squad. There he pushed me away and shouted, "Raus! Raus!"

My doubts, suspicions, and bad thoughts about my cousins had proven unfounded. Isaac had managed to get me a job working aboveground with a construction company. When we were given our food in the afternoons, Shlomo would come by and give me half of his food. His contribution was ultimately very important in prolonging my life. He would also give food to a fourteen-year-old boy who had been a neighbor of Shlomo's deceased mother.

This new twist in life gave me a different perspective on the others around me. Although I still doubted and distrusted nearly everyone, I regained some feelings of human emotion that had disappeared with the deaths of my mother and sisters at Birkenau.

The first time my cousin brought me a small portion of his food, I was flooded by many different sensations all at once: for one thing, I felt shame, and, for another, my pride was wounded. As I thanked him for his kind gesture, remembering that I had once thought that they might be German collaborators, I began to sob uncontrollably. Tears that I had held back since that night at Birkenau began to flow, and through them flowed all the pain and desperation that had been heaped up after so much time. Afterward, I went over to a corner and finished eating.

My cousins understood my emotional state and let me eat by myself. When I finished licking the plate, they told me that they had seen me unload a truck of potatoes in exchange for some food. Yes, an ss soldier, who looked gaunt and half dead himself with the thin, white face of a rat, had offered us an extra portion of food if we would unload his truck. No one stepped forward nor said a word. I was more naive than the rest, so I agreed to do the job for the reward. Immediately, I set to work with vim and vigor, stimulated by the idea that my efforts would result in a prize; besides, after breathing, eating was the second most important aspect of staying alive. Once I had finished, I went over to the ss to request the promised portion of bread. He looked at me ironically with those little beady eyes and then knocked me to the ground with a blow from the butt of his rifle. His German shepherd pulled on its leash and growled. I got up, bleeding from the nose. I don't know what kind of expression he saw in my face but he let the dog loose and shouted, "Jacob! Jacob!"

The dog leaped on me and I fell to the ground. The repeated biting didn't pierce my flesh through the ragged uniform, for I was nothing but skin and bone. When the ss called his name again, I realized that the dog had a Jewish name while I was nothing more than a number: A-7393. Between the dog Jacob and the Jewish dog A-7393 there was an enormous difference: the former was trained to attack while I was simply a number, a piece of garbage with no name.

My cousins had watched that incident and I didn't know it. Nevertheless, they calmed me down and gave me some good advice on how to stay alive at Jaworzno. They finished by adding that the blood from my nose was irretrievable and that it was best to save it in order to conserve life. "To stay alive, you must eat, go to your bunk, and rest as much as possible." They were speaking to me like a brother. Their intentions coincided with my fundamental goal, the one I had vowed to follow during my trip to Jaworzno.

In the meantime, work went pretty well until the fall of 1944. My job, working for the construction company by the name of Holtzmann Stahlbau, consisted of assembling metal frames for buildings and riveting them into place. Due to the cold weather in the fall, the construction work got to be so difficult that once again I was on the edge of death; it wasn't because I had looked for it but rather death seemed to have become enraged with me, even though I kept repeating, "You will not trap me. You will not trap me."

The freezes at night made it impossible to touch the metal structures. If I picked up a metal beam in the early mornings, my fingers would freeze to it and rip off the skin. Since the rivets had to be heated up for riveting, I was able to warm my numb hands. We worked under such precarious conditions that many prisoners, most of whom were debilitated because of hunger and dizziness from anemia, would suddenly fall from high beams, smashing to the ground below. Sprawled on the frozen mud, they looked like mutilated puppets.

Around eleven o'clock every morning, silver airplanes would purr happily above us as they glistened across the sky. I was always hoping that the war was about to end and that the Allies would liberate me from my unbearable situation.

"They'll be arriving before winter begins," I would repeat to myself, seeking the strength to resist the cramping of my body.

If the cold had become unbearable, it was the hunger that decimated us. Of the 14,000 Greek Jews from Thessalonike at that camp, all but 280 had already died of sickness and hunger. Some of them even resorted to eating asphalt, trying to deceive their stomachs for a few minutes; but then they would slowly die in excruciating pain.

Our daily ration of food, despite the long, arduous hours of work, consisted of 250 grams of bread with a little watered-down soup. Sticking to my decision to survive at all cost, I figured out that the best way to obtain the most calories would be to go to the end of the line, not to the front, because the heart of the soup was always at the bottom of the pot. I was right, so from then on I would stand at the end of the line and receive a heartier soup.

But despite the additional bit of food that I got for doing occasional work, or getting food from my cousin, not many months passed before I was anemic like everyone else. Our bodies had become walking skeletons — with sunken eyes and ulcerated mouths and covered with welts and shrunken flesh — we looked like we were wearing clothing three sizes too big. Because we were nothing but skin and bones, we had incurable sores on our hips from the wooden bed frames. We had no mattresses. Trying to find a comfortable position on our sides, our bones scraped against the wood and cut our skin; hence, we could never get a full night's rest. The sores on our skin would get larger because of how skinny we were, and our bones would stick out of the sores like fingers.

An intellectual from Budapest, a refined man who expressed himself well, was among the prisoners in my barracks. He was one of those who kept us alive by constantly repeating that we were all going to survive. It was always the same old song and dance; eventually, he even convinced himself of it. But that fall he died.

In fact, with winter upon us, the intense cold brought death to many prisoners. Practically every day we would wake up to the news that one of us had died. When a person's body would begin to swell, we knew that death was imminent. We would have to haul the corpses outside for the head count; from there, they would be piled onto the backs of trucks, taken to Auschwitz, and tossed into the ovens, thus ending torture and martyrdom.

I could feel the cold approaching. But my cousins interceded and helped me to get transferred to a job indoors. I began in the mechanical section of the Siemens factory, located inside a mountain. From the outside there was only a large hill with weeds on top, but inside there was the feverish activity of war materiel production. I was responsible for rewiring electric motors that were used in the coal mines. As soon as I finished rewinding a motor, another prisoner would varnish it and put it in the oven to dry.

The shop foreman was Polish and, for some reason, he felt sorry for me. On one occasion, after noticing my sad state of malnutrition, he left a piece of a sandwich on one end of the work table. When I saw the bread at noon, I didn't touch it for fear it was a trick. Fear was stronger than hunger. But on the third day, I saw the Polish man signal with his eyes that the sandwich was for me. Even though he must have been good-hearted, he never a exchanged a single word with me or with the other prisoners who worked in that section.

Among them was a Catholic priest from the parish in Jaworzno: Father Bayer. He was young and easygoing. He didn't say much and his attitude was quite different from the other intellectuals. He had a practical way of encouraging the others: a gesture, a certain expression, or when he would lend a hand to bandage a wound. He was no ordinary prisoner because he wore a beret instead of a cap. We had heard that the Germans put him in the concentration camp because he had spoken out against Fascism in his sermons. I always got along well with him. But later, amid the confusion of the arrival of the Soviet offensive, Father Bayer disappeared. I found out later that his parishioners managed to get him out of the camp, saving his life.

By the time we were well into winter, I was suffering from great anxiety. Just as death had begun to prevail at the Jaworzno concentration camp, our will to continue fighting for survival had diminished. Things got even worse when the prisoners began turning against each other. Once again I found my soul filling with distrust, silence, and terror.

Despite the dim light in the barracks, it wasn't uncommon to see prisoners robbing each other of their food. Like wolves waiting in ambush, the prisoners on the top bunks would spy on those below them. The victims of these thefts were those who were sick with typhoid or TB. Soon it became common practice among the prisoners to sew their ration of bread into the lining of their uniforms, but when they would fall asleep or succumb to fever, the stronger prisoners would rip out the lining and steal their cache. The weak, sick prisoners were dispossessed of their belongings like carrion being ripped apart by hungry buzzards. Some prisoners were even strangled by the thieves who wanted to avoid being discovered. A person's life was now worth less than a piece of bread.

That winter we would wake up every morning and notice that those who had died during the night had been stripped of their shoes, socks, and what little food they had on them. In December, prisoners began dying like falling snowflakes, frozen, starved, and frail from the strenuous work and the continual suffering. The stronger prisoners simply clung to life, showing little compassion for the less fortunate. Even though the Soviet army was getting closer, the cold and misery made life in the camp intolerable. As tension grew, it was everyone for himself. While silence became the norm among the prisoners, foreshadowing death, the Kapos applied their hatred with intensified insanity by torturing us all the more. The beatings were so widespread that absolutely no one escaped the whip. The fear of death accelerated greater mistrust. Everyone was immersed in pervasive anguish — afraid of catching typhoid fever, afraid of being beaten or losing his teeth, afraid of being choked to death by a fellow prisoner.

The day of 22 December was memorable for all of us. The Soviets were about to reach the concentration camp. The camp's kitchen was hit by large cannon fire. There was hysteria, but lots of toothless smiles. Paradoxically, our jubilation became a bad omen: what if we died before they arrived!

With the coming of the Russians, a state of alert was announced: weapons were hauled out under the Kapos' frantic whipping, people were running wildly around the barracks, dogs barked, and sirens screamed. During the brief moments of chaos, we made our way to the bombarded kitchen. Extra guards were put on duty, but the machine guns were pointed toward the inside of the camp.

We crawled through the shell holes in the kitchen walls and began pillaging. But we only took bread and cheese. Anyone found stashing food would be executed on the spot, so as soon as we got back to the barracks we satiated ourselves, leaving no evidence. However, some prisoners ate too much and died as a result.

The firepower of the Soviet forces decimated the concentration camp. While many prisoners died outside in the snow, others died inside from overeating. The wounded in the snow moaned for hours; by nightfall there was only silence. No one had shown any compassion for them.

The next day, everyone remained quietly inside the camp; no brigades were sent outside the compound to work. It seemed as if we had been forgotten, for we just stayed in the barracks listening to the bombardment of the cannons and the rattling of machine-gun fire. We concluded that liberation was not far away, and we had to figure out how we could avoid being assassinated before the Soviet troops arrived. We didn't have the slightest idea of the horror that awaited us.

9

We remained inside the barracks for two days and two nights. The feast that resulted from pillaging the kitchen, while it did bring death to those who suffered from fatal indigestion, provided the necessary strength for the rest of us to continue waiting in silence, broken at times by the retching and choking of the dying. I thought only about survival and feverishly clung to life as I waited for the Soviets to arrive.

We could hear the large artillery shells exploding all around us. Intermittent machine-gun fire would wake me up during those brief moments when I would manage to doze off. I felt better knowing that I didn't have to go to work and that I could recover my strength by resting. Hardly anyone moved around inside the barracks, although from time to time someone might go to the bathroom near the main door or drink some water.

The agony of those who were dying made us doubly nervous. Whenever they asked for water hardly anyone would get close to them and take a chance of catching typhoid. Those who had indigestion suffered terrible pains and died a slow death. Those who had typhoid agonized over their fever and hunger pangs; since they were unable to make it to the kitchen to steal some food, and since other prisoners had stolen their rations from them, they would cry out for a piece of bread. Despite our willingness to help them, however, we didn't have a thing to eat. Everyone had stuffed themselves without thinking about tomorrow.

On 25 December, the camp was enveloped in peace and calm: the gentiles were celebrating the birth of Christ. For us, peace meant silence, for there was no artillery fire in the distance, nor was there any noise in the camp, except for a barking dog from time to time. It had snowed during the night and the camp was buried in whiteness. The cold was intense: we could see our breath when we exhaled. As the sun came up, the only interruption of peace in the barracks was the sound of our chattering teeth. Unable to ward off the bitter cold, we simply lay on our

bed frames without any blankets or woolen clothing and curled
up the best we could.

Most of us would just doze off. Time passed very slowly and our anguish intensified. Around noontime, when the sun had produced some warmth in the barracks, the prisoners began to perceive that something strange was occurring. The more optimistic ones stood on their bed frames and looked outside the windows. The lack of activity throughout the camp created the air of abandonment. Since we heard no trains or trucks moving, we deduced they wouldn't ship us out in retreat, yet the ss guards continued manning the guard towers with their machine guns. The more pessimistic prisoners were saying that the Nazis were waiting for Christmas to be over before they liquidated us. Others, however, believed that the Germans wouldn't assassinate us with the Russian army nearby, because a massive slaughter of so many prisoners would be proof of the Nazi atrocities.

Freezing temperatures kept the corpses from smelling. A similar situation in the summer would have been unbearable. By the afternoon I began to feel hunger coming on again. I had gone two days without eating anything, and, despite my efforts to preserve my energy, my stomach, unaccustomed to the recent feast, was hurting. I drank some water and fell onto the bed. After hearing the conversations of the other prisoners, I feared our destiny had already been sealed. But we had to resist. I wasn't able to think very well, but I meditated on one single truth: killing is the ss's daily work. The forces that had worn me out and made me a wretched soul, the loss of human values, the distrust, the slaughter of my family, the hunger, and the humiliation—what was the source of all this evil? Who were these people who had turned to assassinating their neighbors and friends? What man had received permission from God to exterminate his fellow man with impunity?

Neither fate nor the ire of God were enough to explain the nightmare that had already lasted five years since the Hungarians had taken over Sighet. While I continued to ponder, I longed for the peace of my native city, the murmuring waters of the Tisa that flowed past our house, the graceful freedom of the horses, the smell of the apple harvest, the swift hares scampering across the fields.

As night began to fall on Christmas, the barracks door burst open. Working quickly, the Kapos ordered an entire loaf of bread called *Festbrot* to be distributed to each of us, as well as enough *guargel* cheese to last us for eight days. I was so hungry that I did the same as before: in one sitting, I ate everything they gave me, without saving anything for the next day. No one could take my food away from me, for I was carrying it inside my stomach.

Soon thereafter, they took us out into the cold and we fell into formation. In the middle of winter, wearing thin and ragged cotton clothes, we began the "Death March" in an effort to escape from the Soviets. The worst part of my situation was the pair of wooden clogs that scraped at my toes.

At Jaworzno there was a blackout throughout the entire camp in order to prevent the Russian artillery from discovering our last-minute escape and firing on us. We were even prohibited from talking, let alone murmuring some complaint; only the wind and the curt orders from the ss stationed at our sides could be heard. As we walked, the frigid wind lashed at our bodies. Our caravan quickly passed through the gate at Jaworzno and headed for the open countryside.

Without looking back and not knowing where they were taking us, we began the most abominable pilgrimage ever imagined. Rumbling down the road with their lights illuminating the snowy landscape beyond the interminable columns of prisoners, the trucks, which ran on gases created from wood combustion, carried the ss guards and watch dogs. The German escort consisted of two soldiers, one on each side, for every five rows of prisoners, that is, two soldiers per twenty-five prisoners. The march was composed of those who were left over from the fourteen thousand prisoners condemned to die at Jaworzno. Even though we were ordered to trot, we were still unable to warm up.

After five hours of marching, fatigue set in and the number of stragglers began to mount. As soon as someone fell behind or was unable to keep up, an ss guard would order him to get down on his knees in the snow. He would point his gun at the back of the man's head and pull the trigger without mercy. No one protested. The first to die were the old and sick prisoners, then the weak ones. We were on the road to savagery once again. By midnight the intervals between gunshots were shorter; more and more prisoners had fallen by the wayside, shot in the head. We couldn't stop to think about what was happening. The blowing snow had begun to stick to our deteriorated bodies.

Even though there was no time to complain or grieve about our situation, there was one prisoner among us who still possessed a spark of goodwill. That human being's flame provided warmth for my frozen soul; I befriended a fourteen-year-old boy who accompanied me for the duration of the march. He was from the lower Czechoslovakian side of the Carpathians. The two of us hunched over together to fight off the cold, and we encouraged each other not to give in to the fatigue. Somehow, we shared our misery with the dignity that only two lifelong friends could do. We were like two old friends, neither speaking nor gesturing to show gratitude, nor displaying any comforting glances, but only providing the company and sharing the feeling that we were together at that critical moment.

We walked for three days and nights without stopping. Our minds and bodies had been numbed through and through. But nothing would detain that column of indigents: not the terrain, not the fatigue, not death itself. During the first day of the march, I had to pop the blisters on my feet with my fingernails. I realized that if I didn't get rid of those wooden clogs I wouldn't be able to go very far; my survival depended on obtaining a pair of shoes. So I began to concentrate on one thing — my feet. Whenever I would pass a corpse on the road, I immediately looked at his shoes. I knew I would be taking a risk by stopping, but I also knew that I had to steal some shoes from someone who was about my height and who had kept them in good condition. A lot of the shoes were hidden in the snow, but most of them were in bad shape, torn, bloodied, too small, or too firmly tied to their owners' ankles.

Driven by the need for some shoes, I trotted along until I came upon a dead prisoner about my height and whose shoes were half off. Here was a dead man who hadn't been carted off yet, and he had given me a gift. I bent down, pulled them off, and brushed off the snow. Hardly stopping, I put the stolen shoes on and threw the wooden clogs away. To steal from a dead person is an iniquity, but there's one thing for sure, that pair of shoes enabled me to continue living.

It appeared that the uninterrupted three-day march was an attempt to distance us from the encircling Soviet forces. We had been in the center of conflict and now we were forced to flee as quickly as possible. By evening of the third day, we stopped and they distributed some bread to us. The march began again before dawn the next morning. During the night, many prisoners froze to death with a piece of bread between their lips. Now they were covered with a blanket of snow. The corpses were also the targets of thievery, but I didn't touch any of them, out of fear of catching typhoid. I advised my young friend not to eat the infected bread.

During the march, the military had ordered farmers along the way to accompany the column of prisoners with their carts in order to pick up the corpses strewn along the wayside. The squeaking wheels played a death hymn. Blood oozed through the wooden slats of the carts and trickled onto the snow. It was like a long, warm, open vein that accompanied us endlessly. Once in a while, the muffled moaning of a dying person could be heard, the bullet having failed to do its job. It seemed to me that the enemy was neither hunger nor the march, but rather the carts into which one was put for the final trip, contributing that blood to the warm artery in the snow.

As we left behind the industrial area of Upper Silesia, we continued our march using side roads, but we also passed through the cities of Katowice, Konigshule, and Gliwice. After about a week of walking, we arrived at the outskirts of Kozle. In order to get through the city we had to cross a bridge over the Oder River. Inertia had set in, keeping my legs from moving. We had already covered about 120 miles with few stops for rest; we were exhausted and my strength and energy were gone. My Czech friend tried to help me along, but I was too heavy for him. I fell to the ground. At that moment he looked into my eyes and I motioned for him to keep going. Returning to the column to continue the march he turned to wave good-bye, forever. I was being left behind. A continual string of prisoners passed by in front of me, but no one stuck out a hand to pull me up or even look at me. I had been sentenced to death because of fatigue, and, by dropping out of the column, I knew what was waiting for me. A guard nearby saw me and ordered me to get to my knees. The prisoners continued to pass by without noticing me. The rifle was pointing at me, all I had to do was get to my knees.

I thought that was the end of my tenacious desire to survive, but, panic-struck upon looking up at the dark hole of the gun barrel, I jumped up and began to run with all my might toward the line of prisoners. When my young friend saw me, he smiled from ear to ear and he gave me his shoulder to lean on. As if my strength had been miraculously renewed, I was able to keep walking the whole day long. Our human convoy continued forward until past nightfall. The night's rest helped me to recover my energy. The next morning we continued toward the city of Breslau, passing through different cities on heavily used routes.

My hands were so frozen from the cold that I couldn't even unbutton my pants. The Czech helped me to open my fly so I could urinate, he tied my shoes for me, and he fed me my ration of food.

New Year's came and went. No one even gave a thought to those insignificant things. The beginning of 1945 found us walking with wet shoes alongside the outstretched bodies of our fellow prisoners, enduring the cold and hunger, and agonizing over a journey whose destination we knew nothing about. The countless days, the landscape, and the pain were all one and the same to us. No one looked to their sides. We forged ahead merely to survive. Despite the harassment of the guards, the beatings, and dog bites, the endless convoy of wandering skeletons advanced ever forward. In one hamlet, the people came out of their houses to yell and scream at us. "Kill the Jews, the sons of bitches!"

They threw hard-packed snowballs at us. Without looking up, we stumbled onward, hiding our fear and trying to shrink out of sight. We simply continued along with heads hanging low. Crossing our arms so we could put our hands under our armpits to keep them warm, we must have looked like bats crippled by a sudden strong light—trembling, quivering, and confused by the infamy that surrounded us. The nickname the Germans had given us in the concentration camps fit us perfectly: *Muselman.* The word, meaning part bat and part man, was used by the soldiers to describe our deplorable appearance.

Our walk toward Breslau seemed endless. Time became meaningless. Practically unconscious, we plodded on mechanically. I quit wondering why my legs just didn't stop holding me up. We were an enormous caterpillar of a thousand legs that simply continued forward, despite being frozen, blinded by the bright snow, faces contorted from the pain and starvation, lips split open, and ears frostbitten.

It wasn't long before even the guards' image began to tarnish—their severe military carriage, their Aryan composure, their elegance, their impeccable uniforms, their shiny boots, their haughty inner strength, their murderous insanity all faded—as if they were entering with us into the same subhuman world, the same space of worthless people and insignificant life.

Bread rationing became less and less frequent, and when they gave us a piece, perhaps by mistake, it was like a scoop of snow in our mouths. We left Breslau and began another journey that would take us to Legnica.

When evening came we stopped to spend the night on a farm. Blurting out commands, the guards pushed us along to get us settled so they could rest. The farm consisted of a run-down house and granary. Nearby there was a well with a watering hole for the animals. The barn smelled of wet hay and old cattle dung. We went through the main doors in groups of ten or twelve at a time, pushing each other and trying to grab a spot where it would be warmer through the night. We had spent so many nights out in the frozen elements that the barn seemed like the most luxurious hotel in the world. Some were saying that we were really lucky. Little did we know that our stay at the barn would soon become a new source of pain and anguish.

They ordered every last one of us inside — space or no space. The stragglers, who were forced inside with whips and gun butts, were plastered against the ones who were already inside. Everyone was piled on top of everyone else. We were so squashed and jammed up against each other that we couldn't breathe. Those who fell to the floor were trampled and asphyxiated. Those of us who were still standing were destined to sleep that way.

Since there was no more space or air to breathe inside that barn, I quickly realized that if I remained where I was, I would soon die from asphyxiation. I looked up and saw the beams of the roof. Some prisoners had beaten me to the idea: they were already perched up there. Nevertheless, the beams provided more space than down below, so I climbed up one of the wooden columns, reached a crossbeam, and was even able to stretch out on it. With the heat that rose up from that conglomeration of people below, I soon fell fast asleep like a hen on its roost.

The next morning, we were jolted awake by gunshots, lashings, and guards shouting orders. The barn door was open and the light of a new day came streaming in. Once again, however, we started reliving the nightmare. We spilled out into the cold air and were ordered to fall into formation for the head count. Inside were numerous dead prisoners, a virtual harvest of corpses. We had to pile them up outside for the count and then fall into line again for a recount. But this time some prisoners were missing, so they threatened to kill us if we didn't tell them where they were hiding. Someone pointed to the well. Several soldiers looked inside and let loose a volley of machine-gun fire into the dark hole, but not a single cry was heard. An officer took a grenade from a soldier, pulled the pin, and dropped it into the well. The explosion made a hollow sound similar to a mortar. Rocks and dirt spewed out of the hole. Finally, there was silence as smoke wafted out of the well like the smoke from a pipe.

Once again, the soldiers pointed their weapons at us and threatened to kill us all. A patrol squad went into the barn, grabbed some pitchforks and began to stab at the piles of hay in search of the missing prisoners. While they did uncover a few corpses here and there and, consequently, adjusted their head count, more prisoners were still missing. An officer ordered the guards to cock their weapons. By then it was about noon and we were still standing near the entrance to the barn. The officer shouted for us to tell him where the others were or they would begin firing. But no one made a move.

The officer gave the order to start shooting. As the bullets began mowing people down, we panicked and scattered every which way. Tripping over each other, falling down, dodging the wounded, jumping over corpses, we ran like winged spirits in search of refuge. During that stampede I lost my young Czech friend and never found out what had happened to him.

Overcome with terror, I fled without looking back. I didn't stop running until I reached the bank of a creek, where I slipped and fell into the mud. I drank some water from the creek and crawled over to a fallen tree trunk. I waited a long time, not daring to move. Then it started to get dark. Spying through the brush, I could see off in the distance a dim light coming from a farmhouse. I tried to walk but I blacked out.

Several hours later, I opened my eyes to see the black barrel

of a pistol pointing right at me. I thought it was a nightmare.
I looked around: there were some cows grazing nearby and I
was stretched out on a pile of hay. A farmer, a short man who
smelled like manure, was standing close by. When I was able to
figure out what was happening, I realized that two men from
the Gestapo were standing in front of me. They ordered me to
get up. When I tried, I couldn't. My leg was in a pool of blood
that had soaked the hay around it. I guessed that in the frenzy
and chaos of my flight I had been shot in the leg but I hadn't
felt it. Now I could feel the sharp burning sensation in my leg:
the bullet had pierced my calf and exited through the front of
my leg.

The two Gestapo officers ordered me to bandage the wound.
They watched me while I tied a piece of rag around my calf
to stop the bleeding. They helped me up and we left the barn.
Accompanied by the two men and walking with great difficulty,
we reached a small village. They stuck me in some kind of jail
cell and locked it.

Discovering that I was alone, I became uneasy. I hadn't been
alone for many months; with no one else around, I felt trapped.
Looking at my surroundings with much trepidation, I sat down
on the cot and set to work cleaning my wounded calf with my
own spit, hoping in this way to forget about my uneasiness for
a while. After adjusting the bandage, I decided to take a rest on
the cot. I woke up several hours later and found a cup of cold
cabbage soup with a piece of fat floating in it. I drank it up and
fell asleep again.

Even though I had no idea where I was, I was being treated
well. I had received food and water and, although no one spoke
to me, I wasn't cold, abused, or overly hungry. I tried to rest
the entire day. During the following three weeks that I spent in
the village jail, most of the time I was flat on my back because of
my wound. My greatest hope was that my leg would heal quickly.
Instead of drinking all the water they gave me, I would use some
to cleanse the wound because I was worried that it might get

infected and lead to gangrene. Perhaps it was the cold and the daily washing that kept it from getting infected, but it took a long time to heal.

In that solitary cloister, I spent my time thinking about my family. I wondered what might have happened to my older brothers who had been sent to the Russian front to work as laborers for the German forces. I remembered how I had abandoned my father and my younger brothers at Auschwitz after deciding to go it alone. I tried to forget that nightmare at Birkenau, but the memory of my mother and sisters would suddenly well up. Nevertheless, those memories gave me the strength to continue fighting for freedom in that devastating world. I used to think that if God was so busy moving each cloud in the sky, each animal in the countryside, each leaf in the trees, and every particle of dust, how could he have enough time for a measly Jew? If he didn't have time to take care of all those details, I sure had better think about taking care of myself. In the end God would decide what was going to happen, but each one of us had to participate in some way.

God wasn't bad, and human beings, in and of themselves, weren't either. The wicked ones were the governments and their social structures that provided the organizational apparatus for death and extermination. Nobody was going to win this war, everybody was going to lose it. Wolves fight to live, people fight to kill. I thought that I would be detained in that village until the war ended because the place seemed so separate from what was happening elsewhere.

When I'd tire of the cot that pained my skinned hips, I would spend hours—quiet, almost motionless—sitting against the wall of the cell perceiving images that were visible only to my sunken, dark eyes. One image that held me captive for hours was the one of the lurking owl perched on the edge of our well. When night fell and they came into the cell to drag me over to my cot, I would remember my father's voice. I could hear him so clearly that at times I thought I had returned to my childhood and was hearing my father speaking to me. "Sanyi, we are still alive, you must fight for us." Then I'd recite the prayer *Shema Yisrael* (Hear, O Israel).

On one occasion, I noticed that I was mixing up the Psalms of David with my own situation; I was carrying on an unintelligible, but irrepressible, monologue. Having been kept penned up alone for so long without anyone visiting me or even saying a word to me, I was becoming mentally deranged. I'd spend my time drawing pictures of our barn in Sighet on the dirt floor with a sliver of wood. Then I'd draw our house, putting everything in its right place, my family too, as if they were all still alive. I'd draw the routes I used to take as a smuggler, and, meticulously, I'd organize a plan on a grand scale.

In my mind's eye I could also see the *cheder* and the classrooms at school. I tried to imagine what life would be like upon my return to Sighet. At other times, I saw an avalanche of faceless Hungarian skulls that would repeat, "When you strike the enemy with the club, don't look at his face."

Before, when we lived in Sighet, we'd go out and pick mushrooms on our days off. We knew which ones were edible, for there were poisonous types that produced hallucinations. And we'd go to the oak forest looking for seeds; when the trees were in bloom, the seeds would sprout from the branches in the form of hanging baskets, like beehives. Inside there were clusters of seeds like wild grapes and we'd pick the fruit, take it home, and cook it until it turned sticky like dissolved rubber.

In the winter, the children would make a snowman, put a cap on him, and stick a piece of wood into his mouth for a cigar. Most birds would migrate south, but the ones that stayed behind would find shelter from the freezing weather near the barns, where they'd eat corn, wheat, and barley.

Life in jail was like the life of a *Stieglitz*, or goldfinch. During the winter months, my brothers and I would set traps, catch them, and sell them to people in Sighet who liked their exotic color and ability to sing. We'd use the sticky substance from the boiled oak fruit to catch them. We put the goo in leather bowls and diluted it with a bit of gasoline. Next, we'd get a small spiny bush and paint the substance all over the branches. Then we'd stick the bush in the snow out in an open field and place a male goldfinch in a cage next to the bush. He would call the females, and with other seeds spread about on top of the snow, the birds would appear immediately. We'd hide and wait for them to perch on the sticky branches. After several had done so, we'd come out yelling and thrashing our arms so they would take to flight; but their wings would stick to the glue and they were caught. Then we'd pick them off the branches, wipe them clean, and try to sell them. We'd always let the females go free because they couldn't sing.

If during my time at Jaworzno I had desired to be alone in the midst of that multitude of anonymous, ghostly beings, now I fervently desired to be around other human beings. I couldn't understand why I wasn't happy with my lot, isolated from the beatings, the death threats, the blistering cold, and the unending forced marches. I guess what brought me the most peace was not having to hear the repeated firing of weapons or having to look at all those corpses. Although the four walls of the cell were oppressive and I needed to see the horizon in order to get my bearings, I also felt protected by them from the cruel, devastating world on the outside. Ironically, despite its pernicious tranquillity and my restlessness, the jail cell was defending me from organized extermination.

I never did find out the name of that village where I had been jailed, but I thought that the people there must have been quite reserved and uncommunicative. I never once heard anyone say anything outside my cell; it was as if the people never talked around there. Only the winds howling in the night made any sound. During the day I could hear noises coming from the streets — carts, oxen, and mules — but it was a village devoid of human beings. Those sounds would make me think of my life in Sighet. Nostalgically remembering my childhood in that city, my heart would sink. The wind, the noises, the silence, the apparent calm outside would distract me and my imagination would bring to life my parents' house. However, those childhood memories gave me more pain than the wound in my leg. And, to top things off, it wasn't healing well; it was just an enormous red gash. Yet I thought that the possibility of my staying the remainder of the war in that village was wonderful; in that way, my leg could heal and I'd regain my strength.

After three weeks of being locked up while my leg was healing, I heard the sound of a caravan of prisoners passing through the village. It was a bad omen, for the pleasure and pain of the loneliness in the cell and the hot meals came to an abrupt end. I was back to marching. Even though it was difficult to stand on my leg.

Nevertheless, someone had decided that I was well enough to move on; the village didn't want the responsibility of harboring a Jew. While an old man spoke to an officer, I looked at them as subserviently as possible. He must have said something about my leg because the officer looked down at it. Then a soldier pushed me into one of the columns of prisoners, and, all of a sudden, I was back where I was before. I noticed that nothing had changed. Everything was exactly the way it was before: the faces, the fatigue, the orders, and the cracking of the whips.

My dreams had been shattered. As we marched toward Gross Rosen, a prison camp located on the outskirts of the city of Gogh, I thought my life was nothing more than an endless nightmare. The burning pain of my leg wound was an insignificant part of that all-embracing nightmare. I had spent so many hours in solitary confinement with the images I had conjured up that everything around me now seemed bizarre and incomprehensible.

However, the fierce pain in my leg and the suffering I witnessed brought me back to reality. Everything turned dark gray:

the snow, heavily trampled by the prisoners and mixed with dirt from intermittent thawing, was a dismal sooty color. And it was impossible to escape the deathly looks on the prisoners' faces and the stolid obedience of the guards. The images and dreams that I had nurtured in jail were starting to fade from my memory like one's reflection in a stream.

But I had come to terms with my reality. It was my only reality, the one from which there was no escaping, that is, being a wandering prisoner. I looked up at the sky. The wind that lashed against my face brought despair: hopelessness enveloped me like a hurricane, hurtling me headlong to where I had been three weeks before—a lonely itinerant walking toward exile.

10

While I had been in that village jail I convinced myself that they might possibly leave me there. In reality, however, I was still A-7393, and numbers, which were still important at the time, had to be continually fed to the maw of death.

Since the wound in my calf had not fully healed, I had to hobble through the snow in order to fall into line with the other prisoners of the convoy passing through that village. As we started out, I saw that winter was still in full splendor—the branches of the trees were laden with snow, the windows of the houses were all frosted up, and the streets had acquired an iridescent whiteness—yet our appearance conjured up images of brutalization, hunger, persecution, inclement weather, and extreme exhaustion. But those things were familiar to me: the four-wheeled carts heaped with corpses, the gaunt bodies of the prisoners, their dazed eyes staring off into space, their frayed uniforms, and their fatigue. As horrible as life in the concentration camps had been, at least there had been a routine of sorts. The never-ending marches over great distances without any apparent objective made moments of lucidity unbearable. The regular hours, and the continual presence of pain allowed life to fall into a routine, despite the horror.

And I fell in with the others as if I had never experienced the brief reprieve in that village jail cell. Both the countryside and the calamities hadn't changed a bit. I really missed the company of my young Czech friend. Deep down I hoped he had made out well in that stampede of prisoners when the soldiers began firing upon us at that abandoned farm.

We had been walking about three hours when I heard someone whisper my name. I couldn't believe it at first and I figured I was simply hallucinating because of exhaustion and weakness. Then I heard it again and turned around to look. Some rows back I saw a man whose face was emaciated from hunger, his skin flayed from the intense cold, and his lips puffy with sores;

he could barely call out my name, but he looked straight at me. I didn't recognize him right off.

"I'm Joseph."

Of course, it was Joseph Fuchs, one of our neighbors in Sighet. I exchanged positions with another prisoner and we began walking together. This encounter with someone I knew made me happy for a brief moment, thinking that now I had someone with whom I could share my hardships, but that euphoria vanished when I saw he was wearing a black ribbon with two yellow circles on his forearm. The deaf-and-dumb wore a similar ribbon, but theirs would have three yellow circles. Those with ribbons got preferential treatment, better work, and more food than the others. The *Halb Juden*, half-Jews or Jews who had converted to Christianity, were treated differently than everyone else because of that ribbon with two circles. More than likely, Joseph had taken the ribbon from a dead person and was wearing it now in order to get better treatment. His deceit, coming from an authentic Jew, made me indignant.

We continued walking side by side, but I didn't tell him how I felt. Who was I to judge others? I had seen fathers taking bread away from their own families in order to stay alive, mothers abandoning their children in order to save themselves, friends fighting over a boiled potato or a leaf of cabbage. The fear of death had turned human beings into animals. While we walked, I asked myself what it was about death that it would change our beliefs and alter our sense of values. Since death had surrounded us and then found its way inside us, undermining us, wearing us down, each one of us would use the most despicable ways to fight it off.

Despite our inertia, we continued forward, always under the watchful eye of the ss. We had lost all strength and were but walking skeletons pushed along by a cruel destiny that would take us to the incinerators. Our appearance was deplorable: our striped, cotton uniforms were rags. The freezing, blowing snow passed through our bodies, penetrating right down to the marrow. We no longer felt pain nor nostalgia, our thoughts were incoherent, nothing made sense, only our souls were suffering from the misery in which we found ourselves. As we walked through a village, the inhabitants screamed obscenities at us, spit on us, and threw snowballs at us. We just looked at them with indifference, not understanding what was happening. I asked myself, Why so much hatred? Why so much evil? What had been our sin to receive such cruel punishment?

I looked up to the sky for consolation. It was covered with dark, dense clouds blowing in the wind and making it difficult to breathe. Not long after we lost sight of the village, the sound of voices, murmuring, sighs, and shouting brought me back to reality. I looked toward the source of those sounds. Next to the roadside, I could make out a barbed-wire fence surrounding a prisoner-of-war camp for English soldiers. I could tell the prisoners were in relatively good physical shape and spirits, only their prisoner uniforms were tattered and worn. Unable to believe their own eyes or fathom the spectacle that was passing in front of them, their faces communicated feelings of compassion and sadness, for we were a macabre spectacle of marching human shadows. They tried to communicate with us, asking questions, wanting to know who we were, and inquiring if were hungry. Some of them threw pieces of bread, or whatever they had, at us. I managed to grab a piece and, after eating it, I could feel that I was returning to life: a ray of light illuminated my soul, and, once again, I made the decision to continue fighting to stay alive and to survive.

After walking a week without any rest, we arrived at Gross Rosen, a camp for prisoners in transit, where we would be regrouped and assigned to other camps throughout Germany. With my friend Joseph at my side, we were thrown into a barracks. The first thing I noticed about this camp was that discipline among the guards was quite lax; in fact, the prisoners looked like unemployed laborers waiting to be hired for work. I wandered aimlessly around the barracks; it was like a Babel of ashen men, the bearers of death from several nations who had been incarcerated by the German army. They would walk around in circles and would ask the strangest questions, as if they were lost in a big city. Our greatest worry was trying to find out where they were sending us next. Men from the same country would huddle together and talk about the Germans' approaching defeat. Joseph and I were also interested in looking for someone we might know. The prisoners' faces didn't reveal much, so we would walk around listening to the accent of the conversations as a guide through that labyrinth of languages. I was going around so involved in listening to the dialogues among that confusion of tongues that I didn't pay any attention to Joseph's question. "Isn't that your brother over there?"

When he said it the second time, he pushed me toward a group of prisoners huddled together near the entrance to one of the barracks. When I looked up, I saw my brother's face appear in the crowd. With all the force that my limping leg would permit, I lunged toward the group of men. Pushing my way through them, I shouted my brother's name. "Saul!"

He turned to look at me and there we stood, face to face, perplexed, hesitant, scrutinizing each other. Suddenly, we hugged and squeezed each other tightly.

Once those first sentimental moments of euphoria were over, trying not to ask about my father for fear of confronting the reality of his death, my question burst out anyway. Saul told me that he was not only still alive but here in this same camp. My anxiety seemed to evaporate: Saul seemed uneasy. Our conversation took an unusual twist. He began telling me about his privations in the camp at Buna; they seemed so similar to my own experiences that I didn't pay much attention to what he was saying. As I observed him, I realized that Saul was older than his years. Confined by barbed wire all this time, he had lost the innocence of a country boy. Cunningness, driven by those harsh times, emanated from his shady eyes. Fearing bad news, I asked him if he knew anything about our younger brother Samuel, whom I had taken for lost among the multitude of skeletons that wandered aimlessly nowhere.

While we talked, he nervously searched for something in the lining of his threadbare uniform. I didn't ask him what he was carrying, but then a troubled look came over his face and he told me that my father had entrusted him with his bread rations. I immediately suspected that my father had typhoid fever because the first symptom of the disease is a loss of appetite, followed by asking someone to keep your food until you get better. I was moved to see that the ration of bread—literally a crumb weighing no more than an ounce—had been sewn to the inside of his coat to prevent someone from stealing it. As if he were trying to reveal the truth of his good intentions, Saul finally showed me several days' worth of bread. But he remarked quickly that he didn't know if he would be able to keep his promise not to eat it. He would lightly pat the bread in the lining to assure himself it was still there. From time to time he would pinch the sacred bread and pop the crumbs into his mouth. In some way, he wanted to implicate me in the pillaging of food that didn't belong to us.

When Saul offered me a piece, I couldn't blame him for wanting to eat it. I understood his quandary, but I told him I couldn't eat it knowing that it belonged to our father. Saul made a gesture of "to each his own" and dropped the matter. Then he suggested we go and look for our father.

We walked past several barracks until we reached the one where my father was staying. As we entered, the darkness frightened me. My father was sitting on the edge of a cot next to another old prisoner by the name of Dudas, a Hungarian gentile who had been arrested for being a member of the Communist party. My father's condition was deplorable. Like an old wall that has disintegrated, his body looked chipped, scaly, and cracked. Hunched over from months of forced labor, only his cheekbones could be made out. His eyes were bloodshot. He was a toothless old man. It was his birthday: 22 March 1945.

We hugged each other and broke into tears. He embraced me with fatherly love, as if he were trying to protect me from harm. Like staring into a mirror, each one of us saw himself in the image of the other. When we looked at each other, both of us remembered the terrible night at Birkenau. The endless affliction and horrible nightmares had disfigured us forever. His listless green eyes gave him away: life was slipping away from him. I was deeply saddened to find out that he was going around exchanging bread for cigarettes.

He asked me to light a cigarette for him. His emaciated face became enshrouded in smoke that would fade away and then disappear. He had turned fifty-two years old that day, yet he looked like an old, sick, miserable beggar. I tried to convince myself of what I said to him next. "Don't worry, Father, Saul and I are going to take care of you."

He responded with a bitter smile, and as he started to finish his cigarette, his words became almost inaudible. "You are young and you will survive. The war is almost over. Your mother is dead, so there is no reason for me to continue living. My life is worthless." His words lost their force as he took the last puffs of his cigarette.

The bell rang to line up for soup. It was five o'clock in the afternoon. We hugged each other again, I knelt at his feet, and he blessed me with serenity; then he lay down on his cot. I wanted to spend a little more time with my father, so I got into the soup line in his barracks, being one of the first in line. When they had finished ladling it out, they counted the spoons and discovered there was one missing.

"There is an unauthorized person here," shouted a Kapo.

In a flash I pushed the soup aside, jumped over some cots, and leaped out the window. I didn't have a second to say good-bye to my father. If I had been caught in the wrong barracks, the prisoners themselves would have lynched me on the spot. When I got back to my area, Joseph was waiting for me in the soup line. I was the last one. The Kapo looked at me with interrogating eyes.

"I was in the latrine," I explained.

While I ate my soup with Joseph, I couldn't get the image of my father out of my mind. With tears welling up in my eyes, I could hear him saying, "You are young and you are going to survive."

It was impossible to imagine then that our furtive encounter that day was the last time I would ever see him.

That night I fell asleep consumed by the meaning of his words. The next day I met my brother at the corner. We had agreed to sign up together at the dispatch office to join the next group of prisoners being transported out.

"I want to see my father," I told him as we finished signing up. But Saul advised me not to go near his barracks because the Kapo and the prisoners would recognize me and I would never escape a lynching. Despite my desire to see my father again, I took his advice, thinking we would see each other again in the transport truck. However, some things are never to be. We agreed to meet in the same barracks in order to arrange our departure together.

The next day, Joseph and I went to the same place where we had met Saul and waited for him. An hour went by. My brother didn't come. The wait made me impatient and I began to imagine all kinds of things happening to him. Each time I mentioned something that could have happened to him, Joseph would try to dispel my fears. A short while later, a stranger walked up to us.

"Who is Sanyi?" he asked.

Joseph nodded toward me.

"Your brother was shipped out yesterday. He asked me to give you the message."

"And my father?" I questioned worriedly.

"I don't know him. All I know is what I just told you."

I extended a piece of bread to him in gratitude, and he went away eating it.

My friend Joseph went to my father's barracks to find out what had happened to him. He returned without any information, saying no one knew anything about him. The family reunion had begun and ended like the flash of a shooting star in the immensity of the night.

A few days later, before we were given orders to leave Gross Rosen, I tried once more to find my father, but I never got any information about him. The prisoners in his barracks were new and no one had any idea where the previous prisoners in that barracks had been sent. Then one morning we were ordered to leave the camp immediately. The wound in my leg was almost healed. For several days we walked toward the city of Gorlitz, while the Germans kept on shooting the stragglers in the back of the head and leaving them on the roadside for nearby farmers to pick up in their carts. All the while, the memory of my father and brother kept coming back to me, upsetting me. I blamed myself for losing track of them, especially when we had been brought together in that place.

After arriving at a train station, they loaded us into freight cars, the tops of which had been removed, while the guards stood watch on catwalks from above. The train pulled out. I hadn't traveled on a train since our deportation to Birkenau, which is why the puffing engine and clickety-clack of the train wheels on the tracks suddenly precipitated profound anguish. Deep in the recesses of my soul, those sounds triggered memories of how our disaster had begun. But the droning sound of the wheels also brought on drowsiness. Some prisoners dropped to the floor, never to get up again: cold and starvation killed them.

The freezing cold gnawed away at our bodies. Not having to walk, however, was gratifying. Bread was doled out from above us by the guards, who were like farmers tossing hay from a loft down to the animals below. But for some of the prisoners, fatigue and sickness were so intense that, despite their hunger, they made no attempt to catch the bread. The stronger ones among us would get double or triple rations, gobble them down, and look furtively to their sides, like dogs, at the other prisoners.

The train came to a halt. We had arrived at Leonberg, near Stuttgart, where, apparently, we were to work in an airplane factory. The doors were flung open, and as we walked out onto the platform wet snow was falling. Waiting in small groups to be assigned, we must have looked like damp lice. When the commandant inspected his newly arrived merchandise, all he saw were our lacerated, injured bodies; our state of deterioration and frailty made him furious. Hence, we were reloaded onto the freight cars and taken to a camp at Mühldorf am Inn.

As we entered the camp, I sensed an air of ruin: no one gave us orders or required us to form work details. Even though we weren't crowded on top of each other and were able to wander about freely, we were still imprisoned in a concentration camp: each one of us still had to survive the best way we knew how. Since we didn't have to work, we would spend the day roaming about the camp from one end to the other, like starving rats trapped in a laboratory cage. The guard towers and the barbed wire were the only obstacles to freedom, and the barbed wire was a constant reminder of what we were: prisoners.

From time to time German soldiers would round us up into work gangs to go out and repair railroad tracks that had been damaged by air raids. I was fortunate to be sent out only once, for it was extremely dangerous work. The day I went, for instance, pilots of the Allied forces happened to see us rebuilding the tracks. Their planes came bearing down on us and opened fire with their machine guns at anything that moved. I managed to crawl into a metal drainage pipe from where I saw the bullets mowing down my companions. Having already survived the worst, now we were being gunned down by our own liberators. After that ugly experience, I did everything I could to make myself invisible every time the Germans came around to form work details.

As I walked around the camp, I noticed there was another camp — one for women — adjacent to ours and separated by a barbed-wire fence. The women were wearing striped uniforms and they had been shaved bald, but they seemed to be in better physical shape. I approached the fence and started talking to a few of them. Some of them were from Sighet and others were from the province of Maramures. A few minutes later more women joined in the conversation.

Since there was nothing to do in the camp, it became very important to Joseph and me to be able to talk to the women every day. They always gave us a little food and we would exchange friendly smiles. One day I saw three cousins of mine — and my old sweetheart! When she saw my emaciated state, Leah Gitel must have been repulsed. Pitying me, she pitched an onion to me and said with bitterness, "Here. Take it. Now there's no difference between us, is there? Now I'm feeding you."

Her skin had withered, she was bald, and her clothing was wrinkled and dirty. I felt no love for her. She was just another person in this cruel world and I simply looked at her with indifference, like a person who, after having stuffed himself on a four-course meal, is offered a dessert.

I could tell from the tone of her voice that she still resented our broken relationship and the open opposition of my parents to our engagement. Her words humiliated me so much that, despite my voracious hunger, I threw the onion back over the fence to her. My cousins, who witnessed the onion being tossed back and forth over the fence, didn't know anything about my earlier relationship with Leah, but they threw a few pieces of bread to me in sympathy.

A few days after seeing Leah, I began to run a high fever in the afternoons. Weakness and the loss of appetite meant only one thing: typhoid fever. I had neither bathed nor changed clothes in four months. Even though I didn't have to work, I did everything I could not to lie down; I thought that if I were to do so, I'd never get up again. My will and fear of death kept me standing up. In fact, I preferred to sleep standing up against the barracks instead of going to bed inside. The worst part about the whole thing was that Joseph came down with it too, and neither of us could help the other. The intestinal hemorrhaging was

brutal and I suffered terrible pain when I used the latrine. But I
managed the best I could to get through the next five weeks.

I had devised a recovery plan by which I wouldn't unnecessarily expend energy, but I could continue eating, despite the internal bleeding and lack of appetite. Most of the day I would sit on the edge of my cot but sometimes the temptation to lie down was so great that I decided instead to sit on the floor of the barracks. I would shake and most of the time I was barely conscious. I would hide my food and eat it only at certain times, mainly because the fever and the pain would let up off and on. Slowly, without really feeling it, I began to get over the disease.

One day when I felt a good deal better I left the barracks in search of food. I went to the kitchen and at the bottom of a pot I found a small amount of warm, leftover coffee. I drank it and swallowed the sediment. It made me feel much better. Then I put the grounds in an empty fruit can. I took it back to the barracks where I forced Joseph, who was still in much pain, to eat the grounds. I found him half asleep, tried to wake him up, and stuffed as much of the coffee grounds into his mouth as he would let me.

The next day I felt much better. I had stopped bleeding and the fever had abated. After so many days of semiconsciousness, I went outside and found myself able to think straight. I was surprised and perplexed to see that the guard towers were empty and the camp practically deserted. Only a small number of prisoners, mostly those who had completely lost their minds, were wandering around between the barracks, acting as if they were in command there. When I had gone to the kitchen the day before, I hadn't noticed anything different. It didn't even occur to me to question why the kitchen had been completely abandoned.

I couldn't believe what I was seeing. In addition to those who had gone crazy, sick prisoners who couldn't get up were the only ones left in the entire camp. I walked over to the wire fence and saw an army tank pass by the front gate. Soldiers were sitting on the turret waving and yelling something at me that I couldn't understand. One soldier tossed a package of crackers to me and I ate them while I wept. I finally understood that they were American soldiers and we had been freed. Without really understanding what was going on, I walked through the gate in search of food. It wasn't long before I reached a highway. I walked alongside the American troops and they looked at me as if I were a ghost. I had walked about three miles when I came upon a castle surrounded by cultivated fields.

Cautiously, I approached the entrance to the property. To me, the cultivated fields meant there must be food around. As I passed by the stables, I heard the sounds of cows inside. I peeked through the window and saw some men attending to the animals. Behaving strangely, moving about clumsily, and laughing like little children, they seemed to be mentally retarded. Their pink, smiling faces made them look like pigs. They had seen me enter the grounds and came out to look me over and touch me. I told them I was hungry. Sniggering, they led me to the kitchen. The cook, an old German, was shocked when he saw how emaciated I was; by then, I couldn't have weighed more than eighty pounds. He gave me cheese, bread, and beef jerky.

Once I had filled my stomach and was feeling quite happy but still not realizing what it meant to be free, I returned to the camp. I was one of the many prisoners who had not been informed of our liberation. I went into the barracks and made Joseph stand up; he had been dozing. As we left the camp together, I told him that I had found a place with an abundance of food just for the two of us. I helped him along as fast as I could. We arrived at the castle and went to the kitchen. The cook gave him a substantial amount of milk to drink. He treated us nicely, as if we were the conquerors, yet we hadn't even fired a single shot.

That night we slept in the barn; in fact, since Joseph was very weak, we remained there for several days. I would make trips back and forth to the kitchen where the cook let me fill up on whatever I wanted. One day I discovered a bottle of cognac. I took it back to the barn, popped the cork, and proceeded to drink the entire bottle. I think it took me several days to sleep off that drunken stupor. When I awoke, I found myself in an American army field hospital. After a physical examination, I was told that my lungs had three scars; they recommended that I get as much rest as possible and eat well. I really didn't need that doctor's advice because anything around me that was edible would disappear instantly. The x-rays had detected TB that I'd caught when I worked in the mines at Jaworzno. For the first time in five months I took a bath and they gave me some civilian clothes.

Joseph also managed to recuperate in the hospital. At the first opportunity we left to explore the surrounding area. Since we wanted to leave the city, we went to city hall where they issued us identity cards and coupons for food rations. The time we had spent in the hospital was boring and monotonous. We did our best to recuperate as quickly as possible in the hope of returning to our homes. People from countries all over Europe were in that hospital.

One night a large group of Ukrainians—collaborators with the Germans and traitors to their own country, Russia—organized a farewell party. They pillaged a freight car that was parked at the train station, robbing it of all the alcohol they could carry. They had invited everyone. There was music and dancing. Those Ukrainians, who had volunteered to serve as guards and executioners in the concentration camps, and their friends had downed so much alcohol that in less than an hour the devastation began. Young men and their wives and girlfriends, who only minutes before were dancing and laughing boisterously, were suddenly losing their sight and rolling about with severe intestinal pain: the booze they had stolen was methyl alcohol.

I barely escaped the catastrophe because the doctor had prohibited me from drinking liquor until I had been cured of my

TB. The party ended abruptly. They were all dead. Corpses were strewn all over the hospital barracks. It looked like the war was still in full force.

The war was over and I was alive, but one-third of an entire civilization had been sent to the gas chambers and gone up in smoke and ashes, taking with it a five-thousand-year-old culture, its traditions, its joys, and its sorrows. The soil of Europe was impregnated with Jewish blood. There would not be enough water in the Rhine and the Danube during the next thousand years to wash out that stain nor to cleanse the murderers of their guilt.

1. Salomon Isacovici, Sighet, 1941.

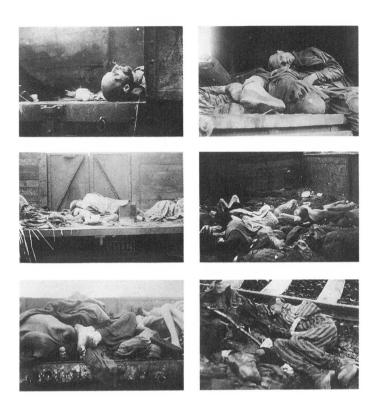

2. Top, facing page. Isacovici family, Sighet, 1936.

3. Bottom, facing page. Salomon Isacovici (center) with Alexander Nedelcovici (right) and another friend, Muresanu, in Sighet, 1939.

4–9. Above. By a railway siding in Leonberg, near Stuttgart, Germany, at the end of March 1945.

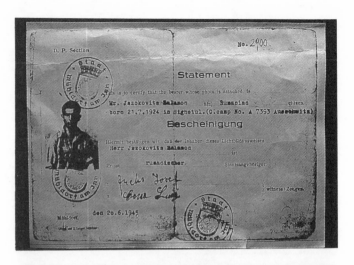

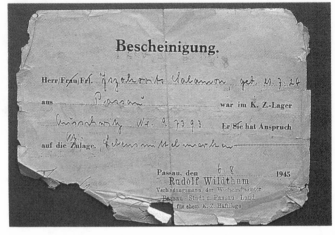

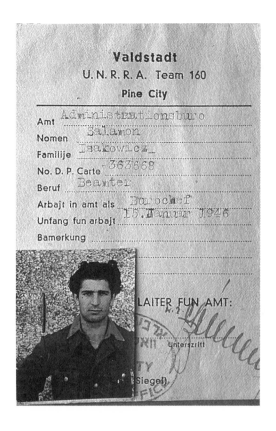

Valdstadt

U. N. R. R. A. Team 160

Pine City

Amt ......Administrationsburo......
Nomen ....Salamon........
Familije ......Isakowicz......
No. D. P. Carte ......363668......
Beruf ......Beamter......
Arbajt in amt als ......Burochef......
Unfang fun arbajt ......15. Januar 1946......
Bamerkung ....

LAITER FUN AMT:

Unterszrift

(Siegel)

10. Top, facing page. Identity document issued in Mühldorf am Inn, Germany, in June 1945, certifying that Salomon Isacovici had been liberated from the concentration camp of the same name.

11. Bottom, facing page. Identity document issued in Passau, Germany, in 1945.

12. Above. Identity document showing Salomon Isacovici as office manager of the United Nations Refugee Relief Agency (UNRAA) camp, Waldstat bei Pocking, 15 January 1946.

13. Above. Displaced Person's (D.P.) identity card issued in Waldstat bei Pocking on 7 April 1946 by UNRRA.

14. Top, facing page. Members of the Hashomer Hatzair kibbutz, Waldstat bei Pocking, 1946. Salomon Isacovici is fifth from right.

15. Center, facing page. Leaders of the Hashomer Hatzair kibbutz, Waldstat bei Pocking, 1946. Salomon Isacovici is third from right.

16. Bottom, facing page. Three of the Isacovici brothers in Paris, 1947. From left to right: Isaac, Salomon, and Samuel.

17. Salomon Isacovici, Quito, Ecuador, 1990.

11

There's no getting around it: the leopard never changes its spots and man is always seeking the eternal return. That's what happened to me. As soon as I was free and began to forget the injustices and sorrows that I had endured in my hometown, the first thing that occurred to me was to return to Sighet. I knew little about politics and even less about the kinds of power that are imposed by one people on another people through ideologies and the propaganda of oppression. I knew nothing about Romania and wasn't even aware that the Soviets had taken possession of half of Europe. I thought it was enough to know that the Germans had lost the war.

And, at the time, it was enough for me to know that I was a free man and that Jews weren't suffering at the hands of the Germans anymore. Innocently, I figured that Sighet would still be the same as before: a city where diverse peoples and cultures lived in harmony. After recovering physically, I convinced myself that life had to start over at its point of origin, the place where it had been severed from me. I reflected on recouping the time that had been lost and continuing our interrupted work, that is, returning to work on the farm. I thought about how I would have the time to organize my life, rest from my weariness, and erase the humiliation from my mind.

Resolved, then, to return to what I considered my homeland and my farm, I stood in front of a map of Europe in order to find out where I was and the best way to get back home. Upon identifying the labyrinth through which I had been led in the "Death March," I became depressed and discouraged. In order to get back to Sighet, I had to cross through parts of Germany, Austria, and Hungary. Still, in thinking about my return, my hopes soared, but I was blinded by the dream that Sighet would be the same as it was when I had grown up there. I had this idea that we were living evidence of what had happened to a people, but I wasn't aware that Europe was crippled, wasted, uninterested in living examples. Europe saw us only as human leftovers, saved from the inferno by mistake. I guess I wanted to be seen by those eyes that thought we were lost forever and be able to say to them, "Here I am. I'm back."

I imagine that I had been feeling something of a hero because, in demonstrating to those who had hoped to conquer us that I was still alive, I was testimony to the perseverance of the Jewish people. I also thought that I had passed the cruelest of tests in life, being one of the Holocaust's living martyrs. I was not aware of how easily people can forget even the most heinous of events and then repeat them in a ritual of death and extermination, when everything begins anew and annihilates itself in a macabre carnival of repetition.

Where was I? The camp was in Mühldorf am Inn, in Germany, near the Austrian border. Under favorable conditions, the distance is still formidable, and with bombed-out bridges, roads, and railways, with no vehicles, not even wagons or old automobiles, the idea of walking that distance seemed crazy. But if the Germans, who had forced us to walk months on end—when we were hungry, cold, sick, and tired—hadn't thought it was such a crazy idea, why would it be crazy now, especially under different, more favorable circumstances? I proposed the idea to Joseph who immediately agreed to walk back with me.

One morning, loaded down with provisions from a military supply depot and walking sticks in hand, we left the camp in the direction of the Inn River. Our objective was to cross the river and reach the Austrian city of Braunau, sadly famous for being Hitler's birthplace. We were like two vagabonds thirsting for new horizons and fresh air. Even though it was frightening to see the devastation that had taken place, freedom and that fresh air inspired us to continue our march. On our travels, we met people of all types, some of whom looked at us with distrust, thinking we were deserters, Nazis, Gestapo agents; of course, we suspected the same thing of them. For that reason we never joined any groups of people or talked to anyone; only to each other. Trying to avoid problems, we would take the less-traveled roads and bypass the towns. We slept on the ground, looking up at the stars, or in some farmer's barn. Thank God it was summertime and the weather was pleasant.

During the long trek with Joseph, the aftermath of the war was present every step of the way: fields were unattended; starving dogs were everywhere; there were dead horses with their bellies ripped open and exposed to the flies; farm equipment was beginning to rust; only the hulks of trucks were left scattered about, for they had been stripped of everything; and junked military equipment and spent cartridges were everywhere. Farm houses and barns seemed about to collapse: roofs had fallen in, walls had cracked, and barnyards were in disarray. Possessions were piled up outside the houses: washbasins, pots, rubble, broken mirrors, old trunks, and broken-up furniture for stoking fires.

We arrived at the banks of the Inn only to find the bridge completely blocked with soldiers and machinery. Joseph and I decided that the best way to cross the river would be to find a ford. We walked up river, trying to avoid any military patrols. After a good distance, we discovered a shallow place where the water was less turbulent. The surface of the river looked like a junk-ridden basement that had been flooded. I remember Joseph remarking that there was enough war materiel out there to start another war: rusty cannons, scrap iron, military machinery, cases of munitions, machine guns, tripods, and mortars.

We took off our shoes, undressed, and put our clothes in jute bags. Shivers ran down my spine as I got into the water, for suddenly I remembered how I would swim and fish with my brothers in the Tisa. I remembered meeting at the river with Leah. I remembered how I would cross the Tisa bringing back contraband items to sell. Now, all those memories seemed to belong to someone else. The suffering and affliction of the concentration camps had brought out the most degraded, beastly part in me, so that now I could only remember any fortuitous aspect of my life before the war as something strange and foreign. We swam over to a pile of junk, rested a while, and then continued across the river. After four or five stops, we arrived at the other side, where the warm air quickly dried us off. Then we got dressed.

As we renewed our trek toward Braunau, we were surprised by an American patrol. We were immediately taken as prisoners and driven to Passau. The city was crawling with military personnel and congested with war machinery. After a few hours, they interrogated us. When I said we were Jews from Romania, a strapping young pock-marked lad spoke to us in Yiddish. Joseph and I showed our identity cards that had been issued in Mühldorf am Inn and our tattooed arms.

Convinced of the truth of our stories, they asked us if we could identify any Gestapo agents, ss, or German soldiers. We answered that we didn't know anyone, but that the ss were identifiable because of the ss tattooed on their upper arms. Many of them were now passing as civilians and were fleeing with false identifications to Latin America and other parts of the world. And now the Americans were looking for victims who could identify those Germans. But we only wanted to forget everything and return home. The thought of revenge never crossed our minds. I think that freedom is an experience that takes time to assimilate; I knew I was free, but I wouldn't be able to realize it fully until I was back home in Sighet.

We had been so humiliated, so painfully punished for who we were, that we were motivated only by tangible ideas, which were like life jackets that kept us from drowning in a sea of insanity. Just as the will to survive had provided the faith we needed to avoid death, now it was the desire to return home that provided the motivating force to keep us moving forward in a mangled, chaotic world.

Once again, we started out by leaving the bridge behind us. We returned to Germany. It seemed to me that no matter how much we wanted to leave that region, invisible claws were always there to carry us back to the starting point, that is, nowhere. Were we really free yet? Even though the barbed-wire fences no longer interrupted our view of the horizon, the invisible lines called borders were preventing us from continuing.

We started out again, trekking through the blue-tinged countryside. Our nomadic path was like a funeral march taking us past tomb after tomb, through desolation, more desolation, and extermination. At night, when I would stretch out in a field to sleep, I couldn't help but make a comparison between the limpid, bluish-black sky above and the misery here on earth. I would thank God that human beings didn't live in the heavens because, if they did, the peace and mysterious serenity emanating from up there would have already been destroyed.

Joseph turned out to be a good traveling companion. I had already forgotten about my animosity toward him for the ribbon he had worn. We'd walk along making small talk, conversing about our adventures in Sighet, about our plans, about our futures. We had tacitly agreed not to discuss the concentration camps. However, always hoping to find a family member who might still be alive, every time we crossed through a region where the concentration camps had existed, we would visit them in order to read the lists of those who had survived.

At every camp, we would add our names to the lists, hoping that someone from our families or a friend who might happen through there would find out that we were still alive. So many years had gone by in which we had existed only as numbers; now we wanted to prove to the world that we were still alive, that we weren't just numbers but real people. Ah, the pleasure it gave me to write my name on those lists: "Sanyi Isacovici, a Jew from Sighet, is still alive in spite of the extermination, the abuse, and being stripped of my identity."

At the Feldanfing concentration camp, a pleasant surprise was waiting for me. As I ran down the list of survivors I came across the names of my brothers Paisi and Isaac. How beautiful their names looked to me! They were alive and had returned to Romania. Now I wasn't alone anymore, I still had some next of kin . . . but in Romania? It was so far away!

We continued walking for three months in search of our roots. When we arrived at the city of Celle, we decided to go to the extermination camp at Bergen-Belsen. Luck was finally on our side. As soon as we arrived we met some women from Sighet. Almost all the young women belonged to the Jewish upper class and Joseph felt very much at ease with them. He immediately fell in love with one of them, and he and I began to see less and less of each other. While we were there, I found out that the Swedish government had invited young Jews to immigrate to its country. Joseph thought the idea was great. His new love quickly made him forget the past. A large number of young Jews accepted the offer. They made plans for the trip and started to dream about the future. Joseph, who chose to immigrate to Sweden, decided to remain at the camp until the right time came along. My goal, on the other hand, was to return to Romania. Hence, our paths led us in different directions—forever.

Once again, I was on my own. We said farewell to each other and I wished him luck and success. I didn't want to question whether I really wanted to return to Sighet; having met people from my hometown had only served to stir up my memories and to push me all the harder to return. Trapped by nostalgia, I would think about our apple orchard, the horses, and the fields of grain. With those sentimental thoughts, I walked from Bergen-Belsen to Hanover where I was able to hitch a ride on a train headed for Munich. The odyssey that was taking me south had, at last, begun in earnest. I had finally stopped going around in circles, looking for familiar names on the lists at different concentration camps. When passing through Würzburg and seeing the cultivated fields, the bountiful vineyards, and the ample forage on the hillsides, it didn't seem to me that this region had been touched by the ravages of war. I submerged myself in my thoughts: sadness weighed heavily on me. I'd think long and hard about what was waiting for me upon my return home, then I would remember the smell of clay and manure emanating from the freshly plowed earth.

I was so absorbed in my thoughts that I hadn't noticed a young, pale, pink-cheeked German lad sitting in front of me. When I glanced at him, he politely offered me a cigarette. I thanked him but told him I didn't smoke. Then he tried to strike up a conversation, but it didn't go anywhere because I wasn't in the mood to talk to a stranger. My own worries and mistrust of others had made me antisocial.

I plunged deep into my thoughts once again: as soon as I arrived home I would begin plowing the fields and planting the wheat. I figured out that now was the time for planting. With the first snowfalls, the fields would receive a protective blanket while the seeds lay dormant until the spring when they would sprout shoots and the whole area would turn green again. The wheat would ripen in the summer and turn golden yellow. The tassels of wheat would undulate, disappearing in the distance, like waves in a light breeze. Those images refreshed me and I was able to ignore my bitterness, my misfortunes, and my worries about the future.

The slowing of the train brought me back to reality. It arrived at a station where I had to switch trains in order to continue on to Munich. That afternoon I got on a passenger train overflowing with people. We went through Dachau, another extermination camp about thirty miles from Munich. Upon our arrival, I ran into a problem. No passenger trains were available. I wanted to leave as quickly as possible in order to begin recuperating from all those months of chaos and ill fortune, but it seemed that destiny was constantly thwarting my return. I finally got on a freight train bound for Austria that was full of young survivors of the Holocaust. No one talked about the past, but everyone's conversations centered on the same thing: a desire to consummate the lives they had started. All they talked about was the work that lay ahead: finishing that wall, finishing that half-read book, plowing the fields, reopening a store that had been closed in the middle of the night, visiting the synagogue that awaited their prayers. Back home, a lit candle that would never burn out awaited each young person aboard that train.

While they discussed their expectations, the slow, monotonous trip seemed to fly by. As we crossed the border, each one of us produced an identification card. When we passed into Soviet-occupied territory, everyone became tense, conversations came to a halt, and each one of us internalized our thoughts.

On that trip I saw entire trainloads of machinery and factory parts being shipped to the Soviet Union. As we looked out the windows, we could observe the small, sad eyes of those who were accompanying the cargo of tools, cranes, transformers, block and tackles, turbines, and motors. During the journey, I made friends with a Hungarian Jew who had an aunt in Budapest. Finally, we crossed over into Hungary. Budapest had reminded me of Leah, but I had no way of tracking her down.

The night we arrived, I went with my friend to his aunt's house. She was very kind to us. I slept on a mattress in the warm kitchen. Staying in a normal home brought me back to reality; I finally understood that despite the war, life continues. Hope was being renewed and people sought to discover the meaning of the future. At daybreak, I went back to the train station to wait.

That same day I arrived at the Romanian border, where I was interrogated for four hours by Romanian soldiers who couldn't quite believe I was from the Maramures region. In a scenario strangely similar to the way I used to carry contraband between Romania and Czechoslovakia, I reentered my country on foot. I was still about 135 miles from Sighet, and I was bringing back two large, heavy bundles that contained leather for shoes and cloth for shirts. As I lugged them, I said to myself, "This will

be my retribution for the time I worked in the concentration
camps."

After having walked about seven miles and deciding to rest, I heard the sounds of a motor. To try to stop the approaching truck, I stood in the middle of the road. I could see the face of a Romanian soldier through the window. I explained that I was headed for home and asked him if he could give me a lift. He said he was going that way and would take me. I climbed up into the cab of the truck and told him straight away that I had no money because I was returning from a concentration camp. He understood perfectly and along the way he offered me a few swigs of his plum brandy. As night came on we arrived in Sighet. I told him that my bundles were very heavy and asked him nicely if he could drop me off in front of my house.

I could not believe it! There it was ten o'clock at night and I was finally standing in front of my house. No lights were on. I crossed the patio, went up the steps, and knocked on the door. A tall man in his underwear came out and asked me in Russian what I wanted. With the little bit of Russian that I knew, I explained with difficulty that I was the owner of that house. He laughed and insulted me: "Jazai! Idy kibenyi mat. Pasli!"

Despite the difficulty I had understanding him, I could tell that he was insulting my mother and telling me to get packing. He angrily muttered insults that I couldn't understand. I backed away, turned around, and crossed the patio, and stood in the darkness of the street, not knowing what to do next. The return of a stranger. During the time I had spent in the concentration camps, I had dreamed of kissing my parents' land if I were to have the chance to return. I didn't remember, not even for an instant, my promise. The city of Sighet had been lulled into frightening blindness. The wind seemed to wail across the Tisa. I was home.

12

It was especially dark outside that night and it seemed even more so in the street alone. My shoes had become too tight: I sensed they were being worn by someone else. When one arrives at a familiar place but finds everything alien and different, one begins to wonder if he is really the same person. That's exactly what happened to me. The impact of being a foreigner in my own city, in my own house, and in my own garden so disillusioned me that I stood there petrified with no idea of what to do next. It was already late that night; the two bundles at my feet and I had no place to go. Feeling threatened and bitterly out of place, I asked myself out loud, "Sanyi, why did you have to come back?"

It was as if a wall had been raised between the person who had grown up in Sighet and the person who had just returned. I immediately turned my thoughts to my brothers. I had to find them in order to figure out how to reclaim our property. I didn't realize that now we owned nothing. As I placed the bundles on my shoulders and started to walk, I remembered that the Strinbelyi family used to live near us. During the summers, they would join us on our porch to sing songs and play games. As I approached the front door, I tried to peer inside.

"Not one light on," I said to myself.

Thinking that no one lived there anymore, I was about to turn around and leave when the weight of the bundles made me stumble against the door, sounding like a mallet had hit it. The figure of a woman with an elderly face marked by goiter appeared in the darkness.

"What do you want?"

"Don't you recognize me? I'm Sanyi, the son of your neighbor Basia," I answered in a soft voice, hoping to set her at ease.

"You're not Sanyi. He died a long time ago."

She slammed the door shut. Terrified by the strange events that had devastated the region, frightened by my partisan appearance, and fearing reprisals, she was retreating into her own

home. When I leaned toward the door and shouted that I was
Sanyi and that I was alive, the old woman kept on repeating that I was dead. I asked her if she would at least tell me where I could find my brothers.

"In the barn at the Medvesz place," I heard her say as her emaciated body shuffled away from the door. Her words — Sanyi is dead and his brothers live in the barn at the Medvesz place — echoed painfully in my head; as far as the people of Sighet were concerned, the young smuggler of the Isacovici family no longer existed. It's a revelation that is hard to assimilate when a neighbor simply will not recognize you, and then says that you are dead.

I kept walking. The sheer weight of the bundles reminded me that I was still alive. And so who was I then? I wasn't Sanyi but a dead man returning from death — without family, without homeland, without neighbors, without any links to the past. At that moment, while I was walking along, I became transformed from an enslaved and tortured Jew, dispossessed of his memories, to something unknown to either God or myself.

Widow Medvesz's house was not far away. After almost a mile, I found myself standing in front of the darkened structure. The fall winds blowing off the Tisa were stronger now. The waves of the river slapped harshly against the shore. By then, it must have been midnight. The chilling, ill-fated cry of an owl sounded off in the distance.

I banged hard on the door of the barn. I needed to find out if I was really alive, and my fists pounded the door with such energy that the door almost shook off its hinges. If only my brothers would recognize me, then I'd know that I was alive.

"Who's there?" someone asked from inside.

"It's me! Sanyi!" I said with a trembling voice.

I recognized my brother Issac's voice; now if he would only recognize me. The door opened and our strong brotherly embrace confirmed that I was still alive. Then Idel and Paisi appeared and the four of us exchanged joyous hugs. Still dazed by it all, I saw my brothers pick up the bundles and we went inside. Mrs. Medvesz's brand of charity meant we slept in the animal stalls. A candle illuminated the adobe walls. There were no cows or horses left. The light created a circle within which the beams above revealed the spider-webbed narrowness of the stall. This was our bedroom and home: a strawless manger with dried dung on the floor, an old plow blade in one corner, riding gear piled up in another, and, at the back, some sacks filled with hay.

Then the figure of a man came looming out of the shadows. It was my Uncle Moses, who had also taken up residence in that animal shelter. He greeted me sleepily. A strong, courageous, older man, he was the only survivor of anyone his age.

Isaac brought us a bowl of cold mush, my first meal back home. As I ate, I reflected that, all things considered, my arrival in Sighet seemed ominous.

We placed some of the sacks together in order to make beds. Idel, who had been the barber, told me that Samuel was alive in Hungary. He'd become involved in transporting salt and it turned out to be a lucrative business for him. No one knew anything about our father or Saul. After exchanging that bit of news and without anyone mentioning their own suffering, we tried to get some rest. Someone blew out the candle and darkness enveloped us. Soon we were snoring, huddled together in our misery.

At dawn, the sun began streaming through a large window into the stalls. I woke up not knowing where I was. Looking around in the semidarkness I began to recognize my brothers' faces. In one corner a sack of cornmeal was standing next to a pile of potatoes.

Down the road, church bells were calling the parishioners to Mass. That familiar clanging sound made it seem like nothing had changed in Sighet. My brothers were shaking off their drowsiness when my uncle brought us a pot of mush and we sat down on our makeshift beds to eat breakfast.

My brothers talked about their military life in Ukraine.
Thanks to his profession, Idel made out by giving haircuts and shaves to the Hungarian soldiers. Since he had spare time on his hands, they put him to work watching over the cattle that the military in the rear guard would transport with them. He led a peaceful life until the retreat from the Soviet front began. Then he stopped barbering and spent all of his time taking care of the stock. At the same rate as the troops sped up their march in order to flee from the Soviets, Idel decelerated his march with the cattle, purposely dropping farther and farther behind. The distance between the German troops and the cattle became so great that one day he stopped the animals, turned them around, and started to herd them back home. After repeatedly making up stories about who he was and what he was doing, and giving away animals to people along the way as payment to keep them quiet, Idel arrived on the outskirts of Sighet with three emaciated, TB-ridden cows. He bid farewell to them, as if they were the three closest friends he had in the world, and walked into Sighet, which was still occupied by the Soviet forces, as if nothing had happened. He set himself up as a barber and waited for his brothers to return.

Isaac and Paisi had also been in Ukraine. As Jews drafted by the military, they had been given orders to dig latrines and trenches, but they never bore arms. When the Soviets began to advance toward the city, the Hungarians decided to burn down the Jewish encampment with everyone inside. Justification? Plague. Incinerate them all! Suddenly one night, Paisi woke up and smelled fuel oil everywhere, and, before the soldiers could torch the place, he and his brother managed to escape. Many Jews died in the fire. If Paisi hadn't happened to wake up, he and Isaac would be dead.

While they were telling me their stories, we ate the cold, tasteless corn mush. As we talked, time flew by, but our stories of the vicissitudes of the war slowly gave way to practical matters. Now that we didn't have anything to call our own, we had to find ways to provide for ourselves. We each took on a task: one of us would look for our cattle and the jewels that our parents had left with neighbors; another would investigate ways to regain our house; another would look for tools. By the time the tasks had been designated to everyone, it was already noon. We ate some more mush and roasted some potatoes, which is all we had. Despite our efforts, our resignation to our miserable state really depressed me. I asked my brothers why they didn't go fishing or do something to alleviate their poverty, but they didn't seem to pay much attention. After a war, one needs a great deal of courage and energy to rise above indifference.

Actually, thinking kept us from dying; we would think about anything in order to stay alive. What was the importance of accumulating wealth, property, and education if it was just going to be destroyed with bombs and bullets? That defeatist attitude was contagious; in their situation of extreme poverty, even my brothers felt that way.

I went for a walk in the afternoon. Out of respect for our mother and sisters, no one had mentioned them in our conversation. After walking a good distance, I found myself in Sighet proper. The Jewish businesses, industries, and farms had fallen into neglect and disrepair. Long ago the shops had been looted, the machinery shut down, and the houses vacated and left disgraced by rubbish strewn all around. The Jewish neighborhood had been reduced to a sad state of penury.

Then I walked outside the city toward a forest of birch trees near the Tisa and, finally, there she was, flowing along lazily, seemingly fatigued. I sat on one of the natural dikes and looked at the little niches where the swallows used to make their nests. The calm waters of the inlets brought back many memories. My eyes welled with tears. Thinking about my adolescence, my work on the farm, the excursions into the country, and my passion for Leah Gitel, I was at once trapped in nostalgia and disappointment. Enveloped by memories, now just fleeting traces of bygone times, I looked up at the sky. As the sun's rays hit the fall clouds, they turned reddish and made me think of the flames swirling up into the sky during that terrible night at Birkenau.

That evening our old maid Anita came by, limping as always because of her dislocated hip; she had brought us a chicken casserole. How humbled and grateful we were for that poor woman's goodwill toward us! During our absence, she had given birth to a baby by a Hungarian and, somehow, managed to endure her poverty with greater dignity than we could.

Before long all of us set out to perform our tasks in order to recover the family's possessions. According to the Jewish calendar, it was Rosh Hashana, the new year, but none of us had the energy or the money to celebrate it.

My mission consisted of speaking to the Soviet commandant about getting the occupants out of our house, which had been converted into a hospital. I knew that I had to conjure up all of my past experiences as a smuggler in order to be able to see him and then to convince him to return our house to us. Taking some of the cloth from one of my bundles, I wrapped it up and went down to the river. I took a bath in the freezing water, which rejuvenated me, and then I got dressed, trying to look the best I could with the same pants and jacket, but sporting a nicely washed shirt. In those clothes, which were all I had, I started out for the city.

After walking around everywhere and bartering with half the world, I sold the cloth. The next step would be the most difficult: purchasing a bottle of vodka. I spoke with some of the old Hungarian smugglers, who told me where I could obtain the liquor. I found a bottle of authentic Russian vodka at the black market. By noontime, I was ready for the interview. While I was walking toward the commandant's office, I went over and over the arguments that I would present to him, remembering that I had to remain serene in front of an army officer. My head was buzzing, and all of a sudden I was standing in front of his office.

I approached the guard and asked to see the officer in charge. The soldier seemed pleasant enough and told me to take a seat.

I placed the bottle on my lap so it would be more visible to the guard. Shortly thereafter, I was ushered into the adjoining office. I introduced myself with all the aplomb I could muster, thinking that someone who had survived a concentration camp shouldn't fear anything. I stated my name and the reason for my visit. Without beating around the bush, I went straight to the point. However, the point wasn't our house: it was the bottle. I wanted to facilitate things by expressing how grateful the Jews were for being saved from the Nazis by the Soviets. It was an obligation to drink a toast to their victory. Noticing my poise and confidence, the officer brought out two glasses. I proceeded to open the bottle and filled the glasses to the brim.

"L'chaim!" he said in Hebrew, making a toast "to life." I was totally taken by surprise, for I had just been beaten at my own game: that Soviet officer, with medals hanging all over his chest, was also a Jew. And here I had thought my directness and confidence had done the trick. We got along immediately because we happened to be Jewish. I told him that I wanted our parents' house back. He seemed to show compassion for those of my family who had died and for those who had survived. After our talk, which lasted as long as it took us to finish off the bottle, the Soviet officer promised me that the temporary hospital, that is, our house, would be vacated and another empty building, closer to town, would be used instead.

By the time I stumbled out of his office, it was already nighttime. I walked down the poorly lit streets happy because we had gained our property back. I spent the next few days looking for work but, after knocking on door after door without any luck, I came to the conclusion that all the local industries had been shut down because their owners never returned from the concentration camps. Since there was no work to be had, I decided it would be better to work on the farm.

My brothers didn't have any luck either. All that was left of the jewels that my parents had left with our neighbors was a gold chain that my mother had worn on important occasions. Of everything that we had owned, it seemed that only the house would be returned to us—if the Soviet officer kept his word. After eight frustrating days of looking for work and trying to re-claim what had belonged to us, a soldier appeared at the Widow Medvesz's barn to inform us that our house had been vacated and we could return to it. We were very happy that night. Since I figured I would be taking charge of the farm chores, the thought that I would be working with plants and animals once again made me jump up and down and clap my hands like a child. That same morning we started out toward our land.

We thanked Widow Medvesz for her help and hospitality, bid her farewell, packed what few belongings we had, and, without looking back, started walking toward our parents' house. In the midst of so much happiness, the prophetic words of my mother echoed in my head: "There's our house, take a good look. This will be the last time I see it."

It was hard to believe how far we had come since she had said that, but it was equally painful to remember it. My mother had foreseen her fate, she had intuited it, and here was her last testament and will: the house, her home.

Like a skeleton that had been stripped of its flesh and dis-infected, there was nothing left inside the house. The smell of formaldehyde and anesthesia hinted at the presence of death throughout. There were no curtains, no furniture, no decora-tions; all that was left were the naked walls on some of which it was still possible to see the outlines where pictures had once hung. We looked through the entire house for something that would remind us that it used to belong to us, but there was nothing to be found.

Filled with aching emptiness, I went out to the patio. There, I saw everything that wasn't ours anymore: the apple orchard to which we had given so much of our care; those young trees whose stems we would cover in the fall to protect them from the rabbits; those older, mature trees whose trunks we would paint with white lye so the ants wouldn't attack them; those irrigation trenches around the trees that we would fill with manure in order to nourish the roots. Along with the cattle, the apple orchard now belonged to our former farm worker George Floreanu. The Socialist government in power had turned all of it over to him because, according to its dogma, the land belonged to the person who tilled it.

The beehives, fortified with beet sugar during the winter months and supplying us with honey in the summers, had been destroyed; the only thing left were some boxes, now vacated by the bees, that were strewn about on the patio, exposing the inner honeycombs like false teeth. As I walked past the edge of the well, I took a look down inside. The water was dirty and stagnant, now unfit for drinking. I remembered the owls, also exiled like the rabbits from that forsaken place.

Even the riding equipment and farm machinery in the barn no longer belonged to us. As we entered the barn, spiders upset by our intrusion scurried away across their webs. And birds that had made their nests among the beams in the roof fluttered about seeking exit through the skylights. The remaining arable land had no current value because it was too late to plant that year, for winter was already upon us. Besides, without seeds, machinery, or tools, we couldn't do anything anyway.

Ten days had flown by since I had arrived home and we hadn't managed to get much done. I couldn't find work, there was nothing to do in the fields, and we had no money. Trying to face the situation, I remembered Alexander Nedelcovici telling me when I was in the ghetto to abandon my possessions and flee for my life. It seemed strange to me that I would think about fleeing from my birthplace, but I couldn't figure out what else to do. While not yet deciding to leave, I told myself it was time to visit my friend.

And that's just what I did. All I had in my backpack was some

leather for making boots—that was all I could give him. I cut off
a large piece, tucked it under my arm, and headed for Alexander's house.

As soon as he recognized me he invited me in, and, in the Yugoslavian custom, he offered me some bread as a sign of friendship. His whole family hugged me as if I was a long-lost son returning home. Alexander seemed more mature now; he had put his clumsy, impetuous adolescence behind him.

They didn't ask me about my life as a prisoner, most of which they had heard about from my brothers. It was a topic I preferred to avoid too, but I did take advantage of the moment to talk about all the problems I'd been having since my return. Alexander advised me to leave and search for new lands because, as he put it, underneath the ashes there will always be hot coals. What he meant was that the war, according to him, wasn't over yet nor had the hatred toward Jews abated.

As I left his house and began walking home, I thought deeply about my friend's advice; whatever the case, either I wasn't ready to leave or an innocent faith in peace helped me to postpone my departure. For the next few days my brothers and I spent our time absurdly and irreverently dedicated to robbery. Since there wasn't even a single stool in our house, we decided to look for furniture that was left behind when the Jews had to vacate the ghetto. There wasn't much left and we didn't think we were committing wrongful acts like the Hungarians who had pillaged those places after the last convoy—all Jews on board—left in the direction of Birkenau. We spent two days finding whatever we could.

By sheer coincidence I came across the same room that housed us during the few days that we were in the ghetto. I had stayed in that room with my parents and my four younger siblings. Poking around among piles of old papers, I uncovered a doll. I picked it up and scrutinized it closely. It had a sad smile on its face. As I shook off the dust and wiped it off with my hands, I had a vision of my little sister rocking that rag doll to sleep. Horrified, I ran out into the street and started walking toward the main plaza.

As I walked, I was stupidly clutching that doll in my hands. Hardly anyone was around. Beyond the benches and the trees up ahead, I could see a man wearing a military uniform limping along. As I continued forward, I was able to make out the man's face. Yes, it was him — Second Lieutenant Vigola Yanchi! — the man who had tortured me for not saluting him. And now he was about 150 feet away from me.

He must have recognized me as well because he immediately began to hobble away, supporting himself with his cane. Squeezing the doll with rage, I started to follow him. By then Yanchi was scurrying along like a rabbit. As I ran to catch up with him, I was amazed at the crippled man's strength. The idea of getting revenge on this sinister old man gave me renewed energy and vigor. I pursued him as far as a busy street where a carriage passed in front of him. Like a kangaroo, the Hungarian lieutenant sprang into the vehicle. I followed the carriage while the driver cracked his whip over the horses to get up speed.

Despite my disadvantage, I felt like I could catch up with him; however, the carriage stopped in front of the police station. Vigola Yanchi bolted out of the carriage and made a beeline inside. I stopped. After a few minutes I calmed down and started back home.

My brothers, who were worried about me, were waiting on the porch. When they saw me arrive sweating and carrying a doll instead of furniture, they asked me what had happened. I told them about my encounter with the Hungarian. After hearing my story, they told me that he had lost a leg on the Russian front. Isaac said he had come around before and, in friendly fashion, asked about me. On some occasions, he even brought food to Widow Medvesz's barn. Since my brothers had left for the Soviet front before my run-in with Lieutenant Yanchi, they knew nothing about the beatings I had received because of him.

Believing that he and I had been friends, they thought his con-
cern for me was genuine, but when I explained the truth, they finally understood what had really happened.

Then I showed them Pesil's doll. I handed it to Isaac and he put it in the living room, as if it were an icon. Quickly there-after we started to work fixing tables, gluing legs, mending mat-tresses, and performing other household chores that would dis-tract us from the torment that we shared that night.

13

No matter if it's war or peace, hair grows just the same. Idel had a good profession and was able to make money at it. Just as he had acquired a good reputation for cutting hair and giving shaves among the Hungarian soldiers, he soon became well established in a shop in the middle of the city. He was the first one of us to make an honest living, especially from his private customers for whom he made house calls. His shop consisted of a small room. His independence was based on some simple tools of the trade: scissors, combs, shaving brush and razor, soap, a mirror, a chair and white towels, all of which he had acquired without difficulty.

One day our friend Baruch Farkas came to the house looking for Idel to cut his hair. He was the one who had brought me food from my mother when I working at the camp in Korosmezö. Somehow, he hadn't been sent to the ghettos, and during the war he fought as a partisan against the Germans. Farkas had always been an impassioned, loquacious man who carried a large knife, even after the war, in order to defend himself against any Romanian who might try to pick a fight with him. But that day he was noticeably quiet and withdrawn. Our conversation was limited to curt responses referring to nothing in particular.

Farkas thought we must have had some news about Schmiel but that we just didn't want to talk about him because of the sadness and the pain it caused us. In reality, however, we didn't know any news about our half-brother. There was silence, except for the scissors whirling around Farkas's head. I watched clumps of hair begin to cover the floor. Finally he couldn't stand it anymore, so he blurted out: "Damn it! Why doesn't someone ask me about Schmiel?"

We froze. When Farkas saw our perplexed faces, he told us how his partisan friend and our sad, down-on-life half-brother had died. The Germans had gunned him down in an ambush at the Iron Gate Dam in Yugoslavia. We were so shocked by the story that we had to wipe tears from our eyes. After a short while, Farkas became himself again and began to sing a partisan song at the top of his lungs:

> Never say you're on your last road
> though bright days be hidden behind gray clouds,
> for that cherished moment is still to come
> and we will be heard: Here we are!

> From the country of snow to the country of palms
> we are here with our pain and our sorrows,
> and wherever a drop of our blood is spilled
> our heroism and courage will sprout forth.

> Never say you're on your last road
> though bright days be hidden behind gray clouds,
> for that cherished moment is still to come
> and we will be heard: Here we are!

> The morning sun will make our day golden
> and the enemy will vanish like yesterday,
> and until the sun begins to shine again
> let future generations rally behind this song.

> It has been written with bullets and blood;
> it's not a song about the freedom of a wild bird.
> Amid the collapse of fractured walls,
> it was sung by a people bearing arms.

The song was a tribute to Schmiel's entire life because he had given it up for us to be free. The song, echoing throughout the house for the longest time, could still be heard when the lights went out at bedtime—lingering and tingling in our ears.

The dawn of the new day brought us back to the reality of our daily existence and common concerns. Paisi, still very much a leftist thinker, quickly secured employment as head of an accounting division in a firm downtown. The Romanians helped him because he was a Communist leader who had assisted in the creation of the Socialist regime. Isaac and I were still without work, and things didn't seem that promising for us. The bridge over the Tisa didn't exist anymore because the Germans had blown it up when they had been forced to withdraw. Even though I might have wanted to continue in my former activities, now there was nothing to smuggle.

The explosion when they blew up the bridge had split open the front wall of our house. Isaac and I were assigned the job of repairing the damage. With some cement and a good ladder, we began the task of fixing the roof; winter was just around the corner and the rains had damaged the attic.

One morning, going on noon, when we were hard at repairing the tile joints on the roof, I noticed the long shadow of a man approaching the house. His awkward gait gave him away: it was my brother Samuel. I flew down the ladder and hollered at Isaac, "It's Samuel, it's Samuel!"

We were overjoyed at his return. I hadn't seen him since we were separated at Auschwitz. He had become a young man, thin but healthy, although an air of mourning, like lost innocence, cast a shadow over his face. He would never be the same again, and he would never recount what he had lived through in the concentration camps. Samuel was laconic and hard-working, but his eyes revealed a new cunning. He had been buying and selling salt in Hungary and had made money at it.

Samuel's return home changed my profession from repairing the house back to smuggling again. He was well aware that salt was highly prized in Hungary, so he immediately proposed that I let Isaac finish the house repairs, something he could do by himself anyway, and dedicate my time to smuggling salt with him. Knowing that I already had experience dealing with border crossings, he felt comfortable in asking me to join him. While Isaac took charge of fixing up the house, Samuel and I bought salt at a cheap price from a salt mine not far from Sighet and began our business in a big way. We quickly resolved the problem of transporting the salt by utilizing the trains coming from

Russia and Poland carrying former prisoners of war who were
being repatriated to their homelands.

We worked independently to avoid creating suspicion and also to expand our operation. We started by smuggling out 220 pounds of salt apiece. We would take the train to Hungary, traveling among Italians, Hungarians, German-speakers, and other German allies. Once in Hungary, we would sell the whole bag of salt to an intermediary and, with our earnings in hand, initiate our return home on the train that would take us to the Hungarian border town of Debrecen. From there, we would walk to Satumare, in Romania, and then thumb rides in trucks for the remaining 145 miles. Crossing the border at Debrecen and walking the 26 miles to Satumare meant possibly running into military patrols who could rob us of our profits.

We would make two trips per week. With the earnings from this work I began exchanging money—usually rubles for money from Europe—with the prisoners on the trains. Shortly before December 1945, the trains from Poland stopped running, which made our work a great deal more difficult. It was around that period, however, when I made my last trip, the one that completely changed my modus vivendi. By that time I was taking more than 400 pounds of salt with me. Upon our arrival in Hungary, the prisoners in my train car decided among themselves to rob me of my salt. The sun was up, but it was freezing cold outside. I found myself in a strange place without any money to take the train back home, so I began to walk to Debrecen.

I came upon a small village with a train station where they would fill the engines with water. Hiding in the bushes nearby, I waited for a freight train to show up. I was dozing off when the whistle of a train suddenly woke me up. Once it had come to a halt, I quickly climbed into a freight car full of boxes of wheat, cereals, and canned goods. I was very hungry, so I opened up a box, took something to eat, and loaded up with some supplies to make up for my loss from the theft. The train pulled into Debrecen that afternoon. Half frozen, I walked across the border toward Satumare. On one street, I spotted a cargo truck that was headed for Sighet. I talked to the driver and exchanged the food for a ride back. I climbed into the cab and made it all the way home. When I arrived, it was already late at night.

But my problems didn't end there. The next morning I learned that my savings had gone up in smoke: the Austrian government had discarded the old schilling and minted new money. In one fell swoop, the savings that I was holding in schillings had been converted into a heap of worthless paper. Once again, I was like before: penniless.

Those were bad times for me; it was no picnic. Upon my return from my trip, I found my brothers upset because the Ukrainians who had collaborated with the Germans were coming through Sighet on their way back to Russia. As soon as those barbarians entered the city they began to plunder stores, rape women, and burn down granaries. A Ukrainian military patrol had moved into our house and forced my brothers to turn our valuables over to them. Isaac, who had been replastering the front of the house, took off running into town in search of Lieutenant Vanka, a stocky but gentle Russian who was always willing to help Romanians. Sporting a PPSH-41 machine gun with a large magazine, he returned with Isaac to our house. As he entered the house, a Ukrainian army captain confronted him.

"Why don't you salute me? I'm a captain," said the Ukrainian.

"I don't salute traitors," Vanka responded calmly.

Suddenly, the captain tried to remove his revolver from his holster, but Vanka abruptly knocked his arm aside with the butt of his machine gun and, in the process, broke it. Pointing the machine gun at the patrol, he ordered them to leave the house. I was somewhere else that night—pondering my sad lot, that is, having to cross the border again—when the same group of Ukrainians returned and broke into our house. My brothers managed to escape out the back windows. Those barbarians

destroyed everything they could find in the house. They
searched everywhere for our valuables, but when they couldn't
find anything and had finished laying waste to every room in
the house, they left to intimidate other people, repeating their
villainous acts.

This Ukrainian savagery precipitated one conclusion in my
anguished soul. The night I returned from Hungary I discovered what had happened: the house was completely turned upside down. My brothers were frightened and depressed; chaos
and violence were everywhere. All of this led me to consider
leaving Sighet for good. And the experience with the Ukrainians was not the only one that would exhaust my desire to remain
in my birthplace. While it was true that their passing through
the city was totally devastating, there were still other nightmares to come. The Ukrainians put the finishing touches on
what the concentration camps had just begun. Many survivors
of the Holocaust, believing it was finally over and hoping to
begin anew, just couldn't understand why they were once again
facing death, this time at the hands of those Ukrainians and
other merciless assassins for whom the war had not yet ended.

That was the case of Laibi Siminovitch, a young red-headed
Jew from Slatina. Two Jewish employees of the Romanian government's secret police, who were traveling in a truck toward
Satumare, stopped at midnight to sleep in the city of Petrosani.
They pulled up to a tavern, went in, and ordered some food. At
a table next to them, two intoxicated men were drinking plum
brandy and carrying on a noisy conversation. The light of the
moon streamed through the window next to them, illuminating
the flushed faces of the two drunks. One of them looked up at
the sky through the window and, beginning to laugh, blurted
out, "Do you remember what that red-headed Jew said to us?"

His friend guffawed as the other continued boisterously, "The
moon is my witness: you're going to kill an innocent person."

Both of them keeled over from laughter and repeated, "The
moon is my witness . . . the moon is my witness!"

Hearing the conversation, the two police agents quickly understood what those two comrades had been up to. A month earlier, Laibi Siminovitch, a survivor of the Holocaust, had disappeared. The agents didn't hesitate for a minute: they grabbed the two sots and rendered them unconscious with two swift blows to the head using their revolver butts. They tied them up and hauled them off to jail. During the process of the investigation, the two men confessed to the crime. They had accosted the red-headed Jewish man in the countryside, on his way from Petrosani to Satumare. It was nighttime. They told him to stop and threatened to kill him if he didn't turn over his money. But Laibi, who was extremely poor, had nothing to give them. When they demanded the boots he was wearing, he took them off and handed them over.

Immediately, they made him kneel down. One of them put his gun barrel to the back of Laibi's head. It was at that very moment when he cried out, "The moon is my witness: you're going to kill an innocent person." There was a single gunshot. Barefoot, Laibi lay crumpled on the ground. His red hair, now tinted with his own blood, shone brightly in the light of the moon. The murder of the young Jew had gone unpunished until the moon had decided to reveal the identity of the perpetrators of this abominable deed. In 1946, the two killers were condemned to twenty-five years in prison.

That's the way it was for those of us who had managed to return from the concentration camps. Weakened by calamity and suffering for being Jews, now despoiled of our belongings and persecuted for our religion, we lived a completely precarious existence. Hatred against us had not been eradicated.

Those of us who had returned with the intention of picking up our lives where we had left off when we were deported were living in a state of desperation. The memories of the past and the continuous specter of the camps had left deep imprints on our bodies and souls. Our neighbors—the gentiles—openly

demonstrated their animosity toward us. They were always saying, "Damn you! Why did you come back? They should have
fried all of you. Maybe the Germans were unable to exterminate
you, but we can still do it."

The situation for Jews in the small outlying towns was so
unpleasant and distressing that many abandoned their farms
to seek refuge in the cities. They would find empty houses and
start their lives anew, but the gentiles' animosity continued to
embitter their hearts. Even so, many Jews were employed by the
Romanian government to help introduce and organize Com-
munism throughout the country, and others were employed by
the secret police; in fact, the agency's first minister was Ana
Pauker, a Jew, who later became prime minister. The majority
of Jews, however, sought ways to emigrate before finding themselves face to face with death again. Kahan, a young Jewish jew-
eler who had survived the camps, for example, was murdered
by Ukrainians when they passed through Sighet. Even though
he had outlived hunger, disease, derision, and abuse, he met his
death at the hands of the Ukrainians who slit his throat when
they robbed his store and made off with his merchandise.

When my uncle Elie Mailech and his two sons, Shlomo Ber and
Smilcu, arrived in Sighet, they informed us of Saul's death. After losing contact with our father in Gross Rosen, Saul had become desperate. Food had become scarce. Because of his anemic condition, walking through Germany was arduous. Then
Saul came upon a dead horse on the side of a road. Ripped
open by a hand grenade, the animal's intestines had spilled out
everywhere and the meat was already rotting. But my starving
brother did not let that stand in his way; he proceeded to eat
the worm-ridden, noxious meat. With neither medicine nor the
antibodies to ward off the poisoning that ensued, Saul fought
desperately to stay alive. My uncle and his sons cared for him
for three days until they no longer had the energy to keep watch

over him. A compassionate German soldier fired a shot into the back of his head, murmuring, "It's better for him not to suffer anymore."

When I was a prisoner, I had promised to return to kiss the earth where I had been born. However, I was unable to keep my promise. During that ashen autumn, my eyes could never focus on the beauty of the Tisa or the surrounding countryside. The owls had long ago stopped perching on the edge of the well, for the granary was empty. My surroundings were terribly alien to me: I was a foreigner in my own land. The war had changed the world's course. Grief and sadness dominated in gloomy silence everywhere. My cherished loved ones—those who had filled my soul with their laughter—had died. What was keeping me from leaving Sighet?

The city had become dreary but turbulent, as if a hurricane had gone through it destroying everything in its path. Houses once inhabited by our people had been abandoned. The Jewish neighborhood, now invaded by weeds, dust, and clutter, was a cemetery of uninhabitable dwellings. The wind would wail like the souls of those executed in the camps. It blew through those hollow places. Crows with purple-tinged feathers were perched on the roof of the shed. Their ominous shrill sent shivers down our spines.

"Wake up, Sanyi! You must leave this dying town," I said to myself as I surveyed the destruction. I realized that life was a precious gift that could not be replaced with anything else. I told myself to turn around and flee from this land where I was born. I should be like Lot, not look back. But where could I go? Which way should I go? What was waiting for me elsewhere?

I pondered those questions over and over, unable to make a decision. However, with each passing day and more and more news of the growing misfortunes of my Jewish neighbors, I had begun to gain the courage to consider leaving the region where I had become nothing but a stranger. My memories had trapped me in my childhood existence, and I knew very well I couldn't make a living from my memories. I had to start my own life, earning my way with hard work. I thought about establishing a new life, but it was going to be impossible in those places that had been abandoned. Each time I heard about more disappearances, tortures, insults, and abuse, I came closer to my decision. My plan was to cross the border and go to Budapest and, from there, walk to Germany in order to make contact with the Israeli Brigade that was fighting for the lands of our ancestors.

Isaac and Samuel agreed with me, but Paisi and Idel were opposed to my taking Samuel, the youngest of the family, which would only serve to expose him to God only knows what other new calamities. He wanted to go with me, but he had to accede to the older brothers' decision. Instead, Isaac would go with me. Then we talked to some cousins and spoke to our friend Baruch Farkas. Everyone concurred that with the new regime in power and the growing daily assaults on Jews, life in Sighet had become intolerable. It would be better to fight for our common cause: Israel, the Promised Land. Our nomadic group included my brother Isaac, my cousins Paisi and Marc, their sixteen-year-old sister Sara, Farkas, and me.

Once the decision had been made, and after discussing the route we would take, we began to prepare for our journey. Each of us secured a knapsack to carry winter clothing, some food, and a few valuables that might come in handy along the way. That was December 1945.

Those modest plans gave me renewed hope. The day we left, it was gray and dismal outside. My spirits, on the other hand, had been lifted and were brimming over. We all carried enough bread to last us until Budapest. When my family had been deported to Birkenau, we left Sighet in grief, but now it was just the opposite: we were leaving with joy.

The truck that was to take us to the border sat idling at the door of our house. Samuel, who would take off after us eight days later but without ever catching up to us, stood there dejectedly next to our older brothers. Idel and Paisi hugged us good-bye. I was wondering what they must have been feeling when we gathered up our bags.

My cousins were already sitting in the back of the truck, along with the former resistance fighter Baruch Farkas. They were waiting for the two Isacovici brothers. Avoiding any outward signs of sadness and not wanting to postpone our departure because it might make us regret our decision, we quickly climbed into the truck.

The freezing cold seared our faces. We six fugitives remained quiet as we watched the church towers of Sighet disappear behind us. A short time later the truck turned onto a terrible road filled with potholes that led to Satumare on the Hungarian border. The Carpathians, surrounded by clouds, began to appear and then disappear in the distance.

It was a cold winter morning, and the smoke from the villages was rising with difficulty, bumping against the low, morning clouds. The trees were laden with snow. The branches of the walnut and birch trees sparkled with frozen dew. We could see our breath. Huddled together, we were feeling no love for our native country; in fact, we were supremely happy to leave that painful place. However, our memories — and knowing that we were abandoning forever the place of our ancestors where we had played as children and experienced our first loves — filled us with nostalgia.

But at the moment, the freezing cold was slapping us in the face and numbing our limbs. In our search for a new life, those sacrifices that we had made didn't mean anything anymore. Yes, we had suffered much, much more in the "Death March," in the concentration camps, in the macabre days of hunger and forced labor, but now it was different: we had freely chosen to face that freezing cold and the pain it caused us. We knew nothing about what the rest of Europe had in store for six Jews whose misfortune and lack of opportunity drove them to begin anew.

As the truck rolled down the road, it was taking us toward a more conscious, authentic experience because we had chosen it. The histories of humanity are made with courage and fear, strength and conformity. Knowing that we had chosen to take this risk, despite what might await us, we felt brave and more human for it, because we preferred to take to the road rather than let ourselves disappear into oblivion in Sighet. We had placed our hope in the decision we had made, moving ever forward, leaving behind our once-revered hometown.

At the cemetery in Sighet, there were tombstones of our family members dating back to 1735. How could they have arrived there if they had stopped somewhere on the way? Fleeing as we were, we too would become progenitors of future generations of human beings, of other families, of other destinies, finally, in other places.

14

Even with the emotion of starting anew in life, I still felt somewhat indifferent about it. Prior suffering in that city had expunged any feelings of patriotism that I might have had. I no longer felt anything for my homeland or any nostalgia for those landscapes that I had grown to love when I was a child. Other impressions were dominant in my mind: discouragement and the idea that Sighet was the origin of my sorrows.

Our destination, Satumare, was on the border. The truck pulled over, and as we got out, night seemed to be descending upon us even though it was still afternoon. The wintery gray clouds were hanging low. We opened our knapsacks and, sitting on a bench, we ate a few good-sized pieces of bread to get ready to cross the border on foot.

The worst problem we had to face was the deep snow. After resting up, we took less-traveled routes that I had discovered during my smuggling days. The snow was knee-deep, requiring us to walk single file. The lead person would open a path for the rest of us, block the wind, and indicate obstacles he encountered. We switched off taking the lead every three miles, and no one wasted any energy discussing unnecessary matters; we were submerged in our own thoughts and tried to imagine what the future would be like. We had many things in common: all of us were young Jews, human residue of the war, disheartened by a life we had not chosen, and exiled from our birthplaces; but we were driven by our strong desire to start over. Of course, no one had any answers about how we would do that, where we could make a go of it, and what kind of luck was in store for us.

By dawn we had arrived at Debrecen. Because of our destitution in a population that was not any better off, we went virtually unnoticed. We made our way to the train station and luck was with us, for within the hour we had boarded a train heading for Budapest. The train car was full of nomads just like us. During the trip, no one spoke to us or asked us any questions; since we were traveling as a group and most of us were males, we were like encircled wagons, ready to defend ourselves.

While the train chugged through snow-covered landscapes, our spirits lifted. Once we were settled in the train car, we took the remaining bread out of our knapsacks and ate it all. Nothing was saved for the following day. Our situation was so uncertain that it wasn't worth worrying about what might happen upon our arrival in Budapest. We needed rest and soon fell asleep on the wooden floor of the train car. By the time we were pulling into Budapest on a cold, bitter morning, hunger was already gnawing at our insides.

Since some of us already knew our way around the capital city of Hungary, we headed straight for the Jewish neighborhood where we thought we could find help from our people. On our way, we walked by a bakery. The smell of fresh bread was everywhere. Farkas had a sensational idea on how to restock our food supply. The bakery was situated in a basement that looked out onto the street. He told us to wait under the eaves of a house because it had started to snow heavily. After a short while he returned with a long pole like the ones used for herding cattle. He tied a knife to the end of the stick with a shoestring. He said he was "going fishing."

Finding a place to sit down, he thrust the stick through the transom of the door going into the basement, and, while unable to see his catch, he poked at the bread rolls with the knife and then pulled them up, still hot and steaming from the ovens. The bread went straight into our knapsacks. In minutes our provisions had been replenished. Farkas set the pole down next to him, as if nothing had happened, and put his knife away.

As we walked calmly toward the Jewish neighborhood we ate the fresh, chewy bread. Upon reaching our destination, the same situation of desolation that we had seen everywhere else took us by surprise. The few people we managed to talk to advised us to keep going because there was no room to be had anywhere. So we trekked back to the train station and waited for a freight train that took us to the Austrian border, which we would have to cross on foot. We took advantage of the fact that it was nighttime. We continued consuming our bread faster than we could walk.

We discovered that we were going to have to climb a mountain and cross into unknown territory. Since there were no signs to guide us and the snow had covered the road, it was difficult to find our way. Although we knew we were headed in a northerly direction, by midnight we were completely lost. Farkas took the initiative, telling us to rest in the shelter of a big rock while he and one of my cousins climbed to the top of the next hill with the hope of spotting a nearby village.

While we waited, we bundled together as best we could. A howling wind whipped around the jagged rocks and lashed snow in our faces. My cousin Sara went to sleep on my shoulder, and although she had covered her face with a blue woolen cap, she looked as if she were frozen to death. Just as the rest of us were starting to doze off, I heard Farkas calling.

Although they hadn't seen any lights, they had discovered a large valley ahead. There are always people living in the valleys. Following him, we started down the mountain. At dawn, off in the distance, we sighted a small farm. Cautiously, we drew near. Total silence surrounded the house, but inside the dilapidated barn cows were mooing. We had been fighting off hunger for quite some time and we were worn out from the long walk. Isaac knocked on the door of the house. A man appeared, his eyes full of sleep; with the door slightly ajar as a shield, he asked what we wanted. Farkas pushed the door open and violently bulldozed his way inside. The man called to his wife, a young, plain-looking blond woman.

There was no fire in the kitchen stove. We sat down at the table and demanded something to eat. When the man refused, Farkas took out his knife and drove it into the table top. Immediately, the couple set to work. The woman crumbled some bread into a soup pot and added some old grease. That was more than we had expected. My cousin lit the fire in the stove and within the hour we were eating a thick, greasy soup that was hot and invigorating.

Isaac, who was not as aggressive as Farkas, explained to the couple that we were only traveling through and that they shouldn't have felt threatened by our presence. We asked them if the city of Graz was nearby. The husband, who finally calmed down when he saw us eating so voraciously, drew a map on a piece of paper, explaining the route we should take. Minutes later we were apologizing to him for Farkas's aggressiveness. We thanked the couple for their hospitality and resumed our march toward Graz. We arrived there just as the year 1945 was coming to an end.

We already knew that there was a refugee camp in the city. Upon our arrival, we asked where it was and found it easily. The United Nations Refugee Relief Administration (UNRRA) camp was run by the American occupation forces. Once inside, we felt very much at home: three hot meals a day, a bed, shelter from the harsh climate, a daily shower, and the opportunity to wash clothes — it was a place to regain our strength. This was not our final destination, but a place to rest along the way, an inn for pilgrims.

An abhorrent event occured in the UNRRA camp that intensely disturbed me. While I was walking through the camp, I came upon a mob of Jews who had recognized one of those gangsters from the concentration camps. With violent hatred and vengeance, they kicked, punched, and beat the Kapo with sticks until his body was one big, bleeding wound. They dragged him half dead to the entrance of the barracks, where he finally died. Were we entitled to kill our enemies? With a heavy heart, I remembered my participation in the clandestine groups in Sighet. I think that I had matured since then because this act by my people repulsed me. I had learned that violence breeds violence, it destroys everything, even our own conscience.

After a week's stay at the camp, our little group was fully re-covered and ready to continue our trek toward Germany. We boarded a train that crossed the Austrian border toward Bavar-ia, where we found shelter at UNRRA Camp 160, called Wald-stat bei Pocking. Once again, we felt right at home. The camp housed mainly concentration camp survivors from throughout Eastern Europe; the majority of the refugees were young peo-ple. The level of camp discipline reflected the organization and discipline of the *kibbutzim*, or communal farms, which were al-ready in existence in Israel, then called Palestine. At that camp, about 130 of us — mainly from the Transylvania region — formed our own kibbutz. The board of directors was made up of 10 in-dividuals: a president, a secretary, a treasurer, and 7 others who took charge of maintaining order among the camp members and assigning daily tasks. On several occasions I was nominated to be president of the kibbutz, but I never accepted the position. All the members of a kibbutz lived in the same barracks.

Refugees and survivors of the war in Europe were arriving in such numbers that every day new kibbutzim were quickly organized to take care of their needs. Upon our arrival, I became captivated by the euphoria of the young people there. There was much camaraderie among men and women alike, solidarity in performing our tasks, and communal living — after all the nightmares of the past, the enthusiasm lifted my spirits.

We were overwhelmed: the human contact was so vastly different from what we had experienced in the concentration camps. In fact, we were living an illusion of paradise — our ex-periences were so different from real life — but dreams are also necessary in order to develop one's hopes.

We would work hard morning and afternoon. At night there were cultural programs with folk music, singing, and dancing. Since my youth was irrevocable, I found myself disoriented by so much human contact, happiness, and dancing. When our leaders talked to us about our culture, they'd constantly refer to Israel. We had to return to redeem it and rebuild it for our descendants. The lecturers were young Zionists, well-prepared leaders. While they talked, tears would well up in my eyes and the spirit of adventure and triumph filled my soul. The long, impassioned speeches brought us to one realization: we had no choice but to work toward the creation of the Jewish state. Their words awoke in me feelings of what it is to belong to a nation, feelings that had been destroyed upon my return to Sighet.

"Yes, Israel will be my country and my destiny," I told myself. This idea turned out to be an illusion, but it was so important to me at the time.

I was assigned a job in an office. The Zionist leaders must have noticed something about me because they made me responsible for those refugees who were arriving around the clock. I'd check their documents, interview them, and assign them to the different kibbutzim. At the same time, I'd give them food and clothing. After one month I was put in charge of that office.

What makes the human heart cling to ideals that are nothing more than mirages? I really don't know. But I do remember going around with a renewed spirit of heroism, feeling euphoric, like the romantic who can't live without love, which is ecstasy. And in the kibbutz, I did fall in love. She was a Lithuanian girl by the name of Deborah Qwint. She was the girl of my dreams, she was vivacious and had a special manner about her. My crude clumsiness, learned in the concentration camps and from living with my brothers, clashed with her delicate nature and sense of courtesy. We worked in the same office together. She had black hair, porcelain-like cheeks, and the figure of an eighteen year old. But her serious demeanor squelched my desire to approach her. At night in the barracks, I couldn't stop thinking about the way she looked while she worked at the office.

However, the communal life and the evening dances made it possible for me to get to know her. During one dance known as the *chora*, I was lucky enough to hold her hand. It was like an electric jolt, stronger than if I had been hit with twenty whiplashes at the same time. I was sweating profusely and I felt like I couldn't breathe. Even though the music had stopped, I kept holding her hand as I guided her over to a corner, where I began talking about my job and about the poor people who were arriving from everywhere, greatly magnifying the importance of my insignificant bureaucratic position. Now, as I look back on it, I must say that I wanted to become something larger than life to her because, frankly, beyond my rapture for her, I had absolutely nothing to give her. But she politely listened to my boring, vain monologue. Then I asked her if she would go out with me. She responded that she wasn't opposed to it, as long as I maintained a serious and honest relationship with her. Despite her youth, she was more mature than me. The more we saw each other, the more I slacked off in my work because I couldn't think about anything but her. All my attention was directed toward her petite but dignified figure. Little by little, our relationship evolved into a sweet, loving, and passionate romance.

But the governing board of the Hashomer Hatzair kibbutz movement knew what was going on. At first they reprimanded me for letting my job slide. Then they decided to send me on a secret mission designed to eliminate the intense passion that was devouring me. But the fact that they would choose me for such an important mission made me proud and gave me the self-confidence that I needed, in the same way that I needed to eat and breathe, especially after having been so humiliated and abused in the camps. Perhaps because of this new assignment I saw myself in Deborah's eyes as her equal, even though she was much more refined and educated than I was.

The secret mission involved leaving the kibbutz and, along with my cousin Paisi, traveling to Czechoslovakia to impart Zionist ideas among the Jews who were dispersed throughout the Sudeten Gebiet region. Neither of us knew the mission in its entirety so that, if one of us happened to fall prisoner to the Soviets, we wouldn't be able to reveal the clandestine movements of those who were fighting for the establishment of the state of Israel.

That delicate mission, which was to contribute to the creation of a new nation, spurred my spirit of adventure. Despite my twenty-one years, I had experienced such an unpleasant life since my carefree smuggling days that I tended to treat important matters with excessive severity.

Our bosses gave us documents enabling us to get to Prague. The commanders of the Zionist movement never showed their faces, they only gave orders for us to fight for the cause, that is, the creation of the state of Israel. Paisi and I traveled by train to Prague. Our contact was waiting for us at 7 Josefoska Street. Once we had identified ourselves with our password, he informed us of the next step: we were to continue to the city of Podmokly, gather up a significant number of Jewish survivors, and prepare them for travel to Israel.

We arrived one afternoon. After we told an agent the purpose of our mission, he immediately and secretly brought together as many people as possible in the local synagogue. In the evening they congregated in the temple as if they were attending a prayer service. When I saw them all there, I thought I was seeing myself before I was sent away from Sighet. The majority were young people with pale, empty faces, people who had lost their ideals. It wasn't that their faces reflected the fear of death in the concentration camps anymore, rather there was a sense of apathy about them, the lack of initiative of the hopelessly trapped.

I gave the most eloquent delivery possible, talking to them as if I were talking to myself. "Here in Czechoslovakia, you are simply migrants in transit," I said. "When the Nazis attacked us, very few Czechs came out to help us. The ground you are standing on right now is not yours, it belongs to the Czechoslovakians. Our land, our country, is the land of Moses, David, and Solomon. Your nation is Israel. Come and help us build a new Jewish state, a place we can call our own because it belonged to our ancestors."

Sudeten Gebiet had been a region inhabited by ethnic Germans, who had collaborated with the Fascist regime during the war. When the war was over, they were expelled from the region and their possessions were distributed among the survivors of the Holocaust and the Czech Jews who had fought with the Czech Resistance against the Nazis, in order to get them to stay. This form of compensation had been intended to appease the Jewish resentment for the harsh treatment they received in the war.

Hoping to convince them to leave and fight for the new state, I appealed to them with the following argument: "What you consider to be yours right now previously belonged to the Germans. Just remember how bitter you were when the Nazis robbed you of your possessions. Now you are doing the same: you're accepting what doesn't belong to you. Don't accept anything out of generosity. We will find prosperity only if we build it ourselves. What you now possess doesn't belong to you, and it's possible that once again they may take it all away from you because neither the land nor the other possessions you've been given as a handout are yours. Help us, instead, in the construction of the new Jewish state. Israel is our homeland, our shield, and our protection."

When I finished my speech, I received a lengthy ovation. But fate being what it is, I found myself not paying any attention to the applause, but staring at a familiar face framed by a kerchief. That young woman, whom I just happened to see in the audience, was none other than my old girlfriend, Leah Gitel.

I was unable to go over to her because immediately following my talk there were questions about how people could leave Czechoslovakia and move to Israel. I had to stay around to relieve their doubts: no one could blame them for being afraid to leave Czechoslovakia. They wanted to hang onto whatever they might call their own — an old shack, a small piece of farmland, an empty store — something that was still a part of them. To abandon even those few possessions that had come to mean everything to them and to join an adventure that required energy and sacrifice was not a decision they could make overnight.

We managed to deal with the onslaught of questions until late that evening. We argued, cleared up erroneous ideas, dispelled gossip, and explained that we would help them pay for the trip; we presented the best scenario possible of what life would be like in a kibbutz in Israel. We ended the meeting by singing a hymn in Yiddish dedicated to the Holocaust.

OUR VILLAGE IN FLAMES
They're burning, my friends, they're burning,
our people are being consumed.
Raging winds, blowing like a hurricane, are shrieking
and dispersing us everywhere;
and nothing but desolation will remain;
after a war there are only deserted, scorched walls.
And you, my friends, simply cross your arms
and watch our people being consumed.
Nothing will be left but ruins and ashes.
And you, my friends,
are here watching how our people burn.

As we were leaving, Leah came up to congratulate me for my speech and the work I was doing. Perhaps because her fiancé was standing next to her, we had an awkward, trivial conversation. During the brief time I remained in that city, I saw Leah alone one other time. Basically, she told me that she wanted to renew our old romance. Her awkwardness at expressing herself made me sad. She was ready to break with her fiancé if I would accept her offer, but I could only feel sorry for her.

My love for Deborah, the Lithuanian with jet-black eyes, protected me from temptation. I tried not to offend Leah, but I explained that our lives had matured in such different ways that it was too late to rekindle a love that had been crippled from the very beginning. I experienced anxiety and regret for having to hurt someone I had once loved so intensely. The day of our departure from Podmokly finally arrived. Hearing our comrades' repeated promises, my cousin and I wondered how many of those hopes would actually materialize. With those thoughts, we moved on.

When we were on our way back through Prague, I visited with my cousins Shlomo and Isaac, the same ones who had helped me out in Jaworzno. As a gesture of my appreciation, I gave them a carton of American cigarettes, which is all I had with me.

We pushed on with our mission. We had to identify new contacts and to continue preaching Zionism. We visited so many towns that my memories of them are now a blur. However, what has always remained in my heart was the friendly welcome that we received from those exiled people. They would congregate anywhere—in a home or a shop—in order to listen to us. We would be deluged with questions, for they wanted assurances that life in Israel would be better than their present lives on Czechoslovakian farms. But what kind of proof could we give them? For me, the closest thing resembling a kibbutz was my recent experience at Waldstat bei Pocking. My image of Israel was based on some old, crumpled photographs. That barren land, the arid deserts, and the rocky terrain that only looked suitable for goats didn't really correspond to the image of paradise that I was describing to my comrades.

My enthusiasm would come and go like a boomerang. One day I would be enthusiastic about our proposal to create a Jewish nation and, the next day, sensing the lack of confidence and fears of my listeners, I would become discouraged. However, between those ups and downs, I had to deal with my own doubts, my desire to see Deborah again, the endless travel, and giving lectures. Time flew by. Almost without realizing it, the mission was over and we were back at Camp Waldstat bei Pocking.

How comforting it was to be back with Deborah once again and hold her in my arms! Happiness was still a big commodity at the kibbutz. New faces, which were arriving every day, brought back old sadness but also new hope. I turned in my report on the mission, but my superiors already knew more about what I had accomplished than I did. I never did find out how they knew so much about our efforts, our discouragements, and our achievements.

Communal life was a great remedy for loneliness. Before long I was nourishing that marvelous feeling of leading a healthy life, living and working out in the wide-open spaces. We lacked nothing, because we'd all pitch in with the planting and the harvesting, and we shared sorrow and happiness. Even so, there was something about that feeling of satisfaction that bothered me. I began to think that a life like that could not last, that it was simply a mirage, because I already knew that reality was something totally different. Israel was in the hands of the British army and to ponder going on an expedition to Israel conjured up great uncertainty.

When I thought about Deborah and the future, that is, the possibility of getting married and having children, I wondered what it would be like to raise a family in a commune. To my way of thinking, the family was the nucleus of any type of communal relationship. Here it was just the opposite: first the commune, then the family.

Every day I would see young people getting married and turning their future over to chance; they had nothing and there was nothing they could offer to their families in order to get ahead in life. Nevertheless, caught up in youthful passion and wanting to break with their past, they turned to marriage as a gamble with the future. It was easy to find fleeting happiness through a mirage, but I always remembered my father saying that marriage should not be based on youthful impulse but rather on obligation and responsibility.

Aside from my job and my youth, what else could I offer Deborah? Everything belonged to the commune. Not even the pants I was wearing were mine. Those thoughts gnawed at me and crushed my spirits.

15

Even though I was encouraged by my contribution to the Jewish dream of recovering our homelands that had been taken from us nearly two thousand years ago, I was still paralyzed by desperation. I feared that life might come to nothing because I had nothing to call my own and nothing to offer Deborah should she consent to marry me.

After finishing work in the office, I'd stroll around the kibbutz asking myself if I seriously thought I could establish a family within a collective farm. As it was, everything depended on the kibbutz, and if I were to get married I would continue to depend on the community for my material and spiritual well-being. They were good people: hard-working, brave, idealistic, and fascinated by a nation that beckoned to them. But when all was said and done, I couldn't reconcile one basic fact, perhaps insignificant to some but important to me: family life takes precedence over communal life.

Absorbed by those worrisome thoughts, I decided one day to bring it out into the open and ask Isaac's advice. I brought it up one day after work. Instead of going out to sing and dance, we took a walk between the barracks. When I explained to him my doubts about those Zionist ideas, he agreed that while the ideas were probably excellent, they weren't necessarily for everyone.

"There are men who excel in religion, others in business, and still others in academia. What's important is not the profession you choose, it's the way you achieve something within that profession," he said.

As we strolled, I reflected not only on what he was saying but also on how he said it; his tranquillity was due to the many years of suffering that had penetrated his soul. Mature now, he wasn't the aggressive braggart he once was.

"In and of themselves," he told me, "those Zionist ideals are wonderful. But it's not for everyone to live them out. It's not the enterprise itself that makes people good, but rather the way each person lives his or her own life. In noble causes one finds people who are evil, while in evil causes one finds people who are noble. Similarly, marriage in itself is good, but a married man could also be a bad person, whereas, it might happen that a man who never marries is still a good person. You see, it's all relative. Listen, Sanyi, you can fight for Zionism, but you don't have to see yourself living in a kibbutz. In your case, life in the kibbutz is not for you because the most important thing for you is your independence."

His advice led me to the conclusion that if I wanted greater freedom, first I had to obtain spiritual independence. In other words, I had to be myself; after that would come the economic independence necessary to start a family. And Isaac and I agreed that in order to become self-sufficient, I would have to earn some money.

As it turns out, my brother was in charge of administrating the bathhouses in the settlement. One day, he received a request from some butchers to allow them to use the settlement's water to clean the beef that was then sold to the members. Butchering cattle was against the law at the time because the government was trying to build up the herds decimated by the war, so it was done clandestinely. After much haggling with the butchers, my brother negotiated a deal with them whereby in exchange for water, they would provide him with meat and hides. From that day forward, I was in charge of receiving the hides and curing them. I bought industrial salt and began salting down the insides of the skins. Then I would roll them up and hide them in niches underneath the piles of coal used to heat up the water for bathing.

Time was passing by quickly. New refugees, committed to the Zionist cause, continued to arrive at the commune. Among them were some of the Jewish Czechoslovakian compatriots who had heard my lectures during my mission. The money they had been given and the new feelings of hope spurred them to abandon their birthplaces and join the brigades that were fighting for our lands. Upon recognizing them, I embraced and congratulated them for the decision they had made.

One night I couldn't sleep. Lying there awake, I began asking myself how could I have deceived my own kind. I had promoted Zionism, but didn't believe in it myself. Then I began to imagine their faces accusing me of deceiving them. Burdened by guilt, I went to see my brother who eased my concern.

"Why are you worrying? You haven't forced them to come here. All you did was open a door for them. They've had the freedom to choose the road they wanted to take. If they want to travel to Israel, that's their choice, not yours. You believe it's necessary to create a Jewish state so that we will not be the victims of genocide. Well, that's fine, Sanyi, but that belief doesn't compel you to commit yourself to the task. You must choose your life and build it wherever life leads you."

How wisely my brother had explained things! His words made me feel much better. Without giving it another thought, I continued to fight not only for the idea of a Jewish state but also for my own well-being, which was to start a family wherever fortune would lead me. I figured out that I could work toward both ends simultaneously. I had been foolish to worry. I renewed my daily strolls with Deborah, and we began to forge plans.

Spring was upon us and romance was in the air. Once again, however, Leah Gitel appeared in my life; she had arrived at the commune with her boyfriend. Since the first thing any newcomer was required to do was to stop at my office to be registered and to receive supplies for the new life in the kibbutz, there she was, standing right in front of me. Meanwhile, I was asking myself what had motivated her to come.

I had always found it difficult to distance myself from Leah; whenever I was facing a crucial decision, she was always there. While I no longer felt a strong bond to her, her presence bothered me like an old wound that wouldn't heal. Once she got settled, it was her intention to win me back. She told me outright that she wanted to rekindle our old flame. She came straight to the point, making it possible for me to be straightforward as well. I explained to her that our relationship was impossible because I was in love with Deborah and I had obligations to the kibbutz. "You have your own boyfriend, Leah. Start a new life with him. What happened between you and me is a thing of the past."

She looked at me with every bit of hatred she could muster, turned on her heel and left. She never came around to see me again. In fact, that was the last time I ever saw her. We had taken different paths and never again would they cross.

It wasn't long before I had managed to stash 135 hides, but I had no buyers. Even if I did find one, I wouldn't be able to accept German marks because they were worthless. While I was trying to locate some buyers, I came in contact with a tanner from Munich whose factory had shut down because he had no raw materials with which to work. We bartered back and forth, and finally I agreed to exchange the skins for eleven gold coins of different nationalities.

Those eleven coins would fetch a lot of money. I also had managed to accumulate several packages of American cigarettes. Since I didn't smoke—after all, my lungs had been destroyed in the Jaworzno coal mines—there was no chance I would use them. With these possessions in hand, I considered myself ready to seek independence from the kibbutz. I told Deborah about my decision, but I didn't propose marriage because I knew she was not in a position to abandon her mother and invalid sister. Her situation presented an obstacle to our plans. Like my enthusiasm for the Zionist movement that had begun to fade, our love was blocked by the reality of the moment. Current events were beginning to thwart our plans and promises.

Fall 1946. The invisible hand of the brigade and the Israeli emissaries continued to work incessantly. One gray, cloudy day we were told that those of us who wanted to go to Israel must travel first to Italy and then take a ship the rest of the way. Why did I sign up? It's hard to explain. I guess it wasn't because of Zionist ideals which by then meant less to me, but because I thought Israel would offer more opportunities to me and my people. In any case, I had decided that I didn't want to remain in that kibbutz anymore. A trip to Italy provided a way out. I had only a few hours in which to inform Deborah of my decision.

Deciding to go to Israel with the other refugees meant abandoning Deborah because she was unable to leave her family behind. What was I to do? Because of Leah, I knew only too well that adage about the poorly sewn seam that will rip apart at the slightest strain. I had to be honest with Deborah. To leave her behind without formally terminating our relationship would be tantamount to committing a crime, because no one knew what kind of luck we would have in our future travels. Tying her down to a distant love — nurtured only by letters — was no solution for either of us. I had to make a clean break, *now*. Dreams would only postpone the inevitable. It would be more honest for both of us to sever our relationship, surrendering our promises to fate.

Finally, when I talked to Deborah, she seemed to agree with me; but while we talked I struggled to remain steadfast. She was much more educated and possessed more vision than I did, so she quickly understood the situation. She said, "We have been greatly persecuted. Our lives together have been splendid. During the time we've been here together, we haven't wasted a minute. Every moment I have been with you has been marvelous, and that belongs to me. No one can take that away from me."

On the one hand, I wanted to flee from the kibbutz; on the other, my love for Deborah was holding me back. But my lot had been drawn: by leaving both the kibbutz and Deborah, no matter what the cost, I was allowing myself to search for options. In order to forge ahead, one has to give something up.

Deborah was not a melodramatic person. After having lived through such nightmares, our genuine willingness to accept the fruits of our lives as they came to us showed that we were able to accept what was possible for the moment. Lacking a clear future, we clung desperately to the present like someone drowning who grabs at anything around them so as not to die.

The clandestine migration began: the encampment became filled with the sound of trucks, and the good-byes, embraces, and last-minute advice marked the beginning of a painful exodus. We felt like the Jews who had left Egypt. We were bound for northern Italy, and we began our trip in military trucks headed for Austria.

The stops along the way to eat something, drink a little water, or relieve ourselves would last only fifteen minutes. The roads were almost impassable, and poverty had vented its cruelty on practically every city and town through which we had to pass. Desolation prevailed everywhere. Even though the reconstruction of Europe had begun, the consequences of disaster were everywhere: we really felt that we were escaping from the darkness of barbarism into the light of civilization.

Our most important stop was Milan where we stocked up on provisions for the remainder of the trip. Despite our painful past, from that moment on the light-hearted spirit of the Italians began to rub off on us. We arrived in Rivoli in September of 1946. As refugees, we were taken to an old military barracks; dirty and repulsive, these were only holding places while we were in transit. Knowing that our situation was temporary, we were willing to put up with anything.

Rivoli was a small but friendly city of outgoing, cheerful people whose kindness and affection conquered us immediately. Meanwhile we tried to make our lives seem normal by organizing a temporary kibbutz. The young people of the city would invite us to their dances on the weekends. We were Jews and gentiles living in harmony as if we were all next of kin.

The dances made it possible for everyone to intermingle. Two members of our group even married a pair of sisters from the town. Their mother was delighted with the marriages because she used to say that Jews, who were always respectful and hard working, made great husbands.

One thing was for sure: the wine, the merriment of the young people, and the courtships that blossomed daily kept our spirits high. However, one thing never changed: every day we ate the same thing, spaghetti smothered in tomato and onion sauce. We grew tired of it. After two months in Rivoli we were ready to go to Israel. Despite the wonderful hospitality of the citizens of Rivoli, living on someone else's land, having no nation we could call our own, and having to abandon our birthplaces made us uneasy. Also, the cold winter had left us demoralized. In December, the first departure of refugees was announced. Once we had boarded that ship, which had space for 170 passengers, we had happily become *chalutzim*, that is, Jewish colonists in Palestine, the future founders of the state of Israel.

When we got to the docks, a ship was already waiting for us. We marched single file up the gangplank and got settled into our cabins. The transport steamer, which had been converted into a passenger ship, was old and shabby. However, we tended to overlook any inconveniences because we were still charged with the spirit of Zionism, born in Waldstat bei Pocking. The captain of the ship was Italian and Commander Armon was in charge of maintaining discipline. The strength of our optimism shielded us from the dangers that we would soon be facing.

Once the turbines down in the hold beneath us began to churn, the ship pulled away from the dock. Above us, flags were fluttering in the breeze and gulls were screeching all around us. The ocean was blue-gray as we floated gently away from the city. Standing next to Isaac and leaning against the ship's railing, I watched Europe become a blur on the horizon. Once out on open sea, we began to get seasick: the Mediterranean had turned choppy, and soon the foaming waves were smashing against the sides of the ship. Pitching and rolling, the ship began to creak. Most of us were not prepared for the high seas and we felt sure the boat was going to capsize at any moment. Between our fears and our seasickness, we quickly became exhausted.

Many of us sprawled out on the deck. The routine was to get up on your knees, crawl to the edge of the boat, vomit over the side, and then return to where you were before. We had become so weak that Commander Armon told us to start singing patriotic hymns in order to lift our spirits.

The situation had become quite precarious. At the time, the British navy dominated the Mediterranean and their PT boats patrolled those waters in order to prevent ships carrying Jews from reaching Israel. Typically, the British would capture the refugee ships on the open seas and escort them back to Cyprus, where the Jews would be taken off the ships and placed in camps totally isolated from the outside world. Knowing that, our captain tried to follow a course that would outmaneuver the British forces.

The refugees who were turned back were housed in army tents on the Cyprus beaches. No one wanted to end up living that way. Our ship was going to have to evade British vigilance. The ships that did manage to elude the blockade would unload their passengers on Palestine beaches with the aid of Israeli liberation organizations.

On the fifth day, a British patrol boat spotted us. It was raining hard and the waves were beating against the sides of the ship, washing over the decks. Even though by then we had grown accustomed to the sea, the danger of disappearing in a dark, swirling body of water frightened us all. Many didn't know how to swim. We prayed for protection from the perilous waters.

Our fear of falling into the hands of the British put our spirits to the test. Some were ready to turn back. Dreading the weather and the pursuit of the British ships, we asked ourselves if it wouldn't have been better to have remained in Germany. As the British forces closed in on us, the combination of a fortuitous maneuver by the captain, the ferocious storm, and a pitch-black night made it possible for us to elude the enemy. Our captain, facing the danger of taking us through waters that were highly patrolled, decided to head for Genoa, where we finally made a landing. On solid ground again, we felt relieved, but the dreadful weather and adversities had left many Zionists pessimistic about going on. One of them was Isaac, who said he wasn't up to facing another sea adventure like the last one.

And then fate brought us face to face with our cousin David, the smuggler from Sighet who had cheated his own people. He was in Genoa, having just arrived from Israel. He filled us in on what was happening there, for he had taken an active part in Hagana, the Jewish army of liberation.

"You guys know me well enough. I've always been able to take care of myself. My wife and children were killed at Auschwitz. During the war, I was sent to the front lines because the Hungarians suspected I was one of the principal activists for the Jewish people. They knew I had been a spy. After the war, I left Sighet and I've been smuggling in Italy. My plan was to get to Palestine where I had hoped to start over with my new wife."

My brother and I listened to him attentively. He was more experienced than we were. When he became a spy for the Hungarians and then the Romanians, he had demonstrated exceptional courage.

"I'm advising you to go somewhere else. Life in Israel is difficult. There is little industry to speak of and it's impossible to find an honest job. Refugees are arriving every day and they find themselves in the predicament of having neither work nor money to go back home. That kind of life is great for the idealists, the dreamers who are willing to take orders. The idealists are the pioneers. They built their own kibbutzim in the deserts and the marshes. There, everyone has to go in search of water, drain the swamps, cultivate the soil, and live in makeshift shelters. The sun is so strong you can only work in the early morning and late afternoon; you almost feel as if your bones are going to burst into flames. And marsh fever decimated us. You can't rest at night because everyone has to take turns standing guard against Arab attacks. I don't recommend it one bit. Of course, you're free to choose what you want, but for me it wasn't the answer."

He answered numerous questions, still trying to dissuade us from continuing our journey to Israel. Besieged by conflicting emotions once again, I found myself doing battle with many diverse thoughts. All I really wanted was a place to call my country. On the other hand, I detested violence and abhorred the thought of becoming immersed in it again. Why put my life in danger after having sacrificed so much in order to save it? I was fed up with confusion and promises, fed up with having no opportunities to get ahead, fed up with the pain, the wandering, and the humiliation; in short, nothing made sense. I dreamed of peace and tranquillity, but I was living in a state of chaos. I had been seeking a place to call my own, but all I owned was the dust on my shoes. I had been searching for a place that would help me organize my wayward life, but in my soul there was only anxiety and turmoil.

As I thought about these things, I remembered the dream I had of starting a family in the land of our Jewish ancestors. I had thrown myself completely into the project of rebuilding the state of Israel out of scattered, exiled followers. I had been enthusiastic about the plan to send refugees to the Promised Land, but the promised land was an uncultivated place that couldn't guarantee us safe haven. These contradictions upset me very much. How many poor people had I plucked from their homeland and sent on this adventure? Was I to blame for the instability of their lives and their helpless situation?

Adrift in questions, I was rescued by Isaac, who helped clarify things. "We have to take care of ourselves and our destinies," he said. "You didn't force the others to become involved in this Zionist project. Each of us has to learn to make choices. All I know at this point is that Israel is not for me. I've fought enough for the Jewish people. Perhaps we're a people who will continue to wander forever. If that's the way God has willed it, then that's the way it has to be."

I began to think that if nothing happens without God's participation and I was still alive, then my first and foremost obligation was to save my own life. I really think that human beings are citizens of the world; nevertheless, how can one get along in life without a country? Wasn't there someplace out there that I could call home? Where could I begin to look?

In the evening, I walked around Genoa. People of all ages and types — many seemingly with insurmountable problems — filled the streets. The worst way to behave, I thought, was to do nothing. But how do you make a decision? And even if you do, will it be the right one? Who can determine with any certainty which is the best road to take in life? Each one of us is responsible for finding his or her own way. What did destiny hold for me? How could my life make any sense when I didn't even know what to do next?

Fortunately, my brother Isaac decided for both of us. One day he told me that he was already planning our trip. Where? To Paris. Well, it was all the same to me. I had been so submerged in doubt that I didn't care where we went. The only thing I knew was that I didn't want to be embroiled in more violence, and I didn't want to return to Sighet or continue my journey to Israel. Once those places were eliminated, I was indifferent about going anywhere else. My gut reaction told me that any corner of the world was acceptable because misfortune would just follow me there anyway. What abominable sin had I committed that I would never find peace in my soul?

I was tortured by the idea that I was paying for having sent my brethren to Israel. That was my sin. When a person is feeling discouraged, it's easy to burden his or her soul with all the sins of the earth.

Our preparations for the trip to Paris took my mind off the contradictions in my life. Our plan was to travel to the Italian-French border, cross on foot, and, once we were on the other

side, take the train to Paris. We packed our belongings and
talked to people who might guide us to the border. We were
strangers and without a guide the journey would be impossible.
My Zionist dreams had already faded. Only in 1968 did I reach
the Promised Land, as a visitor rather than a pioneer.

16

At first, the prospect of traveling to Paris did little to raise my spirits. Since 1944—the year I was deported to Auschwitz—I had done nothing but tramp around Europe. In the course of three years, I had been to Romania, Czechoslovakia, Hungary, Austria, Germany, Italy, the Mediterranean, and now I was going to France. But after working two days to get a group of people together, I began to feel better about things. I finished packing.

As a youngster growing up in Sighet, I had led a provincial life. Later, like a frail leaf propelled aloft by a strong wind, I had been blown from place to place, a mere plaything of the uncontrollable forces of the time, and I had continued on an uncharted course in life ever since. Was I just kidding myself when I thought that all this was going to come to an end when we reached Paris? Could it be true? I doubted it.

Our traveling group consisted of almost the same people who had left Sighet together—Isaac; my two cousins, Marc and his sister Sara; a new friend named Arie; and myself. In a way, Arie was taking the place of Farkas, who said he would catch up with us in Paris. In the meantime, a Romanian Jew from Bucharest, Domnul Marinu, finally agreed to guide us across the border. Although we had to negotiate the price with him, it turned out that he was already taking other groups across the border who were headed for Paris. We struck a fair bargain. Following Marinu's orders, we all met and boarded a train that would take us to the border. That was in December 1946.

After leaving Turin, the train began following the Mediterranean coastline. From the car windows, we could see the rocky formations of the coast jutting up violently out of the sea. The train snaked its way through long tunnels and arches carved into the rocks, as if we were headed straight for the center of the earth. We could see on one side the sheer walls of granite and, on the other, down below, a gray-hued sea. Continuing along the coast, we arrived at the last city on the Italian side of the border:

Ventimiglia. When the train finally pulled into the station, dusk had fallen in the city.

We waited until dark in order to continue on foot into France. As we began to head up and over the spur of a mountain range, we followed a trail used by sheep herders. The land was dry, and the moon gave a silvery sheen to the rocky terrain. Our guide Marinu told us to remain silent so as not to alert any border patrols in the area. It had been snowing when we left Turin but now we enjoyed a welcome warm spell. Our heavy winter clothing became a hindrance to us, and we began to sweat as we made our way over the rocky terrain.

With daybreak, the fog began to dissipate and we found ourselves in crisp, clear sunlight. From our vantage point, Marinu pointed toward a bay of water down below. There, nestled between the mountains and the sea, was the city of Menton, completely bathed in white. We sat among the boulders and ate a few pieces of bread for breakfast. Then the guide gathered us together for our last set of instructions.

"When you get to Menton, take a bus to Nice. In Nice, go straight to the train station. Buy your tickets to Paris and make sure you get on the first train out. If the police detain you, do not be frightened. Just tell them you are Jewish survivors of the Holocaust. But do not tell them you are going to Paris. Instead, tell them you are coming from Paris and you're on your way to Italy in order to get a boat to Palestine."

Then we made our way through a damp forest; the smell of pine and cypress trees filled the air. We had finally crossed into France. We came upon a road that snaked its way down to Menton. As we were walking along, we suddenly noticed that our guide had disappeared without saying good-bye. His mission had been completed, and successfully, too. The rest was up to us.

We could tell that this area hadn't been affected by war. The farm houses, peacefully situated among the pine groves, seemed almost stately. We made our way into the middle of the town and immediately boarded a bus for Nice.

There, the trees and shrubs were as well kept as a palace garden. Under well-groomed trees, elegantly dressed people in white linen suits and black-ribboned fedoras and sporting silver-handled canes were sitting peacefully at tables on the terraces of the cafés. They glanced at us with disdain because our garb communicated poverty and wretchedness. We stood out like sore thumbs. We were refugees.

I was wearing a beret and a German navy coat that hung down past my knees. Those café patrons pointed at us with a nod of their heads and laughed at the parade of the scum of the earth. But we must have reminded them that there were other people in the world who were unable to live with the same dignity and composure as they did during the war. We reminded them not only of the suffering and hunger that so many had experienced during the scourge but also of the fact that they hadn't lifted a finger to prevent it. Our presence briefly disturbed the smug peace of their immaculate souls.

Following our guide's instructions, we continued toward the train station. As we crossed an intersection, however, a traffic cop spotted us and motioned for us to stop. It was around ten o'clock in the morning. The policeman wanted to see our ID cards. We didn't have any so he led us to the police station. Fortunately, our guide had made us throw away anything that might implicate us in the event we would be arrested. We had already destroyed our Turin tram and train ticket stubs. Hence, nothing we were carrying in our pockets would reveal our direction of travel.

Curious bystanders and store owners who were just opening up looked askance at us. Their haughtiness made me feel ashamed. They were making us the butt of their jokes. Then I asked myself why I had to feel ashamed. If they had an ounce of dignity, they would've realized that they were the ones who should have felt ashamed. We were the victims of their system. Picking up my pace with confidence, I stuck out my chest and cocked my head defiantly as if I were a king on a float in a parade.

My thoughts must have coincided with the others because all of us became jovial and happy.

Upon arriving at the police station, we were asked to empty our pockets onto a table for examination. I plunked down two tubes of toothpaste inside of which I was concealing my eleven gold pieces. I had learned that trick during my smuggling days in Sighet. Then they searched our clothing. We had hidden nothing: we were clean. After the search came the interrogation. I was the only one who spoke a little French because I had learned some in school. For almost an hour I kept repeating the same story until they grew tired of it. "We are Jewish survivors of the Holocaust. We are coming from Paris. We lived on Severe Street, District 15. We are headed for Italy where we will take a boat to Palestine."

The guide had made up that story, which was almost true, except that we were doing it in reverse. In order to determine if we were telling the truth, they called Paris and found out that the street and district, in fact, did exist. But they were unable to locate the street number or the name of the hotel where I said we had been staying. Finally, the police decided we should be sent back to our point of departure: Paris. A representative of the Jewish community in Nice arrived. Again, there were more questions, but this time in Yiddish. And I responded with the same answers, in Yiddish. The representative was able to confirm that we were indeed Jews, and he turned to the police, "I think the best thing to do in this situation is send them back to Paris so they can get their papers in order."

A secretary prepared a document for us to give to the Police and Immigration Office in Paris and wrote down the address on a piece of paper. Then we were escorted in a police van to the train station. Suspecting that we would try to sneak away and continue our journey to Italy without our papers, they had a policeman remain with us at the station, making sure we stayed on board the train until it actually pulled away from the platform. It never even occurred to them that our real intentions were to go to Paris. Their suspicions and diligence only served to ensure that everything went perfectly! In fact, it didn't cost us a cent to get to Paris. At eight o'clock the next morning we rolled into the Gare de Lyon train station. It was January 1947.

Being the country bumpkins that we were and dressed like vagabonds, the capital city of luxury and culture overwhelmed us. Our guide had told us to ask for directions to get to place de la Republique. I approached a man carrying suitcases and asked him directions. He pointed to the exit and told us to go down the steps. Once outside, I saw horse-driven carriages like the ones in Sighet. A woman selling newspapers told us to keep going down the steps. When we reached the bottom, we still didn't know where to go, so we went back up the steps once again. Then I asked another street vendor how to get to place de la Republique. Again, he said to keep going down the steps. I wondered how we were going to reach our destination by going under the ground. I just couldn't figure it out. So I handed the address to a coachman and he charged us 500 francs in advance.

As the carriage jostled along the streets of Paris, we were filled with amazement over the monuments and the feverish activity in that marvelous city. Caught up by the surprise and wonder of it all, we hadn't even realized that if we had kept going down under the ground toward the bottom of the steps, we would have entered the subway and paid 100 times less to travel the same distance as we did in the carriage. And none of us would have ever imagined that the ride in the carriage would take almost two hours while the same trip in the subway was a fifteen-minute ride. Nevertheless, we finally arrived at our destination. We immediately saw that we were in a Jewish neighborhood. The appearance of the stores and businesses was familiar to us. Even from a distance we could tell that the women shopping were from Eastern Europe. I inquired about a cheap place to stay. The majority of the people were just like us and had been through the same experiences. We were given friendly advice and precise directions on how to use the subway in order to get

to the Saint Paul station and then find rue Rosier, where there
was a large Jewish community with a synagogue that would take
us in for the night.

Feeling unsure, we went down the steps to the subway and
purchased our tickets. Suddenly, we began to laugh at our pro-
vincialism and told ourselves that now was the time to become
cosmopolitan. We had paid for our ignorance of modern civilization with the carriage ride, and we just had to laugh at our
country innocence.

We stayed at the synagogue for a week, during which time we
attended all the religious services. Without any money to spend
or friends to help us out, we would spend the major part of our
days scouting the neighborhood, trying to familiarize ourselves
with our new way of life and figure out how to get organized.

The synagogue happened to be the place where the most diverse groups of people would congregate. Not only did they
speak many different languages but each one of them had a
different, mysterious, frightening story to tell. It was precisely at
one of the prayer meetings where I noticed a tall, emaciated man
whose face was partially hidden by the tallith around his head.
At first I didn't pay much attention to him, but his attempts to
avoid me, his efforts to make himself invisible, gave him away.
So I began to observe the man more closely. Something about
him seemed familiar. At first, all I could see was the covered
face of a tortured man hiding under his tallith. But when the
cloth slipped off his head, I recognized him immediately: Steg,
a Kapo from Jaworzno. As if an arrow had pierced his heart,
the Kapo turned to me and, trembling, murmured, "For God's
sake, please don't turn me in."

He had already recognized me. Suddenly I remembered the
Kapo who had been beaten to death by a group of fanatics at
Graz. I thought, What had been the point of such a barbarous
act? There's no sense in spilling more human blood. If I'm not
in control of my own life, how could I ever exercise control over
another?

I looked straight into his eyes and responded, "Don't worry, I won't."

Then I returned to my prayers and forgot about him. But when I looked up from my prayer book, the Kapo had disappeared. I guessed that he didn't think he was entirely out of danger because someone else could have recognized him as well. I never saw him again.

To begin living normally in Paris was an enormous challenge. To become a resident, I had to have an ID; and in order to work I had to have residency status. It was a vicious circle that I had experienced before, so I had to lie. Without the proper documentation it would be impossible to rent a room somewhere. Competing with one another for the distinction of greatest poverty, the hotels in the area were nothing more than miserable flophouses. I ventured into one hotel, which I judged might be cheap from its sordid, deteriorated condition. I explained to the desk clerk that my ID card was being processed. Indignant and threatening to call the police because of my illegal status, he maneuvered to raise the price of the room. After considerable bartering, he rented me a room and then handed me a certification of residency with which I could then obtain my ID.

Happier than I could ever imagine, I went to the police station and requested residency status. With the support of the Jewish community in Paris, I finally managed to obtain provisional residency. With those documents in hand, I set out to look for work. Each city district had a government employment office and employers hired people through the agency. The next day I found my way to the end of the line, waited to fill out the forms, and after a few days I landed a job. Although I wasn't happy about the type of job, it meant survival.

I worked in a factory making tourist souvenirs. I polished tiny metal replicas of the Eiffel Tower, the Arch of Triumph, the Arch of Strasbourg, Saint Denis, and others. In addition to being tedious and tiring, the copper dust floating in the air was harming my lungs that had already been damaged in the mines of Jaworzno.

After a month of work, I changed hotels because the one where I started out seemed to be infested with more rats than the city sewers themselves. Now that I was earning more money, I felt I should move to a decent, cleaner place. The hotel I found was at 86 Saint Louis en L'Ile Street. But then I felt compelled to find a better job. This time I worked in a factory that made fire extinguishers and gold-plated frames for women's purses. Since I had learned soldering years before, it was easy to pick up the trade again and quickly fit in. The owner, Michel Gerst, was a dynamic man, able to recognize the hard workers among us. As soon as I met him I felt sure that he was the one who had built up the factory from scratch; his calloused, hardened hands were proof of it.

The section leader, Mr. Paul, supervised my work on a daily basis. Even though I was a mere cog in the grinding wheel of apprentices and workers, I applied myself diligently. On the up side, I took advantage of all my prior experience and current energy, earning a little extra money and working hard with the hope of moving up the ladder of responsibility; on the down side, I was making minimum wage and there seemed to be little opportunity for advancement. The work was demanding and I did the same thing over and over. To get ahead, I was going to have to learn as much as possible in the shortest amount of time.

Day in and day out, I'd stop working at midday and walk down boulevard Mennilmontand to the street market where I'd buy a baked apple and fresh eggs that I'd take back to the factory and cook there.

But thanks to my brother Isaac and other Jewish survivors in Paris, life wasn't always so boring. I even made friends with some of my co-workers, and from time to time they would invite me to their homes to eat on Sundays. Then one day a Jew came up to me and asked my name. He said he knew someone with the same last name. I asked him to describe the person. From what he told me, it sounded like he was talking about my brother Samuel. I asked him if he would do me the favor of setting up a meeting with him at the synagogue. The next day Isaac and I were there waiting. At the time we didn't know that Samuel, despite our older brothers' refusal to let him leave Sighet with us, had run away from home and had gone to Paris. It had been months since we had last seen him.

He finally showed up, dressed elegantly in a fine suit. We couldn't believe our eyes: this was the young boy we had left behind in Sighet. We hugged each other, and then he invited us to have some wine in a swanky bar nearby. Because of the way he was dressed, it was easy to see that he was earning much more money than we were. Not once did he mention his work; he simply told us he was going to school and lived in Sèvres. Later, he walked us back to our hotel, leaving us ever more curious about what kind of work he did. But he had refused to talk about it.

After that we would meet about three times a week. He was always putting on airs, insisting on paying the tabs, and one could tell that he didn't mind doing it. We decided to start checking around on our brother's source of income. We inquired at his school and they said he attended very infrequently; then a friend of ours told us that he was a gigolo. Since he was tall, muscular, and friendly, the women were always after him. He used them for his own benefit.

One day when we met with him we decided to confront Samuel straight out. I told him he needed to think about what he was doing. His face expressed not only maturity, but a certain jadedness — his youth certainly had been stolen from him. Without a doubt, he had become much wiser about the ways of the world. I began to wonder what had happened to him in the concentration camps to make him rebel against his strict moral upbringing. Basically, Samuel was the product of a series of circumstances that had degraded him. In a calm voice, he said, "I don't have to work very hard. I have all I need."

Deep down, I think he was laughing at our orthodox moral rigidity, but we still asked him to quit living off of his women, to finish his studies, and to begin to build a profession. He responded, "Look, we are nothing more than the dregs of society. I'm simply repaying society for what it did to me. You say I'm not honorable? What about those who chained me in slavery and treated me like a dog in the concentration camps? Are they honorable?"

Isaac and I begged him to remember his mother and sisters who were martyred at Birkenau. We asked him to think seriously about his immoral way of life. But Samuel kept defending himself with the argument that he had suffered physical and moral exile. Suddenly I became so indignant that I got up from the table and punched him as hard as I could. Despite his size, I managed to knock him out of his chair. I waited for him to retaliate, but he simply stood up smoothing his jaw and said, "Don't do that again or else."

Then he sat down and burst out crying. His martyred soul finally surfaced in a sea of tears. He looked like a small child, nose running and all. While he was sobbing, I asked him to forgive me. After a while he calmed down and said we were right. He promised that in honor of his sisters, parents, and brother Saul, he was going to turn over a new leaf, end his loose, licentious life. We found him a job in a jewelry shop. He learned the profession so well that when he immigrated to Canada, he set up his own jewelry store that sustains him to this day.

Life in Paris had changed all of us. Isaac worked at ironing clothes. As for me, I had begun to enjoy the carefree life of that exotic city. Paris is the tropics of culture and art: exuberant, attractive, sensuous, and overflowing with vitality. I decided to make the most of my position at work. Mr. Paul had already noticed my desire to get ahead and soon he took me under his wing, teaching me how to read and interpret technical drawings. I learned how to use the machines in the factory, and before long I understood the entire process. After six months, the factory owner put me in charge of production, quality control, and shipping. With this promotion he also raised my salary, but it didn't amount to much in terms of trying to save money and think about my future.

What I disliked the most about my job was having to work for someone else, not being independent, and feeling trapped within the four blackened walls of the factory. I had grown up in an environment of freedom, under the guidance of my parents, and I felt cheated to have to take orders from someone else.

What I liked to do was get together with Isaac, my friends Jacob Friedman and Farkas, who had just arrived, and other Jews who were living under similar conditions. We'd go dancing on Saturday afternoons, and on Sundays we'd walk around the city and visit museums and tourist attractions. Frankly, I liked Paris and quickly grew accustomed to our lifestyle and easy-going pastimes. If I wanted to go out and dress stylishly, I simply sacrificed a few meals. And when I didn't have enough money to go out, I'd take walks along the Seine and meditate on the possibilities that might materialize while I was living in that city. I had no savings. The future was uncertain. To start a business, I needed capital. If I quit my job, I would only end up doing something similar or possibly worse. And Paris was an expensive city. It was true I was earning enough money to survive, but there was no way I could start a family.

Is this what I wanted? A monotonous existence? But Paris was so dazzling. The Seine would come alive with the reflection of the city lights dancing across the water. But they weren't real, they were only a reflection. Trapped in a similar illusion, I thought my life couldn't become real until I somehow became independent, became my own person, and made a contribution to our wayward, dispossessed people. Paris was only a beautiful dream.

17

And Paris meant love and romance; in fact, that's where I began a love affair. Despite the distances and the obstacles, however, this one would become everlasting. After arriving in Paris in early 1947, I became accustomed to eating at a restaurant on rue Rosier, where many Jewish refugees would gather. They went there to pass the time while they waited for their visas that would allow them to immigrate to other countries. The restaurant served inexpensive home-style cooking, and while its disorderly and run-down appearance is not worth describing, the best thing about it was the companionship that the customers shared, all of whom had known misfortune like me.

It was understandable that no one wanted to talk about the past three or four years. Our conversations always came to an abrupt end whenever the years between 1942 and 1945 came up; it was as if those years had never existed or had been ripped off the calendar. Groups of young people would discuss the future while they shared a bottle of red table wine. Not only would we talk about our childhoods but with each successive glass we would humorously exaggerate our adventurous pasts to the delight of those listening.

That's the place where I met Frida. It was a cold, rainy, winter afternoon, and we were inside warming our bodies and souls as we talked about our dreams for the future. Then the door opened and there appeared three redheads that the fading late afternoon light seemed to turn to flames. The two women and the man looked so alike, it was obvious they were siblings. The striking red sheen of their hair immediately distracted me from what my friend Farkas was saying.

After staring at them for a while, I asked my brother if he knew who they were. Farkas intervened saying he could introduce them to me. He called them over to our table. When I stood up, my feet turned to lead. Frida, the older of the two girls, had a mischievous grin. She looked me over from head to toe. I was wearing a blue German officer's overcoat that had been through it all; it hung almost all the way to the ground and I looked so deplorable that I became embarrassed.

We all sat down at the table and I quickly forgot about my perturbed state. Conversation and wine restored my confidence. Frida was petite and her abundant red hair was nicely done up. Her clear, lively eyes told me she was a strikingly sensitive person. As much as I tried to take my eyes off her—I kept fiddling with my glass to make the wine swirl around inside—I just couldn't look away. You could tell she was educated and had a fine upbringing, all of which clashed noticeably with the habits of a factory worker who made fire extinguishers and metal frames for purses.

Thanks to that initial contact, though, I made friends with Frida and her brother and sister. But Frida was cool toward me and my gallantry. Although she wasn't unfriendly, Frida never let on that she was the least bit interested in me. Our friendship was sincere, but she didn't seem to want to develop a close relationship. Still, I began to fall in love with her. One day I walked her back to the hotel near place de la Republique where she lived with her family. Her parents were courteous and wanted to know all about my employment. Since they were also Romanian, mutual feelings and shared experiences made it easy for me to gain their confidence.

It wasn't long before we were dating frequently. We'd meet after work and I'd walk her home. On holidays, we'd go to Versailles, the Bois de Boulogne, or take a river cruise on the Marne or Seine. Despite the fact that we saw each other almost every day, that redhead didn't seem interested in getting serious. I had already declared my feelings to her, but she didn't seem interested in reciprocating.

One Sunday on the subway after an outing, I recognized another Kapo; this time it was Simon, who had been at Jaworzno. I was standing up. I made out his face over several shoulders of nearby passengers. I pushed through the crowd and tapped him on the shoulder. "Simon!"

The man turned around, became quite agitated, and lashed out, "You are mistaken!"

"You're the Kapo Simon. You were at Jaworzno," I told him.

Since his denials were starting to create some commotion in the subway car, I stopped insisting. As soon as the train pulled into the next station, the Kapo got off, scurried through the crowd, and disappeared. I was upset.

"Who was that?" Frida asked.

"A Kapo from the Jaworzno concentration camp," I replied, still hot under the collar. At that moment, as the subway car was pulling away, Frida took my arm and said, "Don't you see, Sanyi, we are hopelessly destined to feel hatred."

I explained to her that it simply wasn't true. I, for example, was head over heels in love with her and when I told her so, she answered back, "Is there a place for love in Europe?" And whereupon tears welled up in her eyes. That was when she told me she had purposely avoided getting serious with me because her family was waiting to get visas to Ecuador and, from there, to the United States. She explained that nothing permanent could come of our relationship if we had to leave each other as soon as her family received permission to travel to South America.

My heart was pounding hard. Frida was in love with me and knowing that made everything else unimportant in my life. I thought their pending trip was the least of our worries. I said, "You and I can stay in Paris. You don't have to go to South America."

We got off the subway and climbed the steps up to the street. Realizing that she, too, was in love, I suddenly saw Paris in all its extravagance. Night had fallen and I escorted Frida home. Back in my room I was unable to sleep. My joy was clouded by my doubt that Frida's parents would let her remain behind in Paris.

On Monday morning, it was foggy and dismal outside. Not bothering to light the alcohol stove that took forever to heat up a cup of coffee, I left my room and started off to work. Things had gotten better because I had been promoted to something like a section boss. Even though I was still pretty bad off salary-wise, life had become slightly more tolerable. I never seemed to have enough money to go to nightclubs or dancing on holidays, but Frida and I were happy just to spend our time walking everywhere, even until we would almost collapse from fatigue. Then we would stop at some coffee shop along the way and discuss our future. Our future? Whenever I thought about it, the future seemed much less certain than the past.

My heart and soul became consumed by Frida. I knew for sure there was nothing fleeting about my love for her. I had thought long and hard about it: we got along well together—sure, we argued sometimes—but the fondness we felt for each other became a lighthouse in a storm. Love had grown out of a winter relationship that had suddenly blossomed into a spring-like, mutual affection with deep, long-lasting roots.

One Sunday we took off on one of our typical walks. I had already decided to ask her to marry me. Then a spring downpour forced us to find refuge in a café. The park next door became shrouded in a delicate, misty drizzle. At that moment I took her hand and asked her to marry me. I can't remember if she said yes right off the bat, but she immediately began to talk about the future, describing our plans with the clarity of a movie projected onto a screen. Those images created the most beautiful movie that I had ever seen. The two of us became the protagonists of our own film and we played our parts however we pleased. When it stopped raining, it seemed as though the lights of the theater suddenly came on without either one of us having seen the words "The End."

We walked out onto the street and took the subway back home. We made our way out of the Metro, pulled along by the crowd desperate to escape the foul underground air. From there we walked hand in hand along boulevard Saint Denis. We weren't in a hurry like everyone else around us. I was extremely happy to be next to the girl to whom I was engaged. Ecstatic knowing that Frida was mine, I absorbed everything I saw around me: fancily dressed women in flared skirts and tiny hats swayed their hips gracefully down the street. In a small square nearby, we saw the Arch of the Glorious Past and, beyond it, a beautiful boulevard stretched out into the distance. We walked down it holding hands. Surrounding the square were numerous small cafés with their bright canvas umbrellas sporting brand names. Many people were sitting at the tables, talking with friends and drinking coffee while cigarettes dangled out of the corners of their mouths. And there was the red and blue kiosk at the corner. We admired the buildings along the boulevard. Seemingly all crunched together, each one was exactly three stories high and had small wooden-framed windows that showed years of exposure to the weather. The walls had turned black from age, but the rays of the afternoon sun that day produced a rich variety of shades of gray on the buildings. The verdigris of the copper rooftops was beautiful in that light.

It wasn't long before the hot Parisian summer was upon us. I would meet Frida at her work and we would continue to make plans about our future together. It was near the end of July when one day after work I found Frida sad and distressed. Her family had just received authorization to immigrate to Ecuador. The bluntness of her explanation corresponded to the sharp pain I felt upon hearing the news. It meant that we were going to be separated from each other.

Immediately, however, I was struck by an idea. "You're not going to Ecuador. We'll get married before your family leaves. And when my visa comes through, we'll catch up with them there."

My idea sounded wonderful. Of course, I hadn't informed Frida's parents of this. And what if they were opposed? What if they stopped the marriage? But then I told myself they shouldn't be opposed . . . they'll be happy that we're getting married . . . they already know me . . . they know I'm Romanian . . . yes, they'll abide by our decision. Those were the thoughts we shared together as we walked to Frida's house, trying to raise each other's spirits, now that doubt and uncertainty had weakened our hopes.

Frida's parents were kind and considerate, and they had always been nice to me. They served me a cup of coffee. At first our conversation seemed incapable of getting past trivialities but finally I came to the point. I mentioned how happy I was about the news of the Ecuadoran visas. Then the marriage proposal hit them like a lightning bolt. Their rejection was equally swift.

"Frida is still a minor and she doesn't have our permission to marry you," said her father. Her mother chimed in, "We came to this country as a family and that's the way we are going to leave it."

Our dreams and plans collapsed like a sandcastle. I wasn't about to give up — somehow I had to fight for my love. But when her father brought up the real problem, I had no response. "In addition, we don't even know you or your family."

Sensing their suspicion of my parents, who were totally unknown to them and forever lost to me, I stood up and left, slamming the door behind me. With tears streaming down her face, Frida raced down the stairs and caught up with me at the front door of the building. She embraced me with deep tenderness and affection. I think I was rather brusk with her, not so much because our plans had been thwarted but because her parents had insinuated that my parents were some low-class undesirables, when in fact their only fault had been to disappear in the midst of the Nazi nightmare.

As I walked out the door, my mind dredged up all those bitter memories of the Holocaust. It seemed that those years of horror were going to pursue me wherever I went, chasing me down like wild dogs gone berserk in search of their prey. What could I tell them about my family beyond their extermination at the end of a horrendous nightmare? Would those Romanians who had never experienced it ever be able to understand even part of what had happened?

I walked back to my hotel. The humid summer air was oppressive. But it was really my heart that was heavy from the weight of the realization that life had suddenly become meaningless again. I had no answers to my questions. Reality often defies reasoning.

I continued going out with Frida, and my love for her only increased. Yet the rest of the world seemed an illusion now, a dead-end street, a series of closed doors. I didn't have the keys to open them or any way to avoid the imposing walls of defeat that had sprung up around me.

On the day they departed, I went to the train station to say farewell. Standing at a distance from her parents, I said goodbye to Frida. Before arriving at the station, I had thought about what I was going to say to her at that final embrace, but nothing came out the way it was supposed to. As Frida described the route they would take to get to Ecuador, I just looked at her stupidly, realizing that my only reason for living in Paris was slipping away forever. I was unable to express my heartache with words. I simply couldn't get them out; all I managed to do was string together a chaotic, disconcerting good-bye of monosyllables, gestures trying to bolster our love, and pleading expressions of a soul uprooted.

I remained on the station platform until the train disappeared in the distance. The smoke of the locomotive left me feeling as empty and transitory as that cloud of soot that had smudged the skyline.

Getting involved in my work once again and returning to my humdrum life with all its insignificant worries numbed my pain a little. One evening, in the midst of the loneliness of my dull existence and feeling trapped by those peeling walls, I put pen to paper and wrote a letter to Frida. All the words I was unable to conjure up at the train station flowed easily and precisely onto the paper. The letter was long, brimming with affection for her, and permeated with dreams. They say that in time hopes wilt and die, but feeling the intangible presence of Frida near me—the image of her was still so fresh in my mind—my dreams had become my new reality.

Bleak desolation returned to inhabit my life once again. At first I would simply shut myself off in my room at my cheap hotel, but those four shabby, dirty walls dejected me to the point that I thought I was going crazy. I had begun to realize that times of adversity were tempering experiences and that, in order to overcome the obstacles in my path, I would have to rise above my frustration and bitterness.

Neither life nor time can be held back. I finally abandoned my cell and took to the streets. As I passed places that Frida and I had visited together, I would ask myself what she might be doing at that moment and suddenly discovered myself shrouded in that unhealthy nostalgia so typical of the lonely.

Somehow I began to value my solitary outings because they permitted me to observe life in all its misery and sorrow. And all around there were the *clochards*, those picturesque Parisian vagabonds who, seemingly happy and carefree, would sleep under the bridges that crossed the Seine. Unshaven, living in the midst of filth and garbage, they would sleep off their misery in a drunken stupor. From time to time, they would smile spontaneously at people passing by and ask for some change in order to buy another bottle of wine. As I watched them, I said to myself, "No one questions their family background. No one demands to know who their parents are."

To me, their presence was more genuine than any of the fancy lights and elegant stores in all of Paris. Their apathy touched everything, even themselves, and it flew in the face of what one normally thinks education and modern society are all about. Sprawled out on top of whatever you might call their possessions, lacking everything, needing nothing, and totally unconcerned, they lived only for the present. Perhaps it was because of my state of dejection at the time, but I found solace in them.

I wanted to live somewhere peaceful and quiet, a place where wars and genocide are unknown. I must leave Europe, I thought.

Time passed ever so slowly for me in Paris. It was like the dirty, stagnant waters of the Seine; from the Pont Neuf bridge I would contemplate the course of those tame waters. Now that no one would be waiting for me back at my hotel, I had all the time in the world to think. I guess that's what they call self-analysis. I began to examine my entire life, starting with the remote past and coming up to the present moment, which — now — promised practically nothing for the future. My life at the time was no different from that of any other French factory worker, except that I wasn't French and I had no family. I would wash my face every morning in a rusty metal washbowl. I would run to catch the subway in order not to arrive late to work. I couldn't even make a cup of coffee because the alcohol burner would never heat up fast enough. Besides, there was never enough alcohol — fuel was being rationed with coupons. At noon I would usually eat a piece of sausage with some bread, along with half a bottle of wine. On my way back from work, I would doze off on the Metro after a long day of strenuous work, only to be met by a single bed and the four dingy walls of that depressing hotel room.

After having been raised in the freedom of the open countryside, having grown accustomed to wide-open spaces with unobstructed horizons, knowing that the borders of my world were the high peaks of the Carpathians, my current life didn't look very promising.

I said to myself, "You're earning enough money to survive, but you don't have any freedom. If you're going to spend your life enslaved to someone else, you're wasting it. You must emigrate." But how was I going to be able to leave Paris with no money, no passport, and no visa? Once again, I had to start all over again, trapped by my unavoidable luck. Like so many times in the past, once again I was being forced to start anew.

Was I going to let myself become hemmed in by circumstances that seemed beyond my control or was I going to rise above them and take control of my destiny? When someone has experienced a life of continual vicissitudes, it's easy to come to the conclusion that events around us control our lives, that we are being jerked around by some ungovernable force as if we were puppets on a string. To dispel the miasma of disillusionment and frustration, one needs more than desire; one needs to make decisions, to dare to seek adventure. After careful thought and with some courage, maybe one can determine which of his or her possessions to discard, and then, with sufficient freedom, formulate a feasible plan of action.

I had realized that I was not happy in Paris. I needed to be with Frida and the only way to satisfy that need was to leave Europe. That was easy to say, but it was a matter of burning my bridges to the past—forever. So, I told myself, "I'll leave whatever I have and start life all over again. I possess nothing and, wherever I go, I'll just start from scratch, without the fear of anti-Semitic persecution. It's preferable to live without fear than continue submerged in the suffocating past." That's how I had summed it up. Now it was up to me to put theory into practice.

I was ready for a breath of fresh air somewhere else. The winds of Europe were still strewing the human ashes of Birkenau everywhere. The anti-Semitic Nazi spirit had not been stamped out. America! The word rang in my ears as if it were the one place that had not been tainted by antihumanitarian ideologies. America!

18

In the summer of 1947 there was a heat wave in Paris. Every day the newspapers would publish articles about people who had died from heatstroke. The month of August was especially bad. Everyone in Paris was gasping for air, and people would strip down to almost nothing and take walks along the river banks in an effort to escape the sultry weather. The entire city, worn out from the heat, couldn't escape it. I certainly didn't. During the weekdays in the factory, languor was suffocating us, and there was no escaping it inside the four walls of my hotel room either.

Someone had come up with a brilliant idea. It was a holiday and my brother Isaac, my cousin Marc, his sister Sara, and I decided to go swimming in the Seine. The river wasn't far from my place. With such heat, a swim in the river sounded heavenly. About noon we scurried down the cement steps where passenger boats would dock and jumped in the water. Although the water was lukewarm it felt glorious. I imagined myself swimming in the Tisa. But we immediately realized that the river, while it looked clean on the surface, was dragging along with it all the filth of Paris. We had hardly swum a few strokes when we found ourselves surrounded by strange objects, from toilets, that were floating along with the current. Some bystanders watching at the railing overlooking the river began to laugh at us. Feeling quite embarrassed and trying to ignore the putrid smell of the water, we swam as hard as we could to the other side of the river. Brandishing his billy club, a policeman was waiting to give us a fine. Our bodies were so filthy and greasy that he couldn't contain his nausea. With a smirk on his face he told us that it was the first time he had seen anyone swim in the Seine. He must have thought we were crazy or, suspecting we were foreigners, imagined we didn't know that the Seine is the city's sewer. He ended up not fining us, but told us to go clean off the filth that stuck like glue to our bodies.

My hotel had just one shower located at the end of the hall. It was occupied when I arrived, so I had to wait until it became free. By that time, a smelly, dry crust of sludge had formed all over my skin. As I was soaping down, I became nauseated with disgust and almost threw up. I think that was probably the longest shower I ever took in my whole life.

Time was crawling by ever so monotonously and my separation from Frida tormented me constantly. I became a kind of hermit. I hardly went to the restaurant on rue Rosier anymore, or rue Temple, where Frida and I used to meet after work. I even stopped going to bars and cafés. One afternoon when I was quite depressed I met with Isaac and Farkas who worked together on boulevard Mennilmontand. We decided to try a restaurant that served North African food. It was nothing more than a down-and-out hole in the wall; the tables and chairs were made of roughly hewn wood and the walls that at one time had been whitewashed had turned gray like an old kitchen apron. The ceiling was low and the cigarette smoke that had discolored the lamps drifted downward encircling fellow diners; amid all the smoke, one would have thought the patrons were angels floating in the clouds. They were dark skinned, talked in loud voices, and the French called them *pieds noirs*, or "black feet."

We spotted a table. We were curious about the place, with its smell of grease and fried food, because we had heard that Algerian food was really good. You could tell immediately that it wasn't a place where we should have gone, but our hunger won over our fear of running into a group of Arabs. We lacked a chair at our table, so Farkas grabbed a chair from a nearby empty table. As soon as he sat down a young Arab came over and aggressively demanded the chair back. Since he was speaking in Arabic, none of us understood what he was saying, but his body language told us very quickly that he wasn't giving us a big welcome. Farkas, who hardly knew any French and certainly didn't know any Arabic, uttered a phrase that he had learned at the factory where he worked, "Ferme ta gueule."

Farkas had told the Arab to shut his face. The Arab suddenly pushed Farkas. The rest of us got to our feet, ready to defend our friend. Within seconds we found ourselves surrounded by as many Arabs as there were patrons in the restaurant. There was a real hubbub. Tables were overturned, chairs were flying back and forth, and punches were thrown at anything that moved. The funniest part about the whole thing was that the women got involved as well. Fearing nothing, they did their share of kicking and biting us. We were the underdogs and quite outnumbered; the Arabs literally swarmed around us and not even King David was going to get us out of this one. Amid the ruckus, and while we were receiving and landing blows left and right, a thought struck me like a bolt of lightning. If the police showed up, they would throw us out of the country. That revelation was enough to convince me to step aside and start yelling at the top of my lungs for us to get out of there because the police were coming. The word "police" worked like magic: within seconds everyone made a dash for the door.

I was one of the first out. As soon as I reached the street, I heard the police siren. Isaac and Farkas must have understood my warning because, pushing and stumbling all over each other trying to get out, they quickly reached the street too. At that very moment the paddy wagon pulled up at the curb, preventing anyone else who was inside from getting out. As the police rounded up the Arabs and pushed them into the vehicle, we started walking down the street, looking like beggars. We were all cut up and bruised, and our clothes were torn to shreds; our pants, hanging on us in pieces, waved in the breeze like flags. Despite the battering we took and all the hullabaloo, we were feeling neither pain nor any sensation akin to defeat.

The fall season was finally upon us. The routine of those long days of helplessness even surpassed the sadness of the hapless leaves falling from the trees. Whenever I daydreamed, I would think about Frida. Every time I would return to my lodging, I would check my mailbox, only to discover that it was empty. But one afternoon I discovered a letter there. I grabbed it and ran up the stairs to my room. It was postmarked Curaçao. I threw myself down on my bed and began to read. I was so anxious to know how she was that I read the letter in seconds. Everything was still all right. All I wanted was some indication that Frida still loved me. Her letter reaffirmed it and I relaxed. I read the letter over and over until I finally fell asleep, still fully dressed.

Like the gusty winds of the fall, the days began to pass more quickly. Another letter from Rio de Janeiro opened up new possibilities for me. I got a map and began to study it. I tried to imagine the uncharted routes her ship must have taken. I couldn't understand why the ship had gone so far south when Ecuador was just on the other side of the continent, in the north-western part of South America. My love for Frida never waned; I continued to be hopeful. I began to realize that if I really wanted to see her, I had done nothing to make it happen. It was as if the winter had frozen me in my tracks. A passport was the necessary ingredient and I didn't have one.

I decided that in order to catch up to her, the first step was to get a passport and then request a visa to anywhere in the Americas. I began going to almost every embassy around and requesting hearings with the consular agents. In March 1948, however, I received a visit from an Israeli emissary. How distant were my memories of the UNRRA camp and those Zionist dreams! The man was young and husky and we talked in my hotel room. He got to the point immediately: I was needed to help fight for the independence of Israel. I was surprised that he had been able to find me because I hadn't participated in any Zionist activities for almost two years. I told him I wanted to think about it. He said I had two days to think about it, and if I decided to go we'd have to leave immediately.

After he left, I went to see Farkas about it. We went to have coffee somewhere. The emissary had already talked to him and, as it turned out, my friend had decided to join the Israeli Liberation Army. He understood my objections: the violence I had

experienced since 1940 had taught me to avoid its pernicious-
ness at all costs; to me, nothing could be gained from wars.
Besides, I was so in love with Frida that my only yearning at
that point was to join her. Our love remained invincible. Our
continual exchange of letters, in spite of the distance and delays
in the mails, only reaffirmed my decision to marry her.

Farkas respected my point of view and didn't try to persuade
me to go with him. Suddenly the days really seemed to fly by.
At work I could only think about whether I had made the right
decision. And then I would excoriate myself for being a traitor
to my fellow Jews and their cause. But the imprint of the past
continued to strengthen my decision to leave Europe. I had already worked for the cause; now it was time for me to fight for
my own interests. The first step was to leave Europe.

When I met with the Israeli emissary again, I told him I had
decided not to accompany him. The idea of returning to "our
lands" didn't convince me. I once had a country that I thought
was mine, but it banished me. I always believed that one's country meant the place that looks upon everyone with generosity,
without discrimination, and provides equal opportunity for all.
Where was that place? Without roots, it's difficult for the spirit
of patriotism to blossom in one's heart again.

I said good-bye to my irreproachable friend Baruch Farkas.
He was resolute and steadfast, an extraordinary warrior, and a
loyal friend. Once again, I found myself alone, but Farkas's departure inspired me to continue visiting the consulates in search
of a visa. By then I had acquired a passport and I was seeking
to obtain an authentic visa so I wouldn't have problems in the
future.

My brother Isaac and his friend Jacob Friedman bought
fraudulent visas and left Paris bound for Venezuela. At the port
of La Guaira they were detained by immigration officials and
thrown into jail in Caracas. After a long investigation, they were
set free, found work, and wrote me about the advantages of
working in Venezuela. My brother Samuel had left for Canada,

having been accepted in a youth immigration program. Although he was just over the age limit of eighteen, I had managed to change his birth date in his records and, somehow, got him in. He left with our cousin Sara.

Meanwhile, my solitary existence in the midst of that anonymous, cosmopolitan metropolis continued only to get worse; for the first time I began to feel vulnerable and afraid. I didn't have any family left in Paris and all my friends had drifted away for one reason or another. The Ecuadoran visa still hadn't been approved.

But my life wasn't all that bad. The factory owner, Mr. Gerst, thought well of me and he proposed that I oversee a project to make refrigerators for export to the Soviet Union. I think he had hopes that I would become interested in his daughter and eventually take over the new business. I rejected his offer because I had promised my love to Frida; besides, I was hoping to leave Europe at the first opportunity. I felt that Europe was a threat to me. Every nook and cranny of Paris seemed to contain traces of my past: widespread fear, expressionless faces, nightmares. It was a general malaise that continued to reinforce my desire to escape. Even if my plans with Frida didn't materialize, I would definitely leave Europe.

One afternoon the hotel owner Madame Delmas was waiting for me at the bottom of the stairs with a letter in her hand. In a teasing voice, she said, "Here it is. The letter you've been waiting for. It's from that redhead."

The letter was postmarked Quito. Frida's letter described her new life in America and how courteous the people were; she also said I should come to South America as soon as possible. I read the letter over and over again. I knew that our love, despite the distance, had not diminished. But the part that made me the happiest was the news that my documents enabling me to emigrate were already in the Foreign Ministry, and soon I would be issued a visa.

With that news, my spirits soared like a bird. I started going
to work feeling happy and I'd stop by the Ecuadoran embassy
on a regular basis to ask about my visa. According to Frida,
it was supposed to arrive at any moment. But new trials and
tribulations would leave me demoralized.

One night in mid-September 1948 I had to be rushed to the
hospital. A pain in my lower abdomen suddenly became unbearable, and I asked the hotel owner for help. She took my
temperature and it was extremely high. I was burning with fever
and blacking out from the pain. The police didn't want to transport me, saying the matter was the responsibility of the hospital.
Madame Delmas threatened them by saying if anything happened to me, they would be to blame. They took me, finally,
and that same evening I was operated on for appendicitis and
peritonitis.

When I opened my eyes in the hospital, the first person I
saw sitting next to my bed was the kind hotel owner, Madame
Delmas. But I couldn't remember anything that had happened.
Except for the "Death March" in Germany, never had I felt so
weak. I could see and feel that march in my mind: everything
that happened, the extreme fatigue, the sordidness of it all. Now
I was feeling the same way. Nearly unconscious and so distant
from what we call life, I thought I was nothing more than a
cadaver. I recuperated in the hospital for the next ten days, during which time I did nothing but plan my trip, now possibly
annulled for not having checked more often with the embassy.

The day I was discharged from the hospital it was cloudy outside, but there was a new surprise waiting for me at the hotel.
Madame Delmas handed me a letter from the Ecuadoran embassy. It instructed me to appear at the embassy with my passport. I was astonished: that little piece of paper was permitting
me to leave France and to be reunited with Frida! I jumped
up and down out of happiness and I became so ecstatic that I
hugged Madame Delmas and lifted her up off the ground, completely forgetting the doctor's warning not to exert myself for

fear of damaging my wound. I felt a shooting pain and suddenly came to my senses.

Bedecked in my best but still shabby clothes, I headed for the consulate. My visa was in order and they stamped my passport appropriately. I returned to my hotel and immediately wrote a letter to Frida, telling her that soon I would be arriving in Quito.

I boarded the ship *Yagielo* in Cannes. All sorts of people were on board, from bullfighters who were going to the fair in Quito to timid emigrants like me, who hid from the looks of strangers, hoping to go unnoticed.

The farther the ship sailed from European soil, I asked myself, What was waiting for me in those unknown and remote places? Would I be able to start over? The confusion and chaos of conflicting emotions choked my thinking. I wanted, on the one hand, to put Europe and the noxious vestiges of the Holocaust behind me, but, on the other hand, I blamed myself for wanting to abandon my ancestors' homelands. Europe was trying to ensnare me, but I wouldn't let myself be trapped by my memories.

The first stop was Algiers. We were allowed to disembark and take a look around. I hadn't yet made any friends on the ship, so I went alone into the city. One had to climb a steep incline to reach the center of Algiers. A totally new world appeared before my eyes. The entire population was Arab, with dark skin and kinky hair. I walked up some narrow, very crowded streets. I tried several times to speak French but no one seemed to understand me, even though it was a French colony. Everywhere, the expression on their faces communicated displeasure and abhorrence. I walked so much that my feet became swollen from the heat. Without realizing it, I had entered into the old part of the city, where all you could see were small square houses painted white, with narrow alleyways off the streets. The people looked at me with distrust.

A little old man who was repairing shoes on the sidewalk spoke to me in Hebrew. He was actually speaking Hebrew to me! I answered back that I understood him but that it was hard for me to communicate with him because for years now I hadn't been able to use what I had learned in the *cheder*. And he answered back, "You are one of our people, but here you are in great danger. You should not risk your life by staying. Be careful, they might lynch you."

Without even thanking him for his advice, I took off running all the way back to the docks. After arriving safely, I couldn't believe how foolish I had been to expose myself to such danger without knowing it. To top it off, my recent surgery was causing me a great deal of pain.

After a few days of sailing, we hit the open seas of the Atlantic Ocean. Clutching the railing, I contemplated the blue immensity of the ocean. Dolphins swam alongside the ship and my past began to surface in my memory. I imagined myself on the banks of the Tisa, remembering the pranks I pulled when I was a youngster. Back in Sighet, I used to see small fish in the river, like those accompanying the dolphins. I remembered the valleys and hills that reached all the way up the Carpathians. And I remembered what I least wanted to see: the violence waged against us and, off in the distance, the bodies of my family floating up in smoke.

Someone put his hand on my shoulder. I was startled out of my trance. When I turned around and looked up, I was confronted by a tall, stocky man. His attire made him look distinguished. A reddish beard sprinkled with gray surrounded a face of strong character. He looked like he was somewhere between fifty and fifty-five years old. The man greeted me in a friendly way and asked me in which language we could talk. I told him that since we had already started in French we could continue in that language.

He was staying on the upper deck, in first class. The man inundated me with questions. He had seen the tattoo on my arm and he thought it would be interesting to talk about the Holocaust. But he noticed that I was nervously trying to avoid the topic: I explained that I was leaving Europe in order to bury the past and I didn't want to dig it up in order to chat with a stranger. I told him that I was on my way to Ecuador to start a new life; Europe hadn't worked out for me at all.

Once we had dropped the topic of the concentration camps, he continued to talk garrulously about his trip to Cuba, where he would take a rest after having worked intensely as a war correspondent in Paris. Years later, when I happened to open up a copy of *Stern* magazine, there was the same man I had met on the ship: his name was Ernest Hemingway. As fate would have it, we had traveled on the same ship together. He was on his way back to his ranch Vigía. Back then I had no idea who he was. After our chance meeting, I never saw him again on the ship. I can only suppose that when he saw the tattoo on my arm he wanted to get information from me, but he didn't get it.

Our second stop was the Madeira Islands. Some native islanders boarded the ship on their way to Venezuela to work for construction companies. By then I had come to realize that the food they served the second-class passengers was not very abundant. Since I was still convalescing from my operation, my body was demanding more nutrition than I was getting from the three daily meals.

I was lucky to have struck up a friendship with one of the sailors who, it turned out, was Romanian. He showed me around the ship, including the engine room, and explained navigation procedures and communications. Before long I was familiar with the ship's operations and the responsibilities of most of the sailors. I told my friend about how I was always so hungry. When he was showing me the kitchen and the storerooms, he introduced me to several people, mainly the cooks, with whom I became friends. Everyday I would drop by the kitchen and they would give me a little extra food. As a result, the rest of the trip turned out to be a perfect way to recuperate my health. The time I spent on the ship turned out to be a marvelous vacation.

Isaac was waiting for me at the dock. He begged me to stay in Venezuela with him because the country was ripe for development and there was work everywhere. But Frida was waiting for me in Quito. When we disembarked in Venezuela I immediately felt the clean air of this new land called America. The sun shone more fiercely. The heat and humidity caressed my body. There were trees I had never seen before: thick-topped palms, banana groves, trees with purple flowers, bougainvilleas. Indeed, this was a new world, like the way it was when it was first created.

From Venezuela the ship made its way to Panama. As soon as the ship reached the dock, everyone was quarantined. We were like cattle that had to be vaccinated. A doctor came aboard to administer blood tests. After two weeks in a barracks, Panagra Airlines flew me to Quito.

At eleven o'clock in the morning on 25 October 1948, I arrived in Quito, the capital city of Ecuador. I walked out of customs with nothing more than the shirt on my back. My suitcase had been lost in Panama. No one was waiting for me at the airport, and it was cold and desolate. Compared to the climate that I had experienced in Venezuela and Panama, the weather in Quito was more like Romania. I had thought that since I was traveling to a tropical climate it would always be as hot as the devil, so I wasn't dressed appropriately. I didn't know that Quito was about nine thousand feet above sea level, in the middle of the Andes Mountains.

I walked toward one of the main thoroughfares near the airport to catch a bus that would take me downtown. As I walked along, two people appeared in front of me. I recognized them immediately: it was Frida and her brother. I ran toward them and flew into Frida's arms. "Well, you finally made it," she said. I still remember that moment: my heart was overcome with emotion and I broke into tears. Yes, I was finally in Quito.

19

Just before descending into Quito, the plane had throttled back and seemed to glide over the city. We had to skirt around gargantuan mountains that seemingly had risen out of the ground only yesterday and were now covered with intensely green vegetation. We started our landing by circling the city. I could even see the Spanish roof tiles on the houses and, looking down from above, the separations between the houses looked like trenches. I thought that the city must have been under siege, startled to think that I had just left Europe looking for peace and here I was about to land in a city at war. But I calmed down once I was on the bus with Frida and her brother and discovered that those divisions were simply adobe walls between the lots.

Reunited with Frida, I was able to forget some of my problems, among them my lost suitcase. When we got to her parents' apartment, I had expected to get the cold shoulder but it didn't turn out that way at all. Her family was hospitable and courteous. I imagined that by then they had given some serious thought to our relationship. Such a long trip and having come from so far away was proof enough that our love for each other had grown much more than they had imagined since the first time I had asked for their daughter's hand in marriage.

That same day I found a cheap place to live on the corner of Tarqui and 12 de Octubre streets. I knew practically no Spanish; what I did know I had learned from the bullfighters who crossed the Atlantic with me on the *Yagielo*. I could sing a few lines of "Se va el caimán, se va el caimán, se va para Barranquilla," but despite those few words which wouldn't even get me a job singing in a bar, I hardly understood anything.

From the very beginning, I was taken by the accent of the people of Quito: they seemed to whistle as they talked, as if they were mumbling some prayer between their teeth. And people would always say hello and shake hands. Humble people would tip their hats to me on the street and courteously murmur "patruncito" — master — upon which I would nod and smile because I had no idea what they were saying to me. The lack of communication was going to be a serious problem.

But the most serious problem was my dire economic situation. My suitcase had been lost in Panama and, without exaggerating, I had little more than the shirt on my back. I had four dollars and two cartons of American cigarettes on me. The Romanian sailor had given me the cigarettes. By selling them I could pay my first month's rent, but I still had to eat and buy some clothes, razor blades, soap, and shoes. Basically, I could make it for two months, so I had to find work immediately. Not knowing the language was a big disadvantage. By communicating with gestures and practically wearing out my only pair of shoes, I finally landed my first job in Ecuador. I began as a welder for the Ecuadoran Iron and Steel Company; I also taught soldering and chroming classes to young apprentices. While learning the language, all I could do was utter monosyllables and make mistakes. After a month on the job I received a small raise.

The Ecuadorans were very friendly and hospitable. Practically no one knew about what had happened in Europe, so no one asked me about my past. Since I was obsessed with trying to forget about what I had left behind, I turned myself entirely over to my work. I had decided to spend two extra hours a day at work, meaning that along with the raise I had received, my weekly salary was going up.

In order to learn a new language, I had to start speaking it; I began to talk as much as I could with those fine people. Since I would mix French and Romanian with Spanish, my co-workers would laugh and enjoyed listening to me talk. After four months I could speak with some fluency, but I still had a foreign accent. By then I was able to understand what the phrase "se va el caimán" meant.

It wasn't long before the Goldstein brothers, German immigrants who owned a soap factory, hired me as a salesman. I figured that by leaving the steel company and doing sales work,

I could earn more through commissions and eventually save enough to start my own business. The soap factory was nothing more than two halves of a metal barrel with handles welded to the sides that hung from a tripod and under which a wood fire would heat the basic ingredients inside—coconut oil and caustic soda.

Within two weeks the number of orders I had secured from neighborhood stores had far outstripped the factory's ability to meet them. That same week, I demanded that the Goldstein brothers put their books in order and pay me the commissions that had come due. They gave me a pittance of what they owed me, rebuked me, and then fired me.

Stimulated by the apparent success of their soap factory, I decided to start one of my own. So, I hired a guy who was working for the Goldsteins, but I offered him a better salary and a share in the sales. Of course, he came to work for me immediately. I rented a space and called my business venture the "Universal Soap Company."

I bought a barrel and cut it in half. One half was for preparing the first-class soap and the second barrel was for the speckled second-grade soap, to which we would add the dregs of the first-grade soap. I constructed a collapsible box that I lined with galvanized zinc to prevent corrosion from the caustic soda. That box was used to prepare the soap mixture. Then I built a tool to cut the soap into bars and also molds to give them an attractive shape. I copied the image of a small fish from a glass ashtray that would be molded into one side of the bar and on the other side would appear the name of my company. I made the molds out of scrap aluminum. I poured the cast metal into clay molds I made with my own hands. They came out looking perfect.

Once everything was ready to go, my employee and I began to mass-produce bars of soap. We would let the soap mixture cool in the collapsible box where the paste would begin to solidify. Then we would cut the soap into pieces, press them into the individual molds and out would come the bars of soap that looked to me like bars of gold. We would let them harden in the sun.

The next morning I was out on the streets of Quito plying the wares I had made with my own hands. Very few store owners would pay me cash on the barrelhead; just about all of them offered only a small advance up front and then agreed to a long-term payment if they were to accept the merchandise. Within the month I went broke because I had no working capital to buy the raw materials. Once again I was back on the street without a job or a cent to my name. I managed to earn a little here and there doing part-time soldering jobs for different welding shops.

Nevertheless, Frida's parents finally agreed to set a date for our marriage. I saved every cent I could in order to have enough money to rent a house and purchase furniture and utensils. Frida had been working as a seamstress. When we would take walks through the main park, La Alameda, near the center of town, we never discussed Europe; it was as if it had never existed.

Finally, the big day had arrived: 23 January 1949. The wedding took place in a restaurant and about eighty people attended. Except for Frida's family, I didn't know anyone there. Someone had loaned me a suit and a pair of shoes, the latter of which didn't fit me at all. I think other than the immense happiness I felt when Frida became my wife, the most imposing impression I have of my wedding was the intense pain of sore feet that made me remember the "Death March."

Our honeymoon lasted one day, less time than it took for the aches and pain in my feet to go away. I escorted my wife to Tarqui and 12 de Octubre streets as if to the most luxurious hotel in the world. The next morning I was already at my new job. As it turns out, I had met a veterinarian at the wedding, and after talking with him for a while we became friends. When I told him I was unemployed, he said I could work for him on his farm in Conocoto. And so it was that on the second day after getting married I became a farmer. I could have earned good money but it only lasted six weeks, and once again I found myself without work. Frida was making only little money as a seamstress. I felt guilty that I was unable to support her and even more ashamed that I had to hit the streets again in search of part-time work as a welder. I was best at utilizing the mechanics I had learned in Sighet and later in Paris; but industry was scarce and even a skilled worker's chances were almost nil.

After four months of marriage, I found a stable job as a tractor driver and administrator of a hacienda way up on a mountain called Pasochoa. The salary was great and we got all the milk we wanted. Working in the countryside fortified my spirits. The beauty of the landscape was breath-taking. The snow-capped mountain peaks reminded me of my homeland near the Carpathians.

My job consisted of overseeing the hacienda staff, including a foreman and twenty-two Indian peons and their families who worked on the land in exchange for small parcels of land. Basically, they worked for nothing and they were required to do menial tasks for the foreman, Segundo, who acted as the head of their families. Work was assigned to every family member regardless of their age or sex.

Up there on those high, barren plateaus, where the wind would sweep fiercely down the rocky gorges and craggy terrain, the spectacular vistas seemed to be in harmony with nature—except for the poverty-stricken condition of the unfortunate Indians. Their faces, like scorched adobe cracked by the harsh sun, their unabated hunger, their innumerable diseases and their servility to the boss—all filled me with the same anxiety that I felt in the concentration camps. These were human beings living out their death. The twenty-two families were scattered about the bleak, cold wilderness where only a little straw would grow. They lived in mud huts covered with straw roofs and no ventilation. They would enter through a minuscule doorway, seeking warmth; there, they lived in squalor among lice and pestilence. Their wretchedness was only comparable to those who had been dispossessed of everything, namely, the inhabitants of the Nazi concentration camps. Like those prisoners, no peons rebelled, no one would dare to look a white person in the eye. They were always staring at the ground and seemed resigned to endure any kind of insult and to carry out the orders of the heartless foreman.

Segundo, a fierce mestizo, was the absolute authority among the Indian peons on the hacienda. He assigned the work not only the way he saw fit but also according to the relationships he had established with each one of them. The treatment they received depended upon the sympathy or disdain he held for them, which, in turn, depended on the gifts and contributions they would make to him. The gifts ranged from chickens, eggs, and guinea pigs, to a daughter of one of the peons.

The children of the peons were required to work as servants in the house of the hacienda owner. Just as I had been unable to fathom how some of the most advanced civilizations in Europe could inflict cruelty on my people, I simply couldn't believe that such deplorable conditions—anonymity, poverty, and slavery—could still exist in contemporary times.

The local medicine man—Juancho Quispe—was the only person who demonstrated any concern for the Indians' well-being. He would prescribe liquor and herbs, taken from the barren plateaus, to the sick and agonizing people. He'd grind up the ingredients to make tonics or rub them on their ailing bodies.

That world was really disheartening, even though one tends to become indifferent, to look the other way, or simply cease to see when he has to face misery up close. Wanting to help in some way, I would buy them medicines—powdered sulphate, iodine, pills—in order to cure their illness. But the foreman reprimanded me saying I couldn't heal Indians with white man's medicine because they only believed in Quispe's ways of healing.

The suffering I had experienced in the camps was no different from what they were living, except that they didn't know any better, nor did they strive to improve their situation. But they had to know life could be better; they were aware of how the foreman lived and they had seen the owner's house, yet their state of peonage made all that seem no more than an impossible dream. You never saw them smiling. When they drank they would fall into a drunken stupor and lose consciousness; cheap booze didn't make them happy either.

Their faces, seemingly sculpted by fire, were as expressionless as rocks. Never once did they tell me about their suffering or misfortunes. They never dared to question the foreman's orders. Despite the harsh treatment and the constant abuse, they still trusted Segundo more than they did me because I was a white man. To be white created a barrier between two worlds, and there was nothing I could do to win them over.

On the weekends they would walk down to the nearby town of Amaguaña in order to buy salt, animal fat that they called *mapahuira*, and unrefined sugar. While in town, they would sit on the ground bundled together in their frayed ponchos around a barrel of *chicha*, a fermented corn drink. Groups of Indians would line up to buy it by the bucketful and drink the alcohol from a wooden cup that they passed along from one to the other until they became stupefied. *Chicha*, which was prepared in a wooden barrel, required corn, cane sugar, and ammonium, making it a highly toxic drink. By nightfall they were stumbling all over the place; the women, reeling and tottering like sacks of grain with their babies strapped to their backs, would stagger back to their huts into which they would tumble and fall asleep on the dirt floor. On Mondays they were useless because they were still unable to get up and go to work.

Suffering from the lack of nutrition since birth and having to start working at an early age, both men and women were worn out and ancient by the time they reached thirty years of age. Those who looked old were simply early to middle-aged men

and women who had been consumed by the endless suffering,
abuse, poor food, and endemic sickness.

Typically, a peon would earn barely pennies a day, women
even less. That miserable salary was complemented by what
they managed to raise on their plot of barren land—where
hardly anything would grow—their guinea pigs, a few chickens, and perhaps a sheep or two. The land was as destitute as
they were and, in order to fertilize it, they would pilfer manure
from the cattle stalls. Then they would plant a little barley, potatoes, and corn. Their principal food was toasted corn and broad
beans. When I tilled the land on the hacienda, their children
would follow behind and compete with the buzzards for the fat
white grubworms that they would take home, fry, and eat. That
"delicacy" was called *cucaíto*.

Happiness did not figure in anyone's life on those high, bleak,
barren plateaus. Even though I had always enjoyed working on
the land, there wasn't much that could induce me to smile. But
one of the most enduring memories I have of that era was learning that Frida was pregnant. Amid the joy of knowing that we
were going to have a child, I pondered my situation and worried
about the lack of medical assistance for Frida in that godfor-
saken place. But I couldn't just quit my job; there was nothing else that paid so well. While I spent a lot of time worrying,
Frida's abdomen began to expand. The abundant rainfall that
year gave new impetus and hope to the hacienda.

Meanwhile, Segundo was doing everything possible to get
my administrative position on the hacienda. To him it meant
the power to pillage the hacienda brazenly and unscrupulously;
naturally, the peons had no part to play in that power struggle.

Finally, it came time for Frida to leave the hacienda and go
back to live with her parents in Quito, in the event there were any
emergencies during the pregnancy. I stayed on, and Segundo's
harassment didn't let up. One night I thought an earthquake
had occurred. All around the house the ground was shaking as
horses stampeded. Every night Segundo and a group of peons

would run the horses around the house to frighten me and to thwart my sleep. A light sleeper because of the nightmares of the past, I would wake up at the drop of a pin. Images of the Nazi destruction would pop into my mind as if they had been fired by catapults. One day I ordered a shotgun from Quito. The day it arrived, I loaded it and waited for the onslaught of the horses that same night. Then I walked out onto the brick patio and fired two shots into the air, for that's all it took to rid myself of the Riders of the Apocalypse. Nevertheless, Segundo's harassment didn't let up: he really wanted my job.

One day I had to inspect a corn field and I left the mule I used for getting around the hacienda tied to some bushes. Nearby, there was grass for him to graze on. Once I had finished surveying the area, I went back to my mule and climbed on. Nervous to begin with, the animal was spooked by a bird and began to buck. The saddle slipped and suddenly I was holding onto the animal's stomach for dear life as he galloped like a bat out of hell. My right foot was caught in the stirrup. The mule headed full speed for the hacienda. I fell to the ground and the animal just kept on dragging me across the tilled soil until he reached a fence. As the mule jumped it, I grabbed a fence post and held on. The saddle came off the mule.

My entire body was battered and bruised. The peons had loosened the cinch in order to make me fall. In great pain, I slung the saddle over my shoulder and walked back to the hacienda. I told one of the servants to catch the mule and tie it to a post. I was so angry that I found a strap and gave the animal a good thrashing. Suddenly a sharp pain pierced my hip. The servant helped me get into bed, where I remained for several days unable to move.

During my third day of immobility, Quispe came around to see me and for the next two days he gave me massages. Then he said, "Get up, *patrón*." As if by magic I stood up and within days I was completely well.

During my convalescence I received a message to return to

Quito immediately because Frida was about to give birth. I went down to Amaguaña and took a bus to the capital. On the way, I was able to observe all the haciendas in the Los Chillos Valley, one of the most beautiful areas of the entire world. It reminded me so much of my homeland! Then I thought about my family and that soon I was going to be a father and start my own. I looked up at the sky. Clouds were floating by. "They see me," I said to myself, "and while they wouldn't be happy with my present situation, this is what life is all about and I'm ready to do whatever it takes for my new family."

When I arrived, Frida was already in the delivery room. I stood vigil in a waiting room with white walls and haggard people. After two hours of waiting I received the news that my son Roberto had been born. I took care of everything at the hospital and went back up to the hacienda. As I traveled back to those desolate, barren mountains, I thought about how my son's birth was going to change my life.

Frida was unable to join me for a while. Loneliness was like a nostalgic cloak that enveloped me. Even though I didn't like it, I had to immerse myself in my work to make time pass quickly. Six weeks later, Frida and Roberto were able to join me at the hacienda. The adobe walls and the frosty plateaus were not the best of environments for them, but Frida never complained. She had told me once that she would follow me to the end of the world, and even though that line sounded like something out of a movie she meant it.

One day I ordered the peons to plow a particular stretch of land on a hill for planting barley. One of them wouldn't obey and said something nasty to me in Quechua, upon which I popped him so hard that he went rolling down the side of a ditch. I was afraid that I had killed him. As I ran down to help him, I prayed that he wasn't dead.

I reached the bottom. The Indian, Nieves, looked up at me and began to scurry away on all fours. I was relieved when I saw that he was still alive. But that incident made me think about the type of life I was leading on the hacienda. I was a long way from what we call civilization, the salary wasn't anything to brag about, and I lived in a hostile environment. I climbed up a hill and looked out over the fields where the peons were working. They were plowing with teams of oxen, gripping the handles of the plows as the steel blades attempted to penetrate the hard clay. The earth didn't want to yield. The rays of the sun bounced off their stolid faces and apathy was the only expression that could be discerned.

I rode my bay horse back to the hacienda. Frida was surprised to see me return so early. I told her what had happened and about my decision to leave. Frida, who hadn't complained once for over a year and a half, jumped for joy. We immediately began packing the few things we owned and then spent a peaceful last night on the hacienda.

By six o'clock in the morning we were already heading down to Amaguaña. Avelino Gualachico, the only peon who ever trusted me, carried our belongings on his back. Two other peons brought along a dozen chickens. By the time we reached Amaguaña, however, only a few were still alive. The peons had broken their necks so that I would have to give them away, which is what I did.

On Monday, I went to the office of the hacienda owner who lived in Quito. I asked for my salary for the last twenty days that I had worked on the hacienda. While he was courteous to me, he sent me away without paying me, saying that I had abandoned my job and broken our contract. That was in March 1951.

The tormented peons and the foreman who was always exploiting them had made me see reality. I had sought refuge at the end of the world and I had wanted to forget the past, but I had come to understand that the past is never completely swept away and forgotten. It is with us always, for better or for worse. Suffering and misery were as much a part of those barren plateaus as the past in my soul. The past can never be forgotten

or erased permanently, it only allows for certain distractions.
Simply put, I had seen up close another facet of humanity, just as terrible as the concentration camps, even though the situation was relatively unknown by most people and of little concern to others. In much the same way that no one wanted to recognize the existence of the concentration camps in Europe, Ecuadorans were denying the fact that some of their fellow citizens were being tortured by the stinging whip of exploitation.

Was God aware of how those forgotten people were subjected to annihilation? Or was it like the concentration camps where everyone just looked out for themselves? I didn't have an answer. At that moment when the setting sun had painted a yellowish tinge on the hills around Pasochoa, it suggested the majestic presence of a superior being whose hand touched every one of us. But for what purpose?

20

Moving to Quito with eight chickens and a lone trunk of clothes was a daunting prospect. We stayed with my in-laws who were delighted to see their grandson. They were pleased that our child was going to grow up near them and not out in the sticks. Four days after quitting my job on the hacienda, I took a trip to Riobamba. One of my wife's uncles, Dr. Joel Nimelman, worked in that city and had invited me down to visit him. After seven hours of travel on a cobbled road, I found myself in a city called the Sultan of the Andes.

My wife's uncle lived behind the Immaculate Conception Convent. We talked about my plans; by evening, he had me convinced that I should stay for a few days to see if I might like to work for him. The next morning I accompanied him door to door on the streets of Riobamba, where he would sell a myriad of items: cloth, socks, wool jackets. Throughout the day, we would go in and out of old, dilapidated, colonial-era residences, which, with their interior patios, had become a bee-hive of multiple-family apartments. Generally, the first-floor dwellings would be rented out to people of all types and differing social conditions, while the owners of the building would live on the second floor.

Frida's uncle had an established clientele, for everyone would greet him in friendly fashion. Despite the poverty of the province of Chimborazo, people were cordial. Dr. Nimelman was very fastidious in his business. He carried an old notebook in which he would note the purchase, the down payment, and the monthly, biweekly, or weekly payments.

By nightfall we had covered half the city and my feet felt like bricks. Dr. Nimelman, in effect, had taught me from a to z about how to become a door-to-door salesman. The largest store in the world, he would say, was the street. I don't remember where or what we ate that day, but upon arriving at his home I was so exhausted that I fell limp upon the sofa in the living room.

During dinner he proposed that I become a door-to-door salesman and offered me his list of established clients. If I'm not mistaken, I think he said, "I'm ready to move to Quito. You're out of work. This is a decent job. The people are loyal and generous."

I really wasn't very happy about accepting the job. Selling merchandise from door to door wasn't the type of work I had in mind. It seemed so belittling to me. That night I thought about my family; I had to consider their well-being. All that night I studied my alternatives, but at every turn the doors of opportunity seem to close. Dr. Nimelman's offer was the only tangible option I had before me.

The next morning I accepted his offer and, taking his place, I became a salesman. There was no lack of advice on how to run the business, how to collect money, lists of clients, references, and other aspects that one learns on the job. Since I didn't have any capital to get started, I went with him to visit several businesses where he introduced me to people who might extend credit to me. I also needed money not only to move my family from Quito to Riobamba but to rent a place to live.

Dr. Nimelman managed to acquire a modest loan for me from a German immigrant by the name of Ainbinder. I used it to pay for my family's trip to Riobamba, the first month's rent, and initial living expenses. And so on a Monday morning I piled my wares on my back and set out to sell them from door to door. Following along behind me was a small Indian loaded down with a diverse array of goods: shirts and ties, cord and rope, dishes, underwear, and chocolates. I crossed the entire city and its outskirts until I reached a slaughterhouse. I sat down on a sandy stretch along the Chibunga River and well hidden behind some brush, I couldn't contain myself: I started sobbing. I felt as if I were paralyzed by all those goods next to me. I was sick with shame. I thought about how far I had come: I was in a foreign country doing work that I considered degrading. It depressed me to think I had left Europe only to end up in such a sad state of affairs. But the image of my wife and son and my obligation to them made me get to my feet, pick up my goods, and head downtown.

As I walked, it seemed as though everyone was staring at me, and my face turned red. I went along consumed by every detail: Which door would I knock on first? How would I be received? What about my foreign accent? And my nerves? But all of sudden I was stopped by a woman standing at the bottom of some stone steps. I was so immersed in my own thoughts that I couldn't understand what she wanted. However, the Indian, who was already seasoned in the business, stopped in front of her, and took out a box of stockings and lace.

That was my first sale of the day and it gave me the energy to keep going. Soon I was knocking on doors and talking to all types of people. I returned home late in the evening. When I took stock of the day's sales, I realized it had been a great day for me. I hugged Frida and described to her each and every sale I had made that day while Roberto wriggled in her arms. I didn't tell her about my weeping and fears—I kept those to myself.

Day in and day out, I would get out of bed reluctantly because I knew I had to go selling door to door. I was never very happy about what I was doing, but I'd always return home feeling satisfied with the day's sales. The people were always so kind to me. Perhaps they understood how badly I felt trying to sell them my wares.

I was treated with such friendliness that after a while I began to feel less hostile toward my job. The Ecuadorans had treated me well. Many times, seeing that I was a foreigner, they would inquire where I was from and ask me about other countries. I always responded that there wasn't any place like Ecuador. I never brought up anything about my past or mentioned racism in Europe; in essence, I always insisted that Ecuador was the most marvelous and peaceful country in the world. And, indeed, Ecuador possessed serenity, tranquillity, an enchanting environment.

With the passing of time, my job became a routine. Through practice and habit, I gained confidence in myself. Like the young smuggler crossing the Tisa in my youth, I had become free,

assured, and self-confident. Everything that I was turning out to
be I owed to those solicitous, understanding, and affectionate
people. Before long my customers had taken a liking to me and
consulted me about their diverse problems. In my own way,
I would repay them by lifting their spirits. I saw that the old
nightmare of the concentration camps, forever present in my
memories, had been a painful ordeal that I had managed to
overcome, making me all the stronger for it.

My second son, Ricardo, was born on 21 November 1952.
Meanwhile, Roberto continued to grow up in his own independent, mischievous way. He would lob raw potatoes from the
balcony down to the patio below and the owners of the house
who lived on the first floor would harvest them without ever
having planted them. I used to tell myself that there are people
who reap the harvest without having to plant anything and there
are those who plant so that others can reap the harvest. But
those who make sacrifices will also be rewarded.

But not everything was a bed of roses in that job. In one of
my more unfortunate business deals, I sold some black cloth to
a future groom on credit. The bride-to-be had been one of my
customers and came to my house one day with her boyfriend,
recommending that I extend credit to him. After the wedding
and only one payment, the husband disappeared, having abandoned not only his wife but also his job as a tractor driver.

One Saturday, though, I happened to run into him at the
weekly fair at Santa Rosa Plaza. I approached him and demanded that he pay off his debt. I think he must have associated
my claim with the disastrous, three-week marriage because he
became insolent and abusive. I couldn't contain myself and I
punched him so hard that he fell unconscious to the ground.
That made us even, after which I calmed down. But, as it turned
out, the man was in the company of another woman. Humiliated, he wanted revenge: he grabbed a butcher knife from one
of the vendors nearby and tried to stab me in the back. But
Luisa Chicaiza, a vegetable seller, saw what was happening and

pounced on the attacker. The other vegetable sellers joined her. They all became entangled in a full-fledged fight and were able to wrench the knife out of his hand. Later I gave some thought to the matter: after managing to escape death in the concentration camps, here I'm almost killed for the price of a piece of cloth.

Some months later, after forgetting about the incident, I met the exemplary husband again. He smiled at me and in a friendly way said he wanted to pay off his debt, which he did. Then he invited me to have a beer. As we walked together, I didn't trust him one bit. After we had each drunk a beer, he said, "I like to have macho friends. I always thought gringos were cowards."

We left the bar, like pals. As we neared city hall, the Calahorrano brothers came up to me defiantly and, joined by the model husband, began to beat me up. I defended myself the best I could, but I was so outnumbered that I was as bewildered as a drunk at a fair. Santillán, a good friend of mine, saw that I was being pulverized, so he grabbed me by the arms and, as he was pulling me away, whispered in my ear, "Let me get you out of here or else they'll string you up."

Despite those occasional incidents, Riobamba had been good therapy for my past. Now that I was far from Europe and the forces of anti-Semitism, the old sorrows were collecting like sediment, settled but unforgotten. Happiness in the family increased one more time on 16 August 1956: our daughter Daisy was born.

Roberto and Ricardo had started school by then. Their comings and goings brought back those hazy memories of my growing up in Sighet. Frida and I had been planning our children's future and we agreed that we had to move away from Riobamba if they were to receive a Jewish education. Without the presence of strong Jewish traditions around them, our children had become perplexed because of what we taught them at home and the Catholic education they received at school.

One weekend I told Frida that I wanted to go for a walk to be

alone for a while. I started down the road toward the Chimborazo volcano. It was an exceptionally clear day and the snow
on top reflected the sharp white sunlight. I took a bus and then
walked until I reached the snow's edge, the point from which
I could experience a spectacular view of peace and calm. The
sun's rays penetrated my soul that ached from so many trials
and tribulations. I had been able to rebuild my life, I was at
peace with my work, and my family was lacking nothing. The
audacity and security of my youth that had been truncated by so
much pain and suffering had come to life in my soul once again.
Like the Carpathian bears that seek refuge from winter in some
cave or hollow tree trunk to hibernate, my soul had also fallen
into a slumber; but now it had been jolted awake by renewed
energy and the feverish decision to create a place for myself in
life. I felt as free as the Andean condor. Firmly in control of my
existence, there was no doubt in my mind that I would be able
to make something positive out of my life. Everything that I had
become I owed to the goodness of the inhabitants of that remote
region of Riobamba.

Like the sleighs pulled along by horses over the foothills of
the Carpathians during the long winters, my life had begun to
unfold with as much tranquillity. To whom or what did I owe
my life when so many of my people had died? Did I owe it to
the bowl of soup that my cousin Shlomo gave me in Jaworzno,
to my Czech friend who assisted me in urinating by unzipping
my pants, to the German soldier who hesitated to pull the trigger as I knelt in the snow, to the Gestapo agent who didn't
blow a hole in my head when he saw I had been wounded in
the leg, to Luisa Chicaiza who jumped on the model husband
and stopped him from knifing me, to my friend Santillán who
pulled me out of a dangerous ruckus, to an endless number of
people whose participation in my life made it possible for me
to continue living? Anyone, without realizing it, can contribute
to the life or death of one's fellow human beings. The smallest
detail can make a difference. Those thoughts consumed me as

I walked back home. A new flame, driving out darkness, had been kindled in my heart.

How could it be that I was still alive? From the balcony of our house, I could contemplate the Chimborazo volcano and other surrounding peaks. The moon reflected brightly off the snowy summits. My eyes soaked up the immense landscape.

I was determined that my children be raised within the traditions of our people. There was no Jewish community in Riobamba. I talked to Frida about it and we agreed that we should move back to Quito. That decision meant giving up something that had taken years to establish and it was doubtful that I would ever be able to collect what my customers owed me. However, if I ever wanted to give my children an authentic Jewish education, I had to make a break now.

We were asleep when all of a sudden the Sangay volcano began to roar. We went outside to witness the spectacle. The wooden rafters of our roof began to creak with the shaking of the earth. The eruptions occurred repeatedly at five-minute intervals. It was as if the center of the earth were palpitating like a heart. Huge mushroom clouds of fire, smoke, and ashes spewed out of the volcano's crater. Ashes carried by the winds sifted down on the city of Riobamba. The eruptions continued for days until finally everything calmed down.

One evening I thought about what had happened; I felt like a primitive being who doesn't understand the rhythm of nature. Would it ever be possible to understand human beings? I was just a fistful of cosmic dust that had been given life and wanted to decipher the incomprehensible mysteries of our existence. Light becomes meaningful only from the perspective of darkness. The volcano would begin anew when darkness had covered the city. Perhaps we are able to see the light only after we've experienced the test of darkness.

With so much work, I wasn't even aware that I didn't laugh anymore. One day Frida took me aside and asked me why I seemed incapable of smiling. She took me to the doctor. He indicated that my facial muscles had petrified. I didn't tell him

anything about my past. What was the use? Would he understand that being able to laugh depended on more than just facial
muscles?

I went home. My children were playing with my goods as if
they were door-to-door salesmen. I went over to them and gave
them each a big hug. I think I smiled at that moment. Frida told
me that, indeed, a smile had come over my face. I had to start
getting used to it.

Then one day it was time to leave Riobamba. This time it had
nothing to do with having to escape. The truck started off and I
began to remember how I had abandoned Sighet forever. My life
was a continual succession of similar events and the goal was to
keep going. Nine years earlier I had been going in the opposite
direction with two members of my family. Now there were five
of us. God had said that our people would be as numerous as
grains of sand in the desert.

We arrived in Quito on Thursday afternoon, 30 September
1960, and moved into a rented house. A few days later I hit the
streets of Quito, again selling wares. I could not have imagined
that within two years I would set up a textile factory, far less that
I would see it thrive. Nor did that long-awaited success mean the
end of my trials and tribulations. Who can foresee the twisting
paths along which life will lead us?

A light begins to penetrate the darkness. I awake in a room at
the Massachusetts General Hospital. As I open my eyes I begin
to make out a silhouette; it's my son Ricardo. Then I see Frida's
flaming hair. I finally emerge out of a nightmare. A good part of
my life has been just that, a terrible nightmare created by human
beings. But after darkness comes light.

I move my lips and whisper softly, "Here I am. I've returned."

In reality, however, everyone surrounding me at that very
moment are the ones who have returned: my family, my life,
my anguish, my suffering. . . . And the light? They are the light.
And they had come back to me.

Perhaps life isn't anything but a departure toward death. When it arrives, I'll be ready.

A tenuous light accompanies the breeze that enters the window. The shadow of the dead contains both life and death, as if it were a single, indivisible unity. Whenever I die, I want to experience the peace of the walnut groves, the apple orchards laden with fruit, the hills coated with white frost, the murmur of the waters of the Tisa. I want to feel the repose of the air over the forest, the rain soaking the furrows, the irrigation ditches, and the lazy tranquillity of the sun drifting through the sky. Isn't that what God is about?

A prayer welled up from deep down inside: "Oh God, even though I'm not worthy of you, even though you hide from me, please give me peace." It was then I discovered something that had been hidden from me for years. God, the one who hurls us through life, is but a great repository of our memories. My memories are little more than bread crumbs in the universal plan, insignificant ashes among the cosmic dust where life disappears and is reborn infinitely.

My vision grows dim. Sleep, death, what does it matter? If we dream while we are alive, why should we be denied dreams when we are dead? As if I were returning from my memories, I pass through time that is constantly renewing itself. And I repeat to myself, "Killing is their daily work." Perhaps someday humankind will understand it all and examine the disaster of generations still overtaken with fear. Is it necessary to subdue fear in order to finally be free?

I repeat, "Killing is their daily work." But I am a survivor, a man of ashes. Ashes of my mother, smeared across the palm of my hand . . . ashes of my people and their history beneath which the coals of hatred still glow hot . . . ashes, like those of the phoenix, from which I have been reborn on so many occasions and against all odds . . . ashes of the Sangay volcano venting nature's inexorable, incomprehensible fury . . . dust and ashes of which I was made and to which I must return.